D0843384

Ethical Decision-Making in Social Research

Also by Ron Iphofen

SOCIOLOGY IN PRACTICE FOR HEALTHCARE PROFESSIONALS
(*with Fiona Poland*)

AN EU CODE OF ETHICS FOR SOCIO-ECONOMIC RESEARCH
(*with Sally Dench and Ursula Huws*)

Ethical Decision-Making in Social Research

Social Research

A Practical Guide

Ron Iphofen

palgrave
macmillan

First published 2009 by
PALGRAVE MACMILLAN

Palgrave Macmillan in the UK is an imprint of Macmillan Publishers Limited, registered in England, company number 785998, of Houndmills, Basingstoke, Hampshire RG21 6XS.

Palgrave Macmillan in the US is a division of St Martin's Press LLC, 175 Fifth Avenue, New York, NY 10010.

Palgrave Macmillan is the global academic imprint of the above companies and has companies and representatives throughout the world.

Palgrave® and Macmillan® are registered trademarks in the United States, the United Kingdom, Europe and other countries.

ISBN-13: 978-0-230-21035-6   hardback
ISBN-10: 0-230-21035-X   hardback

This book is printed on paper suitable for recycling and made from fully managed and sustained forest sources. Logging, pulping and manufacturing processes are expected to conform to the environmental regulations of the country of origin.

A catalogue record for this book is available from the British Library.

A catalogue record for this book is available from the Library of Congress.

10   9   8   7   6   5   4   3   2   1
18   17   16   15   14   13   12   11   10   09

Printed and bound in Great Britain by
CPI Antony Rowe, Chippenham and Eastbourne

Contents

Case Examples – List of Boxes

Acknowledgements

This book draws on the experience gained from several projects and consultative activities. I wish to acknowledge the insights, comments, concerns and mentorship gained from all the colleagues I have worked with on those projects. The projects include updating the Social Research Association (SRA) guidelines between 1998 and 2003 and subsequent mentorship for the SRA; the EC-funded RESPECT project conducted under Framework Programme 5; consultancy to the Scottish Executive Social Research on their system of ethical assurance; training sessions and consultancy conducted for the UK Government Social Research Unit and the National Centre for Social Research (NatCen). The essential idea for and the elements of the checklist, the template for research proposals and other templates draw on a variety of text sources including Brent and Thompson (2000), Sieber (1991) and many others and has subsequently been refined as a consequence of work conducted in the projects listed above. It has been progressively informed through my membership of the Research Ethics Committee of the National Disability Authority (Ireland) and the Research Governance Committee of the North East Wales NHS Trust.

The suggestions, ideas, cases and insights developed here have been drawn from many sources including face-to-face, telephone and Internet discussions, seminars and lectures. There are too many people who have influenced my views to list them all here, but those whom I wish to acknowledge with particular gratitude for ideas, guidance, inspiration and motivation in our collaborative work on research ethics include Sally Baker, Jerome Bickenbach, Siobhan Campbell, Sally Dench, Anne Good, Ursula Huws, Immy Holloway, Roger Jowell, Mary van Lieshoult, Anthea Tinker, Malcolm Rigg and Ceridwen Roberts.

How to Use This Book

This is not a book on moral philosophy, nor is it a textbook on research methods. It is a guide to 'thinking through' the problems of conducting ethical research in social science. Some moral problems are, of necessity, discussed, some dilemmas confronted and some possible solutions suggested. Similarly the problems entailed in adopting a variety of techniques and methodological approaches will be considered without claiming a comprehensive coverage of all methodological approaches in the social sciences. The book aims to be of practical help to social researchers in resolving ethical dilemmas in research with human subjects. Some of the requirements of ethical scrutiny are laid out and a system for an ongoing review of the elements in any research project is offered. For a more extended consideration of any of the moral and methodological issues raised, further reading and other useful sources are suggested. Neither does the book offer in any detail a historical overview of how these issues have been dealt with in the past. It is intended to be of rapid practical help to researchers.

To be of maximum practical use the book is structured around an 'Ethical Review Checklist' which can be found towards the end of the book and can be used by anyone planning, monitoring or conducting a research project and who is concerned to ensure that they have fully considered the range of ethical issues that could arise in such a project. The checklist acts as an *aide memoire* both to the issues covered more fully in each chapter and to assist a comprehensive consideration in advance of the kinds of moral problems that might arise in any social science project. Each chapter refers to referenced pages in the checklist.

Scrutiny procedures and specific systems of ethical review vary from country to country, but there are similar basic principles that have to be addressed regardless of local institutionalised review procedures. The balance between the methodological and the moral is something that social researchers worldwide must have in mind. I hope therefore that the book will inform debate on ethical research among social scientists globally.

This book does not adopt what has been called a dominant 'biomedical ethics model'. It is hard to escape the terms and assumptions of this model since it is in this field that most of the debate on ethical research has been conducted since it was from this field that the most ethically disturbing research originated. Consequently the literature derives from and builds upon this arena, as do the more formalised systems of ethical scrutiny. However, I specifically argue for consideration of the particular problems of social research throughout the book and for the need to enhance systems of ethical scrutiny by incorporation of insights from social research. To ensure clarity on the terms and concepts used in this book, readers should check out the 'Short Glossary of Key Terms and Concepts' towards the end of the book.

In a similar vein the sectionalising of issues into chapters with different topics implies that these are discrete categories. Ethical decisions are rarely confined to one issue area. There are considerable overlaps and consequences, often unanticipated, of making decisions in one area that affect others. There is also a danger in assuming that all research goes through the same 'stages' in the same sequence – any experienced researcher knows that this is not the case. There is no uniformly agreed 'research process' given the variety of methodological models throughout the social sciences and the unique and unexpected events entailed in any one project. While there can be some elements of planning and patterns to research, there are too many variable influences to allow such a rigid view. So it should not be assumed that each of the items in the checklist has to be necessarily addressed in the order presented – they are arranged for maximum convenience. Formalised ethical scrutiny does require as much anticipation as possible of ethical dilemmas at the outset. But not everything can be predicted or anticipated in research, so there must be opportunities to re-visit the formal scrutiny procedures as 'emergencies' arise or to fulfil the ongoing requirements of research governance. So, although there is a need to complete as much of the checklist as possible before research has commenced, there will also be a need to re-visit most of the items as the research progresses.

Throughout the book there is reference to a range of illustrative case studies. These can be found in boxed sections in which the cases are described and subsequently discussed. These represent an attempt to apply the principles of ethical decision-making to contemporary cases (using examples from professional mentoring and others reported in news media). Some references to 'classic' well-known cases are also included to illustrate longstanding ethical dilemmas – but these are so well summarised and reported in other literature that I felt no need to repeat them all here.

Although the cases used here appear in different chapters, each could be used to illustrate a range of different, but connected ethical dilemmas. And any experienced researcher could come up with many more cases of their own – so the cases presented here are not assumed to be exhaustive of all possibilities.

Sample proformas or templates for use in seeking informed consent, providing information to participants and so on can be found on the book's website and will need to be modified for specific research projects.

The rest of the book is structured around the questions, dilemmas and concerns to be found in the checklist, because checklists on their own offer no substitute for reflective thinking by responsible researchers. Consequently the book attempts to offer full consideration of each issue and suggestions for the grounds upon which they may be resolved. Where there are dilemmas, these cannot be resolved within this book – since by their very nature dilemmas call for judgements and informed choices to be made and all such decisions ultimately lie with researchers themselves and in relation to the substantive research they are conducting. There are many existing ethical codes and guidelines that cover the range of professional associations that make up the social research community. (Links to these can be found before the reference list at the end of the book.) There is no intention here to simply replicate information found in those codes; and preliminary reading and familiarity with such codes of practice are essential for researchers' professional credibility and to ensure standards in practice. However, some of these guidelines are quite generic and so do not contribute to more specific 'real world' ethical decision-making; while other codes are so specific to a particular sphere of research practice that it is hard for their general usefulness to be appreciated. This book is aimed at helping researchers to interpret both the general and professionally specific codes in application to the particular problem or the dilemma confronting them. In this way the researcher can gain confidence that their judgements are reasoned and reasonable, and their choices fully informed.

I also hope that members of ethical review committees will read this book to gain awareness of the very practical problems confronted by the researchers who present their proposals for review.

For ease of use researchers could simply copy the checklist and relate each of the bullet points to the project they are conducting or plan to conduct and, if they need any assistance in thinking any one of those items through, they can return to the section of the book that deals with it. The checklist and the main text are cross-referenced by page numbers. But the sequencing in the main text does not match exactly that of the checklist. Since the checklist is meant as an *aide memoire*, its sequencing is determined by the normal processes of formalised ethical scrutiny (i.e. the kinds of things a research ethics committee is concerned with and the sequence in which they are likely to monitor them). The body of the book follows the logic of the ethically aware social researcher who, regardless of the need for formal ethical scrutiny, asks ethical questions of their endeavours from the outset and through-out the process of conducting the research. Consequently one could simply choose to start reading the book from the beginning and become involved in the fascinating 'moral maze' entailed in the conduct of research in social science.

1
The Problem of Ethical Decision-Making in Social Research

A practical simple definition of ethics is that they are '... a matter of principled sensitivity to the rights of others' (Bulmer 1992). This means that behaving ethically requires careful consideration and regular attention whatever profession one practises. In recent years concerns have been heightened by a range of misbehaviours by those we believe ought to behave more responsibly – the actions of doctors, scientists, lawyers, the police, teachers, civil servants, journalists and politicians have all been under moral suspicion (Neuberger 2005).

It might be due to such misbehaviour that moral awareness and concern has been discussed more publicly recently. It might be that modern mass communications enable us to find out about such behaviour faster and in more detail than was the case in the past. Or it may be that intelligent debate about ethical behaviour has grown to be something expected of an educated citizenry. The social responsibility of large international economic corporations came into the limelight after the Enron scandal – but there had already been a growing movement towards ethical investment which challenged the policies of such corporations. With the global financial crisis that emerged in 2008, concerns about the 'loose' ethical practices of a range of previously trusted financial agencies have grown even further. The institutionalised prejudices of police organisations in terms of racism and sexism have received particular attention and the judiciary has found itself judged and reproved about lenient sentencing for crimes considered to be morally particularly reprehensible. Tabloid journalism has received condemnation for many years but even the more serious media, those that make claims to 'liberality' and independence, have been subject to insightful and rigorous analysis for the complexity of the latent prejudices they contain (Smith 2001).

Health-oriented research in medicine, pharmaceuticals and human biology has posed many ethical dilemmas throughout the twentieth century, and this continues into the twenty-first in the fields of genetic modification and the use of human embryos. No longer can these developments be considered in the cloistered isolation of the laboratory away from public and political gaze. Politicians recognise that public awareness of moral sensibilities requires that they demonstrate their concern and maintain vigilance over such developments. Whatever the promise of innovative science and technology, heightened moral awareness will increasingly require public scrutiny of the implications of research activities.

Is there a particular problem in social science?

Few people believe that there has been any systematic abuse of respondents and/or commissioners by the social research community or that corruption and unethical professional behaviour is a feature of social science in general. This does not mean that 'problematic' events or incidents have not occurred. It could mean that, if they do occur, we do not often get to hear about them. As a mentor for the UK Social Research Association (SRA), I have heard examples of threats, bribery, corruption, barely justified deception and a range of pressures being put on researchers to contravene other fundamental standards of proper behaviour. Such behaviour rarely makes headlines since the consequences affect only small communities of interest and never entail large amounts of money by the standards of such abuses in other professional fields. But there is enough going on to be concerned about and it is in all our interests, as practitioners, participants, research subjects and receivers of the benefits of social research, to ensure that such practices are kept to a minimum and, if at all possible, avoided.

Whenever research has an effect upon the lives of humans, ethical problems will emerge and there is the possibility that, unless we are on our guard, more serious issues could arise in the future for social research. As a professional community social researchers have to attend constantly to the ethics of their profession and be seen to be doing so. Integrity is vital to the 'trust' between professionals and society that enables good practice to be sustained. My aim here is to lay out some of the fundamental problems associated with behaving ethically as a researcher and to offer practical advice on designing ethical social research, on gaining permission to conduct research and in ensuring that research continues to be conducted ethically.

Some years ago in a review meeting for a European Commission (EC) project on setting and maintaining standards in socioeconomic research (the RESPECT project), we were addressing the issue of research ethics specifically and one of the expert reviewers commented: 'I don't care if the researcher is a good person or not – what matters is that they are a good researcher.' I want to argue that, as far as behaving ethically is concerned, it is difficult to separate good behaviour as a researcher from good behaviour as a person. Ethical practice in social research is about being a 'good' researcher at the same time as being a 'good' human being.

My argument rests on the idea that we must try hard not to fragment morality. One either cares to behave ethically or one does not. Of course, even as moral beings it is certainly possible for humans to decide to be 'more moral' in some areas or with some people than with others. (One might even treat that as an ethical decision – thus I might be more 'economical with the truth' with someone who I know has told me a lie, than with someone I believe to have been honest with me.) I would have to ask: Why should a person who behaves unethically in certain spheres of their life have any reason to behave more ethically when conducting social research? If they allow a lesser morality in other spheres of life, why should I trust them to conduct ethical research?

It is for just such reasons that some commentators advocate a more careful monitoring system and administrative procedures for checking on the ethics of research projects. It is, of course, true that no procedure for ethical regulation can be adequately foolproof. If an unethical researcher decides to manipulate an ethical review system, then it is relatively easy for them to do so. While I advocate adopting careful and comprehensive systems of ethical scrutiny, I am not a supporter of what some opponents of increasing bureaucratic control regard to be 'ethical fascism' – the unreasonable interference in the conduct of free social scientific endeavour. The problem is how to permit free social scientific enquiry while ensuring such freedoms are not abused. Perhaps like all freedoms this too is relative.

There is an interesting parallel with the concept of corporate social responsibility. Milton Friedman has suggested that corporate social responsibility is a distraction from the main purposes of corporations – which is to make a profit. Thus, he argued, it would be unethical to seek to do something other than the publicly stated goals of the organisation, which is why people invest in it. In his view corporate executives are employed to seek profit, not to be good people. Others have extended this to suggest that business morality can be separated from

the morality of personal or home life. Thus an unscrupulous asset strip-
per might create unemployment in a community and still go home to
ensure the care and well-being of his own children and family.

If we were to apply the same logic to social science we could say that
we were basically good people at home – but when seeking to advance
social scientific knowledge we can treat human beings as exploitatively
as we wish to since they are our vital data source – and we would only
be doing so in the interests of, say, advancing knowledge, producing the
commissioned deliverables for our funders and so on. To do so would
be to elevate methodology above morals. I suspect that scientists who
conduct research on animals have pets at home for their children and
would baulk at suggesting that such pets would make ideal laboratory
experimental subjects.

I hold the view that, in any research engagement with the world
(social, psychological and material), it is hard to separate how one
behaves as a person and the standards one should maintain as a professional. There is no reason for me to trust anyone who is able to
parcel up humanity into those we can do things to and those we can't.
The kind of scientific experimentation conducted in Germany and its
occupied territories, between the early 1930s and 1945 under National
Socialism, comes to mind. Some actions simply have to be seen as inherently wrong but most actions require addressing the moral problem and
dilemmas that being human and being alive entails. We cannot be 'concerned' in some geographical regions, or about some people and not
others, and think it matters less. Thus, for example, deliberately taking
a human life may be seen as generally wrong, although there may be a
time when, subject to much reflection, concern and attempts to avoid it
we may find ourselves condoning the killing of people – in self-defence,
in a 'just' war or as part of a system of self-selected euthanasia.

A responsible researcher is one who understands and examines the
ways in which the moral and the methodological principles of their
work are interwoven. A technically and methodologically 'good'
researcher who behaves unethically may contaminate the research
field in ways that might undermine further research by themselves or
by their colleagues. A technically incompetent (or 'bad') researcher,
who nonetheless behaves well as a person, produces research that, if
unsound, is disrespectful of persons (of society and of the community)
by wasting people's time and allowing poorly evidenced claims of
knowledge, policy and practice to be pursued.

This point of view fits into an ethical theory known as 'virtue ethics',
which argues for the need for people to be 'of good character' and, in

such a way, good ethical decisions should follow (see Baggini and Fosl 2007: 94). But as a *sine qua non* of social research this points up immediately the dilemmas inherent in research practice – being good as a researcher and as a human being necessitates making choices between alternative courses of action and, therefore, is often a form of compromise. My purpose here is to help social researchers make those choices in an informed way. One of the keys to professional integrity in social research is to ensure sound ethical practice at all times. Given the nature of social research, whereby researchers are often in face-to-face contact with their respondents/participants, and/or handle personal data about them, I argue that it is vital that each researcher takes full responsibility for the management of their own ethical practice. 'Ethical awareness' among researchers, managers and commissioners depends on constant reflection on the ethical implications of their work, continuous professional development with regard to ethical practice and the existence of a system of peer mentorship which can provide advice and guidance when difficult decisions arise.

In order to maintain a climate of trust in the practice and outcomes of social research, it is inevitable that systems of ethical assurance will be established and will need to be maintained by all those engaged in work of this nature. The trust of the public, professional colleagues, those who commission and fund research and those being studied requires an effective system of ethical review, clear lines of responsibility and a manageable degree of independent overview. However, it is also the case that no administrative system, no matter how well conceived, can guarantee sound ethical practice among all researchers. Similarly, unnecessarily cumbersome systems of ethical review can hinder the operation of valuable research enacted in the public interest. All too often institutional caution has taken precedence over ethical concerns and ethical review has been confused with risk aversion, damage limitation and managerial line accountability (so-called research governance).

When we refer to ethical principles within a profession, such as social research, we are thinking of 'a set of standards by which a particular group or community decides to regulate its behaviour – to distinguish what is legitimate or acceptable in pursuit of their aims from what is not' (Flew 1979: 112).

It is this combination of institutionalised overview and risk assessment and limitation, individual responsibility and the fulfilling of professional obligations that frames the discussion throughout this book.

The autonomous professional and the accountable researcher

A major problem facing modern professionals lies in the many lines of accountability they have to deal with. As professionals and as moral beings, some degree of 'role mix' is inevitable – leading to multiple allegiances. Health professionals, for example, face clinical accountability to their professional institution and their colleagues, to the service organisation which employs them and, of course, to the patient. They are also likely to be expected to fulfil non-clinical obligations to their profession (such as keeping their knowledge and skills up-to-date) and to their employing organisation (such as keeping accurate case notes and comprehensive administrative records). Similarly, various lines of accountability apply to welfare and social care workers and to civil servants in general. Professionals in these fields will be also aware of the allegiances they hold to the general public or the taxpayer who pays their salaries.

Even at this level – of the health professional or civil servant – it is never easy to prioritise ethical issues, since they all present dilemmas or difficult choices. It might seem simple to advocate a fundamental principle such as 'first do no harm'. In the field of public health such a principle is never easy to apply in practice – the law requiring a notification of infectious diseases undoubtedly restricts the liberty of any person carrying such a disease. Vaccination carries a risk to each individual vaccinated, but the interests of public health require the balancing of such a risk against the reduced risk of infection to the rest of society. Some harm may have to be risked with individuals, in the interests of protecting or doing some good for the rest of a community or society. So the degrees of harms and benefits to both the individual and the community as a whole, first, have to be estimated and then balanced against one another.

If we add the act of conducting research to this, the additional ethical dilemmas merely compound treatment issues since the health professional *as a researcher* adds many more lines of accountability to those they already serve. As health *researchers* they raise obligations to other researchers in their field, to patients again – who now also become 'research subjects' – to science in general in terms of the advancement of human knowledge and to society in terms of human benefit.

Civil servants commissioning or conducting research confront such dilemmas regularly. Their allegiances may be torn between the department that employs them, a government minister wishing to explore certain policy options, the public in general and their principles as an autonomous research professional. (For a discussion on the dilemmas of professional accountability in formal organisation, see Bovens (1998).)

The potential for 'divided loyalties' has to be addressed so that all involved in the research are clear as to the researchers' value hierarchies (Bell and Nutt 2002). This is something which is carefully watched for by those responsible for the ethical review of health research. It is seen to be of primary importance that patients, clients and those in the care of the health services are not harmed by the research and that their individual treatment is not affected in a negative way. It is something that will have to be considered more fully by government researchers in the social care, social welfare and employment fields.

Fundamental competing principles

Behaving ethically when conducting research requires the researcher to plan a route through a moral maze. To engage in ethical research one constantly has to make choices within a range of options. These options involve competing principles, often in tension with each other, and which present us with moral dilemmas that are common to all research – not just social science.

Being a 'good' social scientist/social researcher means both not doing harm – or at least minimising it – (i.e. non-maleficence) and, hopefully, doing (some) good (i.e. beneficence). To be beneficent entails a range of actions with the scientific intent of improving human knowledge about the area of human behaviour under investigation. This might mean describing, understanding and explaining the phenomena of interest. Good research might also produce benefits in the form of improved social policy in the topic area under study and advice on 'best practice' drawn from systematically produced evidence.

Being non-maleficent requires that, as a consequence of being a beneficent scientist or researcher, one is careful not to harm people when intervening in their normal daily routines and activities. Just the simple intervention of the research engagement alone might be seen by some as disturbing. People may not like being observed or being asked questions about their thoughts, attitudes and actions. Sometimes that intervention changes people's lives in unforeseen ways and, sometimes, such change might be a deliberate part of the scientific process – an intervention which works like a scientific experiment. For example, we might ask people to do things differently to see if the difference produces an improvement in their lives or the lives of those they associate with.

The choices one makes as a researcher are about getting the right balance between being a good scientist and not unduly interfering in people's lives. If the goals of science are not valued relatively highly, or if they are not considered worth pursuing, then no interventions in the lives of human beings could ever be justified.

Things do get a little more complex, however, if some people think the goals of science worth pursuing for how they improve our knowledge even if others don't – especially if it means 'too much' interference in people's lives and, therefore, is perceived to be, to some extent, harmful. Whether research is then conducted depends on the relative power of those supporting the research set against the power of those opposing it.

For example, college and university students used to be one of the most frequently studied groups in the population. Lecturers, who hold the power in such situations, often used them as research subjects and could justify their actions on the grounds that the students would also be learning about research while going through the experience of being the subjects of research. Students had little choice in the matter and could feel obliged to participate in the research – they rarely objected.

It is not necessarily the subjects of research who seek to oppose it. There are plenty of groups in society that hold moral objections to some of the topics studied by researchers and/or to some of the methods they use. Thus, for example, some religious organisations once objected to the study of homosexuality on the grounds that it was a moral perversion and should simply be condemned – they did not believe that it was worthy of investigation in an attempt to understand 'alternative' forms of sexual behaviour. They argued that such research led to condoning homosexuality. Similarly some people hold that no study should be covert or deceive the subjects being studied on the grounds that deception is wrong – whatever the purpose – even if that purpose is the advancement of human knowledge.

Whether such contentious research ever gets done, then, depends on the relative power of those supporting it against those opposing it. Research on genetically modified (GM) food crops offers a useful example. Ecologically oriented groups in the 'green' or organic food movement hold that such studies are potentially a fundamental threat to the environment since GM experiments cannot adequately be localised. Scientists working in the GM field and many governments currently support such work and so it continues to be conducted – subject only to damage from occasional 'guerrilla' tactics from the more ardent ecologically conscious groups.

Equivalent examples in the social science research field are harder to find since it is often more difficult to see the consequences for society of such research actions or interventions. At least we can say that if both the *observers* (researchers and other interested groups) and the *observed* (people being studied) agree that the intervention should be allowed in the interests of scientific advancement then some part of our first set of moral dilemmas is on the way to being solved.

But agreeing to research, in principle, must then be qualified by further fundamental ethical decisions. Whether the proposed research actually goes ahead will then be dependent upon three further sets of questions:

What precisely is the research being done for?
Who is doing it?
How do they propose doing it?

These broad questions can be represented as concerns of 'purpose' (which we are discussing here in Chapter 1 and further in Chapter 2), 'profession' (which will be considered in Chapter 3) and 'practice' (which comprises the rest of the book from Chapter 4 to the end).

Each of these questions poses a further series of potential ethical dilemmas which may conflict or lie in tension with each other. These will be examined, in turn, in each of the subsequent chapters.

Cultural variation and the language of morality

There may be some researchers who find it hard to understand these problems from within their own cultural perspective. In some political and cultural climates the power of a researcher working for the government might be seen to override all other concerns of morality. (That certainly was the case in Nazi Germany.) But global sets of standards on research ethics require, to some degree, a global moral order – and there isn't one yet. Indeed some commentators hold no hope for there ever being one, while others wonder if a universal moral order is necessarily a 'good thing' (see discussion in Rachels 1978: 15–29). It is hard for those experiencing Western-style, multiparty, representative democracies to understand the norms and values extant in, say, a one-party authoritarian state. But this should not preclude researchers from operating in such cultures – otherwise the discipline of anthropology would never have been developed. In fact, the globalisation of research professional activities can aid in the spreading of cross-cultural principles and, possibly, even the seeking of a set universal ethics within the field of research.

Politics is not the only constraint on research ethics. Language is even more subtle in embedding moral assumptions about how to conduct research that deserve to be challenged – but these are often so latent that they may not be confronted directly. To illustrate, one reviewer for this book charged it with adopting an excessively biomedical model due primarily to the use of the terms 'template', 'protocol' and 'research subjects'. This, of course, was not my intention – if anything I am seeking as neutral a vocabulary as possible so as not to be accused of imposing the biomedical/health model on social science. As a result throughout the book care has been taken to advocate terms suitable for generic and for specific purposes. There is little else I can do about someone else's vocabularistic prejudices.

A rapid review of raised ethical awareness

One way of quickly coming to an understanding of ethical decision-making for social research methodologists could be to consider approaching ethics in the same ways as one approaches experimental validity and reliability. In other words, one should ask: What are the 'threats' to the principles we are attempting to balance? Thus:

- What threatens our autonomy – as researchers and as subjects of research?
- What might threaten our interests?
- What are the threats to the interests of all 'stakeholders'?
- Are there any threats to participants' capacity to consent to participate in research?
- What threatens the possibility that research can be of benefit to 'us' (as individuals, groups or members of a particular society)?
- What are the threats to making sure that research does not do us any harm?

By asking such questions we soon see that all members of society are, to greater or lesser degrees, 'vulnerable' as either researchers and/or subjects of research. We might all have to be involved in attempting to minimise our vulnerability. Each of these potential ethical threats varies systematically for individuals, groups and other categories of population members.

If we take 'chronological age' as a determining variable, we tend to be less autonomous when we are very young, or when we are very old – life allowing some measure of increased autonomy in our mature (middle) years, when we have enhanced access to those physical and material resources that permit or facilitate such autonomy. Age is similarly a factor in determining our capacity to consent to participate in research activities. Once again the very old and the very young may be assumed not to have adequate cognitive capacity to give fully informed consent. One could do the same for a range of variable characteristics of groups or individuals. The learning disabled, the mentally ill, those with physical disabilities, varying levels of educational achievement or economic resource and so on.

In fact, it is vital when doing such 'rapid' ethical review to remind ourselves who precisely are the stakeholders in research activities. It is evident that researchers themselves, the funders or commissioners and the participants are the more obvious stakeholders. But then in making claims for broader societal or communal benefits, we must include society at large, our own communities of interest – professional, geographical, ethnic and so on – and the communities of which the research subjects or participants might be considered representative. Thus, whatever the sampling strategy adopted, the older person, say, being interviewed becomes 'representative' of the community of older people in general, and a child becomes representative of children. That is not to assume any necessary homogeneity in that community, but as evidence bases are constructed and policies devised on the basis of that research, the researched subject can be taken for, and may see themselves, as representing their community of interest.

Variable dimensions of ethical choice

Another way of coming to rapid ethical decisions is to consider the variable factors which underlie moral judgements. Thus, for example, let's say we conduct research we believe to be of benefit to the individual and the community. It is clear that sometimes actions that benefit individuals have no benefit for the community – indeed they may even harm it; and the corollary is also the case – community benefits may be at the expense of individuals. Ideally we would seek to benefit both, but if they are in conflict, we have to make the ethical choice about how to balance out the benefits. The same process could be gone through for the need of protecting the individual and/or community. Protection for one may be at the expense of adequate protection for the other.

The extent of this multidimensional problem can be seen as we consider other variable factors. Thus should we consider the law over and above the acts that individuals commit – in other words, whatever the moral intent or consequence of an act, if it is illegal should we reprove it? And that raises two more dimensions: Are intentions more important than outcomes, and which law should we hold in higher esteem – local or international, or, even, should custom and practice be seen as more valued?

Attempts to simplify the analytic questions produce quite complex multidimensional matrices, but one could begin by at least listing the variable factors to consider when making moral judgements. Each of these factors may be considered to lie along a 'good/bad' dimension and they include:

- *Agents* (people)
- *Actions* (the things they do)
- *Intentions* (the reasons or motives they have for doing them)
- *Outcomes* (the combined consequences of their intentions and their acts)
- *Rules* (the laws and customs they choose to follow or to disobey)
- *Responsibility* (whether or not they assume or are accorded accountability for their intentions, actions and outcomes – with some assessment of the rules they claim to have followed in doing so).

Given the interconnectedness of these factors, such judgements are necessarily complex. Thus, for example, a general principle of beneficence says nothing about *who* should or might benefit.

Variation in methodological perspective

The range of approaches and research methods available to the social scientist derives from an equally broad variety in theoretical tradition and, consequently, in methodological assumptions. The implications this has for ethical decision-making are to raise even more complex dilemmas than that found in, say, biomedical or non-human participant research. These traditions adopt divergent views on the nature of the human 'subject' and the form that social scientific investigation should take. At the more positivistic extreme, controlled experimental designs are sought which require treating the subject as object. At the other end of the scale might be included participatory and/or emancipatory research, where the researcher deliberately chooses to forgo control of the research and passes it on to the participants who are the focus of the project. Between these extremes lies a range of hotly contested views about how best to study all aspects of human society – which is partly what makes social research both interesting and challenging.

Studies of social groupings range from necessarily 'distancing' mathematical representations of social networks to highly participative community-oriented projects which require researchers' physical, emotional and moral 'proximity' and, consequently, intense involvement with people. Studies of individual thought, motive and action cover the territory from algebraic codifying of role and expectation states to phenomenological, intersubjective insights into the unique experiences of persons. While ethical decision-making will vary in emphasis between such approaches, the underlying competing dilemmas remain fundamentally similar: How will this research benefit society, communities and/or individuals? What harm could this research cause?

Throughout this book such variety is taken for granted as part and parcel of the rich methodological and theoretical tradition within social science. The substantive ethical choices implied by the adoption of a particular perspective will be highlighted both generically and in the illustrative use of case studies.

Sample case studies

The exercise of ethical review and the raising of ethical awareness require thinking through the possible consequences and impact of any research on its participants, on researchers and upon the community or society. Sometimes we will need to draw attention to the potential tensions between promoting the well-being of the individual and that of the group or society at large. The best way of doing this is to refer to practical examples. Interspersed throughout the book is a series of case studies, which can bring alive the tensions in ethical decision-making in social research. Some of the cases are familiar, classical examples, others contemporary and less publicly familiar. These are not exclusively social scientific cases since a lot can be learnt from the comparative analysis of the ethical dilemmas being confronted in other areas of similar research. The book itself will be contributing cumulatively/progressively to the reader's own analytic framework within which such an examination of the case study examples can be conducted.

The first case is drawn from sports science (see Box 1.1).

Box 1.1   Adidas Research at Loughborough University, UK

There was a lot of discussion about the nature of the football used in the 2006 World Cup (soccer) competition in Germany. The ball seemed to swerve unpredictably in the air after being kicked. A study was concurrently being conducted by researchers in Loughborough University for Adidas – the makers of the ball. The deal struck with Adidas required that the researchers kept the findings from their study confidential. Since this commercial company were sponsoring it, it could be argued that they had a right to keep it secret, despite the popular interest in the outcome of the study. Some would argue that the design characteristics of the ball could be changing the nature of the game. If this were the case it would make it even more vital that the results were aired publicly.

(see *The Times Higher*, 7 July 2006: 6)

To apply the matrix and the good/bad dimensions to the case, we need to consider the following variables:

Who are the 'agents'?

The people or stakeholders involved in a case such as this, at least, include sports product companies, organisers of sports events, players, coaches, managers, spectators, purchasers of sports products and, of course, the sports science researchers who developed the ball. We may even consider that sports companies other than Adidas have a stake here – although they did not develop the ball, it would have consequences for their future products.

What 'actions' are at issue?

Apart from watching and participating in the sport, the stakeholders listed above find employment, gain economic returns, take leisure and develop their profession in regard to this social activity. Any technological developments will, therefore, have consequences for how they engage in these actions.

What are the 'intentions' of all key stakeholders?

Given the aforementioned actions, the reasons they have for doing them include not only having fun and making money, but also advancing their career. Some may be concerned with the general cultural consequences of this development – such as whether it will change the nature of the sport in any fundamental way.

What are the 'outcomes' of the research described?

Such outcomes refer to the combined consequences of their intentions and their actions. It would be quite complex to outline all the outcomes for all the stakeholders, but to take just a few: the spectators might find the swerving ball to bring a little more unpredictability into the game and, hence, increase the excitement gained from watching. Players might perceive both the opportunities to enhance their skill range and also face the new challenge of anticipating the ball's behaviour. Researchers in other sporting spheres might be encouraged to investigate further technological changes to sporting equipment and so on.

What 'rules' apply in this case?

Developing a new technology in a sport might challenge the existing laws and customs of the game. The definitions of what constitutes a key element of the game – that is, the ball – will have been changed. It is akin to changing the regulation size of the football field. It might only result in more conversational items for the pundits – but it also might lead to considerable extra costs for the amateur sections of the game.

Where does the 'responsibility' for such consequences lie?

Clearly the product manufacturers who commissioned the work have responsibility, but so too do the researchers who agreed to take it on. Whether or not they assume or are accorded accountability for their intentions, actions and outcomes – with some assessment of the rules they claim to have followed in doing so – remains open to debate. Researchers will often say that if they had not taken the commission, then others would certainly have stepped in to take it on.

Questions such as this raise issues about the balance of interests. How can one balance the commercial interests of the football's designers, the duty of the researchers to their profession and their funders and the broader public interest (with further commercial ramifications) that is associated with a highly popular and lucrative spectator sport?

A more problematic issue is raised by the following generic question:

Is it ever ethically acceptable to investigate unethical behaviour by employing unethical means? For example, in a study of how human beings lie or deceive each other, is it permissible for researchers to lie and deceive in order to find out more about lying and deceiving?

The ramifications of such actions have been fully considered in Bok's (1979) *Principle of Veracity* in which she argues for a strong moral presumption against lying – even when you can get away with it. However, she does also allow that lying could be morally acceptable if there were 'good enough' reasons for doing it. She suggests a procedure whereby first one 'introspectively' considers the value and the dangers of deception, and then 'actively' seeks the views of a reasonable public – the latter views acting as a check on the former, introspective ones (see Fullinwider 2007).

For social research purposes and in order to come to a decision about the ethics of such a question, we might typically say: 'It depends' upon the dimensions raised earlier.

Why would we wish to do such research?

Questions of 'purpose' involve the following: What are the aims and outcomes? What is it for? What gains can we anticipate for society?

Who is doing it?

Questions of 'profession' are about who such people are, what training have they received and what allegiances do they owe to their professional colleagues to ensure they do good work? Can they be trusted? These are all issues surrounding the profession of social research.

How is the research done?

'Practice' questions express concerns over methods employed, research design and techniques for conducting research in an ethical manner.

Each of these questions might be answered in terms of degrees. There are variations in purpose or intent – from being 'just curious', through 'explaining human behaviour in general', to 'helping change aspects of human behaviour which might be damaging and hurtful to others'. There are wide variations in professional competence and views about how to organise the profession. And there are wide variations in method or research practice, some of which may be inherently more ethically acceptable than others.

Each set of issues must be considered in detail, and then balanced against each other, to establish the boundaries of ethical social research and the approach that a 'reasonable public' would find acceptable. That is what is meant by the balance of harm and benefit and what the rest of this book is about. The benefits of research must be shown to accrue to society and the groups and individuals in it – the harms must be anticipated and minimised and that may depend upon the perceived vulnerabilities of those being studied.

Any discussion on ethics reveals just how complex an area of debate it is. Wide differences of opinion, values, norms and standards emerge when ethical dilemmas are confronted. The whole field is replete with 'tensions', contradictory principles and judgement calls – there are no absolutes and rarely any simple solutions. This book cannot be as comprehensive as one would hope for two reasons – it is hard to anticipate all the ethical dilemmas that one might confront in one's research career, there will always be unexpected problems that need resolving 'on the hoof'; secondly, the societal and global moral order is in constant flux so that old customs and values might disappear, while new ones come to the forefront leading to constant change in the moral lives a researcher must confront. What I hope this book will do is sensitise the researcher to ethical issues and moral dilemmas so that they respond thoughtfully and professionally to such problems as they arise.

2
Research Rationale – Justifiable Interventions

(See page 4 of checklist.)

All human participant research interferes in some way with the lives of other human beings. Such interference may only amount to taking up an individual's time – the 'harm' caused, at the very least, requires the subject to devote some of their precious time to an endeavour that was not freely chosen or instigated by them. That is, it is a sacrifice of time given over to a researcher's goals and objectives. Or even if the research data are gathered from naturalistic observation, whereby none of a subject's time is diverted and unnaturally taken up, the publication of the findings may disturb the public perception of their sense of a 'natural' social order. If there were no research outputs, and so no other potential consequences for subjects' lives, there would be little point in conducting the research in the first place.

For such reasons alone it is regarded as appropriate that a rationale is given for engaging in the proposed research. It is a way of addressing the following question: Is this research 'necessary'; does it really have to be done; do the data already exist somewhere else and have you looked for them? In other words, is there a justification for conducting it as primary research?

A justification for conducting any proposed project is a way of demonstrating that the research will offer benefits to scientific understanding, to policy and/or to practice that make the resources spent engaging in the study worthwhile. It also offers an opportunity to clarify the benefits accruing to the research subjects or the communities or groups of whom they may be considered representative. It may, indeed, offer the subjects themselves some direct benefit.

Research goals

The contemporary concern for ethical research behaviour originated in the post-Second World War trials of Nazi war crimes (The Nuremburg

Code 1947). The behaviour of Nazi medical scientists was judged to be unethical and led to the establishment of a general agreement that the ends of research can never alone justify the means. Thus, merely wanting to understand more about human beings is unlikely to be a sustainable justification for research activity. Most social researchers will have a fundamental scientific curiosity about people and society – although the idea of substantive 'blue skies' research remains a long sought-after ideal in the social sciences. (There is little chance of commanding the sorts of funds provided elsewhere for blue skies work such as in subatomic physics.) The ethical judgement involved here has to do with whether or not 'blue skies' research with no immediately evident added value constitutes 'responsible' research activity when research resources are being competed for in terms of all the other resources needed for fulfilling other societal goals, when the pressure for relevance is high and when time and energy are also in short supply.

The possibility that there may be some form of human/communal/ societal benefit from research does act as an overarching principle. Many people will participate in research if they believe it could benefit their group, community and/or society. It might be impossible to estimate a value to society accurately assessed separately from the interests of the researcher. But perhaps the researcher is not best placed to make a judgement that balances the costs against the benefits to subjects. After all what researcher would not see some general benefit to the work in which they have invested a great deal of personal energy?

Thus, for example, if feminist researchers engage in research to fulfil an emancipatory or empowering project for women, this is likely to have an effect upon how they do that work and the outcomes of their research. Gillies and Aldred advocate 'locating research in terms of its objectives and outcomes, by fully articulating the motivating political intentions' (2002: 38). But this goes back to a seminal paper of Howard Becker's (1967) in which he advocated a very clear statement of the relationship between researcher and researched such that the goals and the anticipated consequences of research for those being studied should be very clearly stated. Becker argued that it is not that we shouldn't take sides – we inevitably will. What matters is that we make it clear, to ourselves and to others, whose side we are on (see also Hammersley 2000).

Some ethical guidelines for research with children even suggest that if the proposed research does not directly benefit the children involved or their community, then it should not proceed (Schenk and Williamson 2005: 15). If such a proscription was applied to all proposals then little research would ever get off the ground. Much research may not directly benefit the immediate research subjects but hopefully will benefit society at large and/or the particular sector that the research subjects represent.

Recently governments in 'advanced' societies have willingly financed some sectors of research above others. Health research has been well supported and subsequently made significant contributions to public health policy and, in many cases, to clinical practice and service delivery. Social research has long been supported by governments in North America and, after a period of stagnation between 1979 and 1997 due to reduced government support, recent UK governments have financed social research to a much greater extent. This may be seen as part of a trend towards 'evidence-based' policy making.

Opportunities to contribute to policy and practice from research look set to continue to grow. It is vital, then, that the contributions made by researchers are sensible, apt and valuable and any ethical problem satisfactorily resolved. Again this raises issues of the sustained responsibility of individual researchers if such an opportunity is not to be squandered. In the same way, since research knowledge/information does constitute a marketable product, outputs are subject to quality assessment, estimates of worth and value for money. Researchers in independent research agencies, for example, are acutely aware of how delays occasioned by ethical review or legal challenges prompted by ethical compromise can jeopardise the 'added-value' of research knowledge. All researchers have to face dilemmas of knowledge production such as the following: Who (agency or group) is financing the research and under what conditions? Why are they funding the work and what do they seek to gain from it?

Whatever the researchers' sector of activity (public, private or academic), there is little doubt that the research product has become an assessed determinant of career progress. For academics in universities across the world, some form of performative assessment of their research attempts to quantify this. For the private sector it has more to do with how well business accounts with commissioners are managed. In public service the research product is primarily aimed at enhancing evidence-based practice. When research success determines individual career enhancement, ethical review cannot solely lie in the hands of the researcher engaged in the project – given their personal investment in successful research products, some form of independent ethical review is seen as essential.

Does this require primary research?

In his trenchant critique of contemporary social science practice, Stanislav Andreski suggested that 'at least 95% of research is indeed research for things that have been found long ago and many times since' (1974: 11). There must, therefore, be some justification for primary research and it can be encapsulated in the answers to the following three questions:

1. Can the required information be found elsewhere?
   If the information is already available then it is unlikely there is a good, social scientific reason for 're-discovering' it. To conduct such research might disturb people unnecessarily. There may be other, political, social or cultural reasons for primary research which might be taken into account by those funding it. For example, government ministers might fund a research project that researchers know is scientifically unnecessary but the politicians believe they have to 'be seen to be doing something' and so require the research to be done. Given that researchers need to continue to earn a living they will be tempted to accept the commission since they will be paid for doing so. They might have to balance their economic survival against the need to disturb individuals by asking questions they already have the answer to within the existing research literature. The weight in the balance might be that the disturbance could be argued to be only slight – so if politicians want to spend money, and if people are not unduly disturbed, then the temptation to conduct the research is strong – particularly, if one research organisation refuses to take on the research, another might need the funding enough to accept the commission and so it will be conducted anyway.
2. Could the project be carried out as secondary research?
   If research has already been done and nothing more than a reanalysis of existing data will answer the questions set by the commissioners, then it would waste time and money to conduct new primary research.
3. Does existing research answer the research question adequately?
   Previously conducted research might not quite address the question or focus of the current research, so a modified version of the research might be necessary to adjust the focus.

If the answer to all these questions is 'No', then the project is viable as primary research. If the answer to *any or all* of these questions is 'Yes', then strong justifications must be made above for continuing to conduct this as a primary research project. If no strong rationale for primary research exists, then a rationale for a secondary research project will need to be put forward.

Secondary research

It is often assumed that secondary research raises no ethical concerns. This can be misleading and may cause even more harm than ethically reviewed primary research. Many of the assessment criteria that follow throughout this book need to be considered for secondary research and, if anything, the more latent consequences of research that does not require active participation from human subjects should be considered carefully. The nature of the data, how they were originally sourced, how they were accessed anew, handled, interrogated, shared and so on all need to be taken into account as does the dissemination of findings derived from secondary analysis.

The most notable examples of secondary research that has a potential for harm lie in historical and archival studies – and that is not just about the harm caused to the reputation of historical figures (see Box 2.1).

One might claim that the real problem with studies such as this is not that they have been conducted but that they pose consequences, when published, that could have serious effects on the lives of a distinct sector of the population in confirming the prejudices of other sectors of the population against them. (More is said about the dangers of dissemination in Chapter 12.) At this point the question might be asked of the proposed secondary research – knowing that such findings could emerge, and that the acts being investigated, even if they took place, occurred centuries ago and hence more damage can be done to a living population by such research being published – that if it were not to be published (kept secret), then what would be the point in conducting it in the first place?

Box 2.1   *Pasque di Sangue*

Ariel Toaff, professor of medieval and Renaissance history at Bar-Ilan University, published a book in 2007 titled: *Pasque di Sangue* (Easter of Blood) in which he claims a factual basis for medieval blood libels against Jews in Italy. He claims that ritual killings, and the acquisition of the blood of the victim (particularly of children), were carried out by fundamentalist Jews in reprisal for persecution of Jews. On the basis of testimony and documentary evidence he claims to have proven the centrality of the use of blood in Jewish ritual. The rabbinical response was to deny such ritual use of blood in any Jewish tradition and that the evidence used in the book was based upon testimony gained under torture.

(Flusfeder 2007)

This problem is not only related to historical or archival studies. An interesting example of contemporary secondary research analysis with ethical implications lies in the field of 'reductionist' economics. Using secondary data analysis and standard statistical analysis there has been something of a growth in the 'economics of everything' (mimicking the sub-atomic physicists' attempts at physicalist reductionism to construct a physical 'theory of everything' – see Davies and Brown 1988). The data thus produced and analysed offer evidence to suggest that there is more risk of death from eating crisps (potato chips) than from terrorism, school teachers and sumo wrestlers cheat in the same ways and for similar reasons, real-estate agents behave like the Ku Klux Klan, the economic structure of drug dealing mirrors that of fast-food chains, a fall in the violent crime rate is directly linked to an increase in the abortion rate, children run more risk of death in swimming pools than from guns and so on (Levitt and Dubner 2005; Frank 2008; Harford 2008). Whatever the merits of such analyses and the rational choice theory of human behaviour on which it is based, the potential consequences – in terms of our views on estate agents, teachers, parents, McDonald's, abortion and so on – are exacerbated by virtue of the popularity among the general public for such accounts. Fortunately not all economists are in favour of the reductionist view contained in this behavioural economics approach and warn of the dangers of such a blinkered paradigm (Marglin 2008).

Other frequently debated examples of secondary analyses with major ethical consequences include holocaust or genocide studies or studies of correlations between race and/or gender and IQ.

On the other hand senses of injustice and concern for transparency in politics and human relations can be adequate vindication for seeking fuller information about historical incidents (see Box 2.2).

Box 2.2   Kent state massacre

Four students were killed and nine others wounded when the National Guard opened fire during a student demonstration at Kent State University in the USA in 1970. The Guard always denied there had been an official order to shoot and theories about why it occurred included the idea that members of the Guard had panicked and opened fire. But an individual who was present at the time researched for 37 years and finally came across an audiotape of the event in the national archives that contained audibly clear instructions from a commanding officer to take aim and fire.

(Goldenberg 2007)

One might justify a researcher's decision to search the archives to satisfy their own attempts to make sense of a senseless act. In some respects then the discovery of 'the truth' becomes the vindication for the search. The ethical problem with secondary research is to balance that discovery against the potential that more harm than good might be brought about by reminding people of the incident. Thus it is the case that: 'Principles guide our perceptions of how to conduct ethical research ... specific circumstances and contexts inform our decisions' (Mauthner et al. 2002: 6).

In some cases conducting secondary research may even be discouraged in anticipation of the potential damage possible to contemporary concerns. The historian, Tony Judt, began researching the aftermath of the Second World War and the origins of the Middle East situation as a reaction to what he perceived to be the unbalanced coverage of both in North America. He referred to a reluctance to criticise Israeli politics as a cultural prohibition whereby 'all Jews are silenced by the requirement to be supportive of Israel and all non-Jews are silenced by the fear of being thought anti-Semitic' (Laity 2008). Consequently his work questions the received wisdom purveyed by the 'victorious' nations following World War II and has lead to him being banned from lecture circuits since it challenges Western European and US versions of history (see, for example, Judt 2005, 2008). The polemical work of Naom Chomsky has been found similarly disturbing in some circles while all such authors prize the search for an accurate reflection of historical actions and events above the 'disturbance' it might cause to contemporary politics and culture.

It is often argued that qualitative research usually implies a different form of relationship with the research subject. This relationship can be summarised under the concept of 'trust' and tends to be of a more humanistic nature than research that produces quantitative data (Miles and Huberman 1994: 292). Quantitative data analysis is at one remove from the human nature of the subject from whom it was generated. Qualitative data remain methodologically closer to the values, meaning, intentions, aspirations and goals of the human subject. In that sense they are more 'personal'. But this does not mean that those engaged in more quantitative data analysis are immune from the need to consider their trust relationship with society and with those from whom the data they are analysing was generated. Nor does it mean that qualitative data made available for secondary analysis remove the mutual 'trust' obligations implied in primary research engagements. Thus personal biographies (even if posthumously conducted and published) raise similar ethical considerations as biographical data gathering from live individuals (Roberts 2002).

Evidence-based practice?

One has to counsel caution about a phrase such as 'contributing to the evidence base' which has become something of a cliché. While researchers want to claim benefits for their activity, they are rarely in control of the use to which their findings may be put. Even government researchers do not implement the benefits of the research – that is up to politicians, policy makers and practitioners. It is here that researchers must beware of becoming hostages to fortune in the claims they make for their research outcomes if they have no control over what others do with them (Roberts 2008).

Researchers have complained about being commissioned to conduct 'unnecessary' research which a government wishes to have conducted to support its policies – and when the research fails to support a favoured policy, it might even be suppressed (Tombs and Whyte 2003). Moreover many researchers take the knowledge of their accumulated research evidence with them when they accept roles on governmental advisory committees. To assume that such evidence is necessarily 'counted' when it fails to fall congruent with government policy is naïve to say the least.

The problem with justifying research endeavours in such a way is that it assumes minimal error in findings and/or an assumption of absolute 'truth' that is rare in social science research given the complexity of the variables involved. In educational research, for example, there are many examples of research evidence being exploited to initiate and/or discontinue policies leading to considerable instability in educational systems and unnecessary stress on educators and students alike. In the UK evidence that purported to find that class size did not determine educational success led to lower public investment per pupil but was based on research that failed to take account of selection bias. In the USA a nationwide project for compensatory education that produced educational benefit for disadvantaged children was discontinued on the evidence of a faulty modelling exercise that failed to adjust for measurement error.

Once again Stanislav Andreski cast doubt on the value of social science 'evidence' some years ago: 'Possessing only a very approximate and tentative knowledge, mostly of the rule-of-thumb kind, and yet able to exert much influence through his utterances, a practitioner of the social sciences often resembles a witch doctor who speaks with a view to the effects his words may have rather than to their factual correctness; and then invents fables to support what he has said, and to justify his position in the society' (Andreski 1974: 31–2).

There is awareness of this mismatch between research findings and policy outcomes (National Audit Office 2003) and it is clear that the onus lies with researchers to ensure their work is targeted at the right individuals and agencies, that it is translatable, that it is fully and appropriately disseminated and that the research activity also explores the best means for implementation or use. Of course what then happens to the research is not entirely in the researcher's hands, but at the proposal stage, they should clearly demonstrate awareness of these principles and show understanding of the implications of their potential findings (see Box 2.3).

Social researchers may need to explore much more fully the nature of knowledge production and distribution if they are to fully understand the consequences of their work.

Box 2.3   An LSE project

There is an ongoing London School of Economics and Political Science project on the nature of evidence:

'How Well Do "Facts" Travel?' is a project investigating the transmission and reception of facts. The project looks not only at whether and how facts travel, but what happens to those facts when they travel. Do they lose or gain status? Is information scrambled, and does this work for or against the facts? What types of mechanism enable transit? The researchers from different disciplines are looking at 'facts' travelling across time, between disciplines, between academia and policy, between the lay public and the specialist professional, and in the physical sense across countries, embodied in people, spoken, written, performed and executed, or disembodied in books, diagrams, and technologies. They examine the idea of tacit and explicit knowledge, the role of 'memes' as units of cultural selection and metaphor – a way in which the language which facilitates travelling facts also affects the facts that travel and becomes constitutive of the way in which people think.

Located at: http://www.lse.ac.uk/collections/
economicHistory/Research/facts/

3
Researcher Identification – Professional Integrity and Track Record

(See page 1 of checklist.)

In recent years there has been a revival of interest in 'virtue' ethics which expresses a concern for the characteristics of goodness seen to inhere in the individual (see Baggini and Fosl 2007: 94). So this chapter deals with the 'virtues' of the researcher. The virtuous researcher is someone the public, their colleagues and their funders can trust, and as Hazlitt warned: 'Those who play the public or their friends slippery tricks, have in secret no objection to betray them' (William Hazlitt *On the Spirit of Obligations* (Beatty 1920: 150)).

Some simple guarantees of accountability can be found when the identities of researchers, their co-researchers, their supervisors or managers and those who are funding their work are transparent. This means that anyone concerned to review a project or thinking about agreeing to take part in it can make a judgement, in terms of these identities, about who they are getting involved with and how these people or organisations might be contacted if it becomes necessary.

Project identifiers help scrutineers to know which project is being referred to and this avoids confusion when complex research is conducted involving different teams of researchers. Ethical scrutiny procedures will seek a simple project name and/or code number for quick reference. A simple memorable project name also helps research subjects to remember and refer to the project they have been involved with.

If one knows who the principal investigator (PI) is then there is a first 'port of call' if questions need to be asked or if something goes wrong. But such an individual can also then be judged in terms of their previous actions, successes and failures – their 'track record'. It may also be vital to know who they, in turn, are accountable to in case the PI does not adequately meet an objection or enquiry.

Responsible researchers and managers should sign their names to the scrutiny procedure – it is the only way that their acknowledgement of their responsibility can be legally confirmed – together with the date they took this on. This might matter if further ethical issues arise at a later date in the duration of the project. In such cases additional signatures and dates might be required for formal acknowledgement of such emergent implications.

In fact, it might be necessary to repeat the questions asked during a project at different stages from its inception through to the dissemination of findings. It might seem complex but even researchers with heightened ethical awareness might benefit from continued attention to ethical details throughout the life of a project – just a simple revisit of the checklist might help to highlight an important issue that has emerged since the start of the project.

This may be particularly helpful in the case of complaints procedures. Research proposals rarely clarify how complaints can be made or the procedures available for dealing with them. This could be provided on this 'ID' page and then repeated on respondent/participant information leaflets or other appropriate *proformas*. If we truly intend to facilitate informed participation, it is vital that participants know that they can complain and by what procedure this can be done.

The individual researcher's responsibility

Whatever formal ethical review is gone through, and whatever the professional codes that apply, the ultimate arbiter of the 'correct' moral decision has to be the individual field researcher themselves. Given the need to prioritise research goals in different ways at different times, in the progress of the research only the researcher in practice knows the details about what is going on and where the research is taking them. They will be the first to notice if harm is being done or if there is a potential for harm to be done as the research progresses. Qualitative data gathering, in particular, is a 'coalface' activity. Often the individual researcher is involved in a direct relationship with the respondent or individual or group under study – either in observing them, asking questions or participating in their daily lives in some way.

Field researchers engaged in collecting and analysing data for quantitative analysis are not immune from this heightened awareness of novel ethical issues arising. As they collect data from respondents, they will already be aware of the 'data reduction' principles they are applying. Thus the response may not neatly fit the available categories and the field researcher will have to decide whether to reject or include it. Similarly they will be aware of whether or not they are putting some pressure on subjects to participate. Furthermore it may be only as they are interrogating data which make connections between various data sources that something is disclosed about a 'data subject' that might not have been apparent from each of the sources alone. Ethical choices and moral dilemmas may arise at any point during the research process and to attempt to pass the problem on to a supervisor, manager or any other agency is to evade it. The coalface researcher and/or data analyst has an insight into the effects of the research process that may not be available to anyone else.

It will become increasingly evident in working through this book and as one gains experience as a researcher that there is no simple decision-tree that one can follow to help in making ethical research decisions. This is because moral views are not 'factual' in the way that, say, methodological, clinical or administrative decisions can be weighed and based upon available evidence. Moral views are judgements that change over and through time. What was acceptable behaviour in any one group, community or society many years ago may not be acceptable now.

This means that there is rarely ever one correct solution to most ethical problems. No ethical code or set of guidelines could be devised to produce the best of all possible outcomes for all stakeholders. Trade-offs are always required. This is not to say that the balance of harm and benefit is always a zero sum transaction (that one person's gain has to be another person's loss). Rather the potential for harm must always be considered and balanced against the potential for benefit. As is fully discussed in Chapter 5 the problem is getting at the right balance of harm and benefit.

The field researcher's problem is to make a 'live' estimate whether that balance of harm and benefit is being achieved. And the judgement of the balance of harm and benefit, frequently, has to be taken in a dynamic situation. A subject of a case study with a biographical focus might, for example, initially be flattered to be asked lots of questions about their life. But as questioning persists it might become more of a burden than they had anticipated – and this might present a particular problem for someone who may already be burdened by psychological or relationship problems, an illness, excessive physical pain or disability.

In fact, it should be a central assumption of social science that human life cannot be treated as a static phenomenon. People experience life as an ongoing social process and it continues to be so even while they are being researched. What may have seemed straightforward and morally uncomplicated at the outset may turn out to be fraught with difficulty once a project is underway. The availability of detailed formal ethical guidelines and the apparently systematic process of ethical review that precedes most research these days imply a rather static view of the research act. Qualitative research is particularly characterised by 'fluidity and inductive uncertainty' (Mauthner et al. 2002: 2). Whether in surveys, focus groups or one-to-one interviews, unanticipated harm (and benefit of course) can emerge during a study when the only ethical decision-taker available is the researcher themselves. Only they can assess whether a particular set of questions is disturbing a respondent to such an extent that they cannot justifiably continue to ask them.

But researchers have no need to feel alone in coming to ethical decisions. They require the support of their employing organisation and their professional associations and, if possible, their assistance in promoting a public understanding of what good quality social research can achieve.

Contaminating the field

In some respects getting any of the ethical decisions 'wrong' can lead to a contamination of the field which has consequences for all research. So this is another arena in which the virtue of researchers must be established and maintained. Researchers have a responsibility to each other, and to ensure their own continuing career and integrity as a researcher, to prevent doing harm that will undermine future research work. It is not that they can always be expected not to make mistakes – but that genuine errors are admitted, remedied and avoided in future.

It is essential that the professional associations that cover the field of social research establish controls over the standards of their members. Scandals in social science are unlikely ever to be as traumatic as, say, those involving the unconsented post-mortem retention of children's organs. But such scandals do illustrate the taint on all research activity that is a consequence of ethically unregulated behaviour. The research field can be contaminated by many factors which include market researchers or salespeople posing as social researchers, researchers posing as clinicians or the over-evaluation of routine human interactions (such as those between patient and health professional, or between educators and students, or customers and retailers). Contamination of the field diminishes public trust in the act of research and in the actions of other researchers, thereby effectively hindering future access to respondents and undermining the value of any knowledge produced.

Another potential source for undermining public trust in social research is scientific fraud. The more serious cases of research misconduct appear to have occurred in biomedical research (see, for example, Wells and Farthing 2008). Most of these rarely come into public prominence – but it only takes a few for distrust in all research to be engendered (Smith 2006 a & b). Fraud, which includes fabrication of data and/or results, and the falsification of findings and plagiarism, is as likely to occur in social science as in any field of endeavour since the pressure to engage in such research misconduct may be due to the need to deliver commissioned outcomes on time, the pressure to publish results and career progression requirements. (See also Chapter 12 for a discussion of the consequences of fraud.)

The key principle here is that the establishment and maintenance of public trust in the profession and, consequently, in the professional depends upon responsible conduct (Dyer 2003).

The role of professional associations

The professional associations that cover the social sciences worldwide are many and varied as are their operations, obligations to and services for members and their public visibility. The ones with which I am most familiar in terms of their ethics codes and guidelines are listed in the *Useful Websites* at the end of the book.

For present purposes the function taken on by professional associations that most concerns us is the provision of these codes of ethics and guidelines for ethical practice. Those associations that hold practitioner registers or apply licenses to practice can apply sanctions that would exclude transgressor researchers from continuing to practice. Others merely operate in an advisory and informative manner, encouraging members to apply the principles as a personal obligation to maintaining the professional standards. Most professional ethical codes supply fairly generic principles which must be 'interpreted' and operationalised by the researcher in light of the substantive research topic and methodology employed. Given their pragmatic import they also cannot be easily linked to specific ethical theories. Thus no professional ethical guidelines in social science can be easily aligned with, say, a deontological or a consequentialist or a teleological theory. Pragmatic codes necessitate a form of ethical pluralism that reflects and assists 'real world research' (Robson 1993). The advocacy of ethical purism (the maintenance of any one ethical theory) is an indulgence of moral philosophers and theologians. As with all pragmatic ethical decisions, the ethical theories themselves can be seen to contradict each other in matters of fundamental principle. (This is discussed more fully in Chapter 14; see the **Short Glossary of Key Terms** towards the end of the book and Singer (1991, 2000) for discussion of the contradictory tensions in ethical theories.)

Researchers cannot claim ethical awareness unless they are familiar with the current codes and guidelines operating in their field of endeavour. There is, in fact, a wide range of such codes and guidelines across the fields, disciplines and professions of social research. They vary in design purpose and regulatory intent and outcome – although there are, necessarily, considerable overlaps in areas of concern and matters of principle. At base all codes recognise the central dilemma of ethical research – the balancing of the potential benefits to be gained with the potential for causing harm. Most codes address the questions raised in Chapter 1: What sorts of benefits are we talking about and who actually gains? What sort of harm could be caused and who might be harmed? To maintain comprehensive ethical awareness, there is much to be gained from reading the ethical codes and guidelines lying outside of one's own immediate field of research. Insights into one's own problems can be gained by exploring the problems and resolutions in other fields that one might not have imagined. For example, I read the Medical Protection Society's *Casebook*, a newsletter, which reports on the causes and consequences of medical error. From that I learned the importance of good, clear communication with research subjects and the necessity of keeping careful records of communications and decisions within securely stored case notes – for researchers these can be contained within a reflective research journal or diary.

Such sources also suggest ways of seeking mentorship from individual researchers, who have faced ethical dilemmas in the past, and from Internet discussion groups.

A major debate within the professional associations has always been about how sanctionable ethical codes or guidelines can (or should) be. What powers of exclusion, reprimand or proscription can be applied by the professional association to any member who transgresses? Some associations have constituted disciplinary committees which can exclude or punish members who bring the association into disrepute. Others believe that ethical guidelines function better in an aspirational manner or as 'educative' prescriptions – advising the researcher on proper behaviour, assisting their judgements, but ultimately leaving the individual researcher to make their own ethical choices.

It is important to note that most of these codes and guidelines are constructed on the basis of a normative prescription or a 'duty-based' as opposed to a 'rights-based' morality. Although one could conceive of an alternate guidance structure based on rights, it would be much harder to apply since rights are more difficult to define and operationalise and, in practice, are more inclined to conflict with each other (Parekh 2004). It would certainly be confusing (as it is with the current mix of rights and duties in European law) to try reconcile a 'rights' approach with 'duties' under the law, to ethics and to the profession. (The traditional UK legal system would have permitted a more open approach since it was largely proscriptive – allowing any actions to be taken as long as there was no law disallowing it. Recent UK and European Union legislation on data protection and intellectual property is prescriptive. The growing human rights legislation complicates that approach, which can be seen in the difficulty of successfully redressing grievances under any human rights legislation.) Thus no individual person has a 'right' to have their data protected. The data controller is instructed to protect data in particular ways; it is by these vicarious means that individuals are protected.

From a rights perspective it would be nice to be able to argue that the public had a right to adequate information about the social reality that we share. But that concept is so broad and so open to interpretation that it would be impossible to legislate for. As a researcher I would love to help ensure that the public were adequately informed and ethical codes and guidelines often strive to encourage researchers to take such responsibility. But researchers tend not to have much control over all the means of disseminating their findings. It would be unfair to researchers to admonish them for not getting out a message that other, more powerful interests were resistant to. (This is discussed again in Chapter 12.)

The comparison of rights-based and duty-based moralities brings out the problem of all ethical principles being in tension. The writers of codes and guidelines are constantly trying to reconcile such tensions – any right to be informed will always be contradicted by a right for data not to be disclosed. It would only take one respondent in many datasets to seek anonymity for the rest to have to be anonymised – thus restricting its availability – even perhaps for tests of validity and reliability to be conducted by other researchers. If people had rights to anonymity they might be more inclined to seek to apply them and most naturalistic observational studies could not be conducted. Thus social research in the interests of advancing knowledge – the reason we engage in this activity in the first place – would be fundamentally limited.

Codes and guidelines and the advice embodied in them need to be employed by researchers to demonstrate their professional status and to help secure the esteem of the public, research commissioners and research ethics scrutineers.

Mentorship and training

One professional device for enhancing ethical awareness is expert mentorship – the sharing of experiences and solutions to problems. Experienced researchers can aid novices in their ethical decision-making by offering mentorship and advice in response to specific issues. When confronting a difficult ethical dilemma it is always a good idea to ask colleagues how they would deal with it, or have dealt with similar problems in the past. Informal mentorship can be more open and more discursive and less concerned with exposure to formal sanctions and professional reproof. It is an opportunity to air one's errors and seek advice about procedure. Internet discussion groups can equally fulfil a useful function here since they allow some international and comparative debate to open up – disclosing different solutions in different countries and exposing the legal and moral context of the culture in which research has been conducted.

Novice and/or student researchers can represent a threat to the professional standing of social researchers if they are released into the field without adequate guidance, support and preparatory training. The increasing complexity of ethical scrutiny and research governance has led some higher education institutions to prevent students from conducting live research projects – instead rehearsing with families, friends and fellow students. This is a missed opportunity for 'learning by doing' and the professional associations could help by suggesting innovative ways for student research to be conducted in 'real' settings. One device is a form of internship whereby students accompany trained researchers on their projects, another is for student researchers to join research teams on collaborative ventures in which they are trained for and closely supervised in specific research tasks. Even if students are allowed into the field by their educational institution, they should be required to follow the same procedures as all researchers (as part of their skills training) and the research subjects should be made fully aware that the project is part of an educational programme (Sieber 1991).

Indeed professional associations may fulfil a vital mentoring role by keeping a bank of examples or case study examples of ethical decision-making which have been categorised according to different research methods, topics and subject 'types'. The UK Market Research Society makes such a repository available on their website. (See the *Useful Websites* at the end of the book for contact details.)

A more systematic maintenance of ethical standards would recommend that researchers should be required to attend training courses and continuous professional development in ethical decision-making. At the very least this could offer a way of ensuring that they have read and considered the available professional guidelines. Training would need to take place at a range of levels of experience – novices may not be able to anticipate all the kinds of things that could go wrong but more experienced researchers may suffer from complacency, the assumption that they are prepared for all eventualities and/or ignorance of the implications of new legislation.

Finding an experienced mentor and the sharing of concerns with others working in the same field is vital to seeking a balanced professional response to ethical dilemmas.

The 'standing' of the profession

The public image of the profession is a much more difficult thing to control. In some respects we are at the mercy of the mass media and politicians in this regard. But the social science professions can certainly contribute to this in many ways.

Government agencies have frequently recruited scholars and intellectuals for diplomatic and security services, but there is little doubt that, if known about, this can compromise professional integrity. For example, the CIA used to recruit from the American Association of Anthropology (AAA) on the grounds that such professionals would possess vital linguistic and cultural insights. A programme was even set up to sponsor students who would subsequently work for the security agencies (see debate in *Anthropology Today* 2004/5). This was discontinued when the Association realised that such plans 'threaten to compromise the ethical foundations of the discipline' (see *The Times Higher*, 16 December 2005: 10).

More recently the US military has employed anthropologists and social scientists during the conflict in Iraq to map what they call the 'human terrain system' (HTS) and to advise commanders on local culture and social networks. Those anthropologists who support such collaboration argue that the military can do its job better – even if that means that they are assisted in targeting the insurgents better (i.e. more effective killing of people). Others complain that this merely means supporting the US Government in conducting a bad mission better. The AAA recently formally discouraged its members from taking part (Jacobsen 2008).

One can see the temptation. Such opportunities offer professionals guaranteed secure employment at high salaries, and some may even be motivated by a sense of patriotism. The overall US governmental research budget for social science, influenced by the Pentagon, has increased substantially. The risk is of a public perception of all social scientists as potential spies and supporters of armed aggression.

As long as the researcher's profession or professional association has not been excessively maligned or seen to be corrupt, then declaring membership of a professional association can only enhance the credibility and trust assigned to the researcher. It implies the researcher abides by a professional ethical code, has received training and has avenues for open debate and sources of expert advice that can be drawn upon.

Sources of funding – relationships with funders and commissioners

The final determinant of the trust that can be accorded to a researcher and/or their research project is related to who is funding the exercise. The responsible identity and moral worth of a researcher is certainly compromised in the eyes of the public and research subjects if their work is being financed by an 'untrustworthy' commissioner. Such a perception is undoubtedly in the eyes of the beholder. Thus if participants are in receipt of welfare benefits, any research conducted for a government agency might be treated by them with suspicion – on the assumption that the research is covertly investigating benefit fraud or that their entitlement might be compromised by the disclosure of additional data. Those opposed to smoking will distrust the motives of any research funded by tobacco companies, in spite of claims to its objectivity (see Box 3.1).

Whatever one's moral judgement on the examples of military-inspired funding offered above they at least relate to funding sources within a country linked to that nation's own goals in international

Box 3.1   Dirty money

Prof. Gordon Graham (Regius Professor of moral philosophy at the University of Aberdeen) speaking at the National Conference of University Professors advocated taking 'dirty money' for research – conscience money, say, from tobacco companies whose products and/or services had been seen as damaging the public. He argued that the peer review process is the best guarantee of such influences not biasing research outcomes. He dismissed ethical codes of conduct as ineffectual in securing unbiased research.

(Fazackerley and Tysome 2004: 1)

policy. Interesting dilemmas have to be confronted when researchers accept funding from internationally proscribed regimes on the grounds that they should be allowed the 'freedom' to choose research appropriate to their own professional and theoretical interests. For example, the School of Oriental and African Studies, within the University of London, has received funding in the past both from the military dictatorship in Burma and the ultra-conservative Iranian regime (Baty 2000).

The manner in which research is commissioned, by whom and how the relationship between researchers and commissioners is managed is a key determinant of ethical practice. Social research is a highly variable service, dependent on the skills, honesty and ability to deliver of individual researchers. In the growing market for social research services the range of knowledge, expertise and the experience of research organisations and commissioners is extremely broad and varied. As with other research engagements the processing of commissioning and funding needs to be managed in as transparent and fair a manner as possible if it is to be ethical.

The Social Research Association (UK) offers an invaluable guide to good practice in this field (SRA 2002). It points out that there should not be an assumption that putting all projects out to fully open competitive tendering is the fairest and most effective form of commissioning. It can result in unproductive time and effort for all parties and does not necessarily attract the best candidates or deliver the best products. A more flexible approach is advocated which includes commissioners ensuring that they are knowledgeable about the range of skills and services available, and about the practices of research organisations and individual researchers, so that they can engage in direct and indirect commissioning – calling for bids and proposals from a reasonably select and selected group of researchers. Even unrealistic timescales and costings (both for submitting proposals and delivering results) are inherently unethical since they compromise the skills, quality and methodological flexibility that are required of professional researchers.

The secret to a good relationship with funders and commissioners is ongoing dialogue and a responsiveness to changed circumstances by all parties. The key elements of ethical concern that require caution include

- lack of clarity over the intellectual property contained with proposals as well as within findings/completed reports;
- obstructive procurement documentation and burdensome ongoing monitoring procedures (which are not usually fairly and fully costed);

- changes to specifications when contracts have been awarded and work is already in progress;
- underfunding a project which is wasteful of time and energy – poor quality results damage all reputations and waste respondents' time as well as offering unreliable solutions to commissioners' problems (budgets have to be adequate to maintain quality);
- the specification brief has to meet commissioners' needs but should not be so rigid in research design that professional judgements are restricted – the funder should not tie down methodology at the expense of the researchers' knowledge and expertise.

Occasionally research commissioners behave in an unethical manner. Researchers can only protect themselves by the careful laying down of contractual relations and obligations at the start of a project (see Box 3.2).

Box 3.2   Unethical behaviour of research commissioners

When acting in a mentoring role I was asked about how to respond when a major corporate commissioner claimed the ownership (as copyright) for the original (un-anonymised) questionnaires as part of a study of their staff attitudes that had been collected by the commissioned researcher. Obviously this constituted 'raw data' and would enable the staff and their responses to be identified individually. The commissioner threatened to sue the researchers for the data, that they would never commission work from them again and to tarnish their reputation with other commissioners. The ability of the researchers to resist such demands depended on the detail of which data, contractually, the commissioner could be said to 'own' – that is, what had been agreed between them beforehand – together with the form of confidentiality and anonymity that had been promised to the subjects beforehand (and recorded in consent forms and formal information letters to respondents); and, finally, what had been recorded as the researchers' obligations to both commissioner and subjects during the formal ethical review process.

Ultimately, if resistant, the researchers might find no work forthcoming from that quarter again – but that may not be such a bad thing. If corporate commissioners can behave in such an unethical manner once, they could always do it again.

4
Research Quality and Design

(See page 5 of checklist.)

> It may be accepted as a maxim that a poorly or improperly designed study involving human subjects ... is by definition unethical. ... In essence, the scientific validity of a study on human beings is in itself an ethical principle.
>
> (Rutstein 1972: 384)

Poorly designed research is inherently unethical since it wastes researchers' and subjects' time and energy if the results are less than useful. It may produce more disbenefits, such as a contamination of the field by discouraging participants from future research engagements, which may be of better quality. Concerns for quality represent an attention to the 'scientific' standards of the project. There is ongoing debate about how much of the research design ought to be considered as part of ethical scrutiny. Some suggest separating science from ethics while others say that is impossible. Undoubtedly there are overlaps between scientific quality, methodology and research ethics. (The consequences of this for ethical scrutiny are discussed further in Chapter 13.)

The experimental 'ideal' in research requires full control of all intervening variables and the ability to validly and reliably observe and measure pre-experimental conditions and the consequences of the research intervention – or outcomes. This is assumed to be the only way of identifying and isolating significant causal phenomena. Of course, that is neither always possible in social research, nor assumed to be 'ideal' when dealing with 'meaningful' subjects or 'unmeasurable' social phenomena. Social experiments are rare and fraught with methodological and ethical obstacles. Qualitative data gathering in particular 'sacrifices' such control desires in favour of accessing the authentic and natural behaviours and attitudes of those being studied. This means methodologically seeking not to deprive participants of their power to act as they would even if they were not being studied.

Fortunately, this is consistent with the ethical purpose of seeking not to take away the power of our subjects, to preserve their autonomy and to behave as democratically as possible in the conduct of the research. But it would be dishonest to imply that the qualitative researcher needs no power to direct the research. They will choose to adopt methods or practices that are intended to help seek answers to the set research questions and, therefore, entail some form of intervention into and direction of the lives of the people being studied.

So questions do have to be asked about precisely what methods the researchers propose using. Might such methods result in unacceptable forms of intervention in the lives of those being studied? Should a competent professional engage in research which compromises methodological principles to prevent potential harm coming to research subjects if that harm is estimated to be 'slight'? Who is qualified to make the judgement that harm might be minimal?

Concern for the rights and well-being of research participants lies at the root of ethical review. Vulnerability is a prime concern and the very young and the very old, together with those with learning difficulties are seen to be worthy of special attention. Vulnerability is linked to the problem of routinely socially excluded participants and one might ask whether or not the potential for social exclusion in research was an ethical or methodological concern (or both). Pharmaceutical trials routinely exclude the old and females – subjects are sought from young, healthy males. And yet those same drugs may eventually be prescribed to old, unhealthy females. In some respects the issue of vulnerability (see Chapter 10) may be traded off against social exclusion. If we exclude individuals or groups from research we are limiting their access to 'normal' social relations, customs and activities that the majority of the population enjoy (i.e. they should have as good a chance as any other member of a target population of being included in research). However if by including them we test their vulnerability and expose them to risks they would not otherwise have experienced, then we would be morally right to exclude them. So to reduce risks to the vulnerable, we may intentionally exclude them. The ethical point is to have good reason for doing so and not to forget, ignore or exclude them only for our convenience or because it would be too difficult to find ways to include them.

When methods are compared there does seem to be a view among some observers that there are inherently unethical procedures. Covert observation is seen by some as particularly problematic since it necessarily implies deception – yet to let people know they were being observed might result in an alteration of their behaviour. Even conventional randomised controlled trials of drugs or other health interventions depend upon the subtle coercion of 'captive' subjects – that is, patients. It is difficult to ensure that patients do not feel pressured into participation in clinical trials' research. In qualitative research it may be impossible to maintain a neat distinction between covert and overt research. Settings are often more complex and changeable than can be anticipated (Murphy and Dingwall 2001: 342).

Advances in information technology have implications for research ethics – even in qualitative research. Enhanced data archiving makes possible the recording, retaining and reanalysing of data, which has, in turn, encouraged the seeking of data retention longer than was previously thought necessary – thereby enhancing the dangers of leaking confidentiality and anonymity. Similarly enhanced data management (data fusion, matching and transfer) captures the popular imagination more than all the other concerns: 'What do they know about me? Who else could gain access to that information?' (Mauthner et al. 1998).

Appropriate designs

Asking whether a design is appropriate is the overarching research quality question since it incorporates most of all the other elements that go into making up a 'do-able' research project. In the first place it requires a clearly stated research question or questions, clarification of the aims and objectives of the research and, if possible or required of the data, a testable hypothesis. The full skills of the social research methodologist are essential here to demonstrate the worth of and/or need for the question(s) to be formed in a particular way in order to answer the set project goals. This will, in turn, depend upon the nature of the data that are available or that can be acquired, and upon the form that the data analysis will take.

All research reviewers will have seen projects that indicate the research to be of a 'qualitative' or 'quantitative' nature – when in fact such a designation must be dependent upon the nature of the data and how they can be analysed. Thus to designate a project as, say, employing 'quantitative research' methods is a misnomer – the analysis of the data may be 'quantitative' – not necessarily the means employed for gathering it. If a research project only seeks data that can be analysed quantitatively, there must be a good reason for doing so contained within the project design. Similarly data that require qualitative analysis cannot only be collected because the researcher has a preference for it. The research question and the data required to answer it must be demonstrably of that nature. Consequently there need be no absolute judgements about the relative merits of quantitative as against qualitative data analysis – the method of data analysis must be justified by the objectives lying behind the research, the most appropriate means of analysing the data and how the findings will be used (see Bryman 1988).

So the techniques of data collection, sampling and so on must be clearly appropriate to the methods adopted. To illustrate: one question that is invariably asked to test the rigour of a research design is the size of the population sample and how it will be selected. There is often an implicit status judgement that random samples are superior to convenience samples due to the level of inference and the assumed quality of the statistic that can be employed with different forms of sample selection. But all samples are really 'samples of convenience' – the issue has to do with preventing the 'inconveniences' of sampling from impeding the collection of the appropriate data. Thus a street social survey taking a random sample must, once the randomising criterion has been established (every 'nth' person being questioned), not choose to avoid the 'nth' person if they happen to be disabled (see Chapter 10). Similarly it makes no sense to randomise a sample for a phenomenological study of what it means to be disabled – the design should ensure that the rationale for a 'purposive' selection of disabled people fitting a theoretically justified category is made.

Another common poor quality indicator that research reviewers will have come across is the announcement within the proposal that the data will be subject to computer-assisted analysis using, say, SPSS (for quantitative data) or NVivo (for qualitative data). What they omit is to explain 'how' the analysis will be conducted: What coding frames will be applied? How are emergent categories to be developed? What procedures for data reduction will be adopted? What techniques of statistical description, inference or correlation will be employed? And so on. (Moreover the producers and distributors of both programmes would be keen to point out that neither precludes the application of the alternative form of data analysis.) Without such information it would be hard to judge whether the methods of data analysis were appropriate.

Literature search and systematic review

All research, whether primary or secondary, must demonstrate the ways in which it builds upon or adds to existing research findings. Only by doing this can the rationale for conducting the current project be justified. Primarily for reasons of 'quality' then researchers must demonstrate that, by conducting an 'adequate' exploration of the literature, they can show the need for conducting the current study and the remaining research questions that it is worth seeking the answers to.

Searches and reviews of existing research literature can vary widely in 'systematicity'. While a stroll through the stacks and perusal of the spines in a well-stocked library is still a delight and a source of serendipity to old-fashioned researchers like myself, its ad hoc nature is no substitute for the methodical and rigorous, step-by-step procedural search for information relating to the topic under study. Such procedures can be more or less protocol-driven and standardised methods are now advocated throughout the social and natural sciences. The terms 'narrative' and 'systematic' are used to differentiate the extremes in this range of systematicity but these should be treated with caution. A narrative review adopts a different presentational style but need be no less rigorous and comprehensive than a systematic one. And if systematic reviews make incorrect or incomplete assumptions, they can be even more distorting of information on the grounds that they appear more objective (see Popay et al. 2006).

Health and biomedical research has systematised this process in the form of agencies designed to source and compile secondary research data for efficient access: the Cochrane Collaboration, the National Institute for Clinical Excellence (NICE) and the Health Technology Assessment (HTA) programme of the National Health Service (NHS) offer some examples. To some extent this is replicated in a range of social science data archives (see Chapter 9).

'Scientific and ethical justification for new clinical trials requires them to have been designed in the light of scientifically defensible assessments of relevant previous research' (Clarke et al. 2007: 187). But not all medical research does that even now and 'just because systematic reviews are popular, it does not mean you can take their content as gospel' (Jefferson and Zarra 2007: 180). They have to be read just as carefully and critically assessed in the same way as any research paper.

So there are dangers in an uncritical acceptance of this approach and in its further formalisation in meta-analysis.

'Meta-analysis is a quantitative approach to integrating findings from a set of related studies. It introduces a level of scientific rigor to the review process that limits bias and reduces random error in the selection, critical appraisal, and synthesis of published information relevant to an important clinical or research question' (Adèr and Mellenbergh 1999: 323).

But even this definition reveals the problems with meta-analysis, which may lead reviewers into assuming that it is necessarily more objective and its findings statistically more significant. The criteria upon which the review is conducted may contain inherent biases. For example, many clinical trials are excluded as valid evidence in a systematic review on the grounds that they have not been 'blinded' or randomised. Thus, many studies that may contain valuable information are treated as not of value since they did not employ a randomised controlled trial (RCT). Notice too the importance of published studies – since most studies with negative findings are hard to publish (see Chapter 12), the meta-analysis distorts by only summarising positive results. More fundamentally, the statistic applied to test the significance must be used with caution on the grounds that the 'samples' from the accumulated studies are treated the same as any other sample and therefore generalisable to a total population when the samples necessarily have been drawn from different populations, in different geographical locations and over lengthy and not necessarily equivalent periods of time. So the retrospective nature of the data and any limitations of the data sources in each of the individual sources must be recognised (Adèr and Mellenbergh 1999: 322).

It has been argued that cumulative meta-analysis can prove to be of great ethical benefit in discouraging further or ongoing work that is unsafe or unnecessary on the basis of the accumulated evidence of a series of trials. Each trial on its own might not have provided sufficiently significant evidence, but once pooled with others, the weight of evidence could be enough to justify discontinuance. But this approach too must be treated with caution on the grounds that large studies tend to dominate and small studies that disagree with large ones beyond the level of chance tend to be ignored and not even published, hence further distorting the accumulated findings. A solution could be more collaborative work between teams of researchers and a greater willingness to share data – one would have good grounds for treating such cooperative endeavours as productive of more robust evidence (Giles 2008: 44–5).

In spite of these caveats quality researchers must demonstrate their awareness of current evidence and the ways in which the current proposal will add to the present state of knowledge. To replicate unnecessarily existing studies would, again, be wasteful of time, money and energy. It does not mean that replication is never justified – the grounds for doing so must be made clear such as changes in the situational context leading to the existing data being outdated, or errors in the existing research subsequently coming to light or the need to replicate the research in successive historical periods, or alternative geographical or cultural locations for comparative and/or longitudinal analysis.

Risks to successful completion

As a quality measure of insight into their design and methods researchers are usually asked to show the ability to anticipate the threats to successful completion of a proposed project. The most basic threat to completion is an inadequate budget. This can include the omission of some key items in the budget that should have been seen as clearly essential to the design. If specific validated and copyrighted questionnaires are to be included, is there a charge for their use and how much is it? Has enough been allowed for postage of questionnaires, return postage and inevitable follow-ups to increase response rate? Or has enough been allowed to cover travel and accommodation expenses? Even desk research can consume finances – while some of this might be treated as overheads (heating, lighting) others might be additional fees for accessing key databases. The point is that quality research proposals have clear itemised budgets that attempt to allow for every realistic eventuality.

The same can be said of realistic timescales. A researcher that claims completion within an evidently difficult-to-achieve time is as suspect as one who underfunds the project. Establishing realistic project timetables requires demonstrable skills in project management and some evidence of this quality may be provided by skilled design and application of conventionally applied project management charts and programmes.

Only answers to these sorts of questions can convince that there is a reasonable prospect of a project achieving its stated aims/objectives.

Experimental design in social research

It is perhaps ironic that the RCT remains the 'gold standard' in biomedical research when such experimental interventions are looked upon rather suspiciously in social research. Much like the view that covert research is inherently unethical, there is a view that experiments entailing social interventions are similarly questionable activities. Some of this goes back to a tradition in social science that questioned the emulation of the natural sciences' presumed ability to 'predict and control' and the consequent critique of social engineering. But it is also expressed as disquiet over social inclusion and exclusion.

The problem is usually formulated in terms of the delivery of potentially beneficial interventions to the experimental group necessarily dis-benefitting the control group. Crossover trials do not immediately solve the problem since sensed relative deprivation may have already been established and with many beneficial interventions, they may come too late to prevent some absolute deprivations in the control group. Other issues for consideration in an ethical review of an experimental design include how the randomisation is conducted and how participants in both groups (experimental and control) are given information about their part in the project – for 'true' experiments information might have to be tightly controlled. In fact it is likely that most social experiments to be of any value are likely to be field experiments and quasi experimental in design.

The chequered history of social experiments goes back to the Hawthorne studies of the late 1920s and 1930s and their durable notoriety in the continued critical use of the phrase the 'Hawthorne effect'. In fact there were many Hawthorne effects from which subsequent investigators learned. Putting to one side the multiple design flaws, the lessons for ethical research have to do with the subjects' awareness of their being observed enhancing the information they received but producing a 'subject reactivity' such that their behaviour could not be considered 'normal' – hence undermining the value of the entire endeavour. It is also quite ironic that another major criticism was of the developing friendship and therapeutic relationships between researchers and subjects – something actually encouraged within the project team on ethical grounds, and in terms of the quality of the responses then received. During the 1940s, 1950s and 1960s this was perceived as lacking rigour and a source of empirical error, while the growth of feminist research methodologies from the 1980s has led to a rethinking of the value of sustained researcher/researched relationships as part of a critique of experimental methods in general (see Madge 1965; Oakley 2000, Chapter 11).

Most recent social experiments have been conducted in the area of social policy research – evaluating the effectiveness of interventions with, say, service user groups. A remaining concern is that although assuming control, recognition and isolation of intervening variables can be accurately accomplished, this is seen as heightened aetiological

Box 4.1   Participation issues

An experienced research group was conducting a social experiment for a trial intervention of a novel social services programme. They decided that participation on the programme/intervention for service users was conditional on participating in the research; in other words, if a person withdrew from the research, they would no longer receive the programme. They were free to withdraw at any time but this had the consequence of them no longer receiving the intervention.

Their argument was that since they did not know if the programme would work or not, to withdraw from it may or may not have had adverse consequences for the subject. They also planned to collect information for the research that would be useful for the service provider, and even move to a situation where the information they routinely collected for service needs would help tailor the intervention. But this would imply that if a subject chose not to contribute the requested information, the programme could not be delivered properly. They also compared this with the view that being offered a new drug in pharmaceutical trials is conditional on the patient participating in the trial.

evidence, the processes by which successful outcomes achieved are not necessarily clarified. That is, we may be able to demonstrate 'that' something works but not precisely 'why' it works. For such reasons experiments might better be employed in the pilot stages of research with more in-depth processual analyses conducted later.

Hence there are few true experimental research designs in social science. When they occur, they are likely to be pragmatic field trials somewhat akin to the drugs trials adopted by pharmaceutical companies testing new drugs (see Box 4.1).

There is some similarity between a social experiment of this sort and a pharmaceutical trial. It would be reasonable to assume that since this is a novel intervention, whether or not it has an 'effect' (positive or negative) is presently unknown – this means that, until the completion of the trial, whether one is receiving beneficial or damaging service cannot be assessed; so one may not be 'depriving' anyone who withdraws from the study of anything that could benefit them. (One may even be allowing them to remove themselves from further potential 'harm'!) This resembles normal drug trials procedure – the subject resumes 'normal treatment' (i.e. what they were receiving before the trial or what they would have received were it not for the trial) and in the social experiment they would be receiving the original service, without the novel intervention.

There is a danger in mixing service audit with experimental work due to data protection issues. Routine data collection (within the terms of the Data Protection Act) is an 'expected' cost of participation in any government service provision. The 'penalty' to the client/research subject for withholding such information can be seen to be 'reasonable'. That is, non-compliance with the accountability/service requirements of the social services agency might entitle the agency to withdraw the provision.

Ethical social research requires that the research intervention is kept separate from the normal audit requirements of the social services. If audited data are to be used for secondary research in a non-anonymised manner, the permission of the service user/research subject is required. If the research intervention is seen as an addition to normal service delivery, then the service user can be treated as a voluntary participant. But, as above, the consequence of withdrawal from the study must be made clear to them – this means they must be just as entitled to 'normal service provision' as they were prior to agreeing to participation in the trial.

But the pharmaceutical comparison does not fully hold since it is not strictly true that the offer of a new drug is dependent upon willingness to take part in a trial. If the new drug has already been fully trialled, then the decision to use it is a 'negotiated' one – between physician and client, and between physician and health service funding agents. During a trial the patient should not be able to know if they are actually receiving the drug or a placebo, and/or the 'conventional treatment' if there is one – neither, of course, is the physician supposed to know this if the trial is properly 'double-blinded'. If a patient withdraws from such a trial, they will neither be receiving the new drug nor the placebo (or 'standard treatment') all of which depends upon the trial design – once again they should then be entitled to receive normal treatment which is what they would have received prior to entry into the trial. A great deal then depends on the nature of the formal health service obligations of the country in which the trial occurs.

Overall the social experiment as proposed above can be considered ethically sound as long as the participants are fully informed of all their options prior to agreeing to participate.

Researchers' competence

Whether or not a researcher has adequate skills or competence can be a rather subjective judgement. But some categories of researchers do need to have more detailed questions asked about their ability. And there are many sources of evidence on which to base such a judgement.

The student/trainee researcher immediately raises a concern. Students must appreciate the importance of conducting well-designed, useful research. Trivial, foolish or ill-designed research could prove a waste of people's time and may be damaging in other respects. It may be appropriate for undergraduates to do research on small samples from which little could be generalised since the major purpose of the exercise is educational. But quality remains an issue and so good design still requires clear research questions, aims, objectives and intended outcomes – including an estimate of the perceived value of the research.

The amateur social researcher could pose much more of a problem. Amateur researchers challenge the status of the independent researcher and threaten a form of deskilling implying this is something that 'anyone can do'. These may include mature individuals trained in other disciplinary backgrounds who assume they already have the skills to conduct social research – such as thinking that there is nothing much to constructing a questionnaire, say, or interviewing people. The achievement of having conducted research over many years but in other fields should not be enough qualification. Once again their precise training in the proposed method or clear evidence of appropriate continuing professional development would help. Training might be given in a specific technique – which would constitute evidence of a particular skill but not evidence of widespread ability to design comprehensive social research projects. Enhancing the 'research-awareness' of practitioners in other disciplines is fine – but it may not be enough to guarantee quality outputs. In other fields such as nursing, medicine, psychology and so on the solution has been to license practice. It has rarely been considered for social research (see Springall 2002).

All of this means it is not enough simply to provide a generic curriculum vitae (CV) or career résumé to demonstrate competence and ability to conduct a specific project. CVs will need to be targeted to the project in hand to reflect the ability to conduct it. The researcher's track record in contracting, designing and delivering completed research projects that are disseminated effectively acts as a reasonable indicator of quality. It is one of the reasons that the citation indices for a researcher's work are valued. It is also why peer review is recommended – the judgement of other respected and expert independent commentators can be a guide to a researcher's ability to deliver quality products and services. However both citation rates and peer review can be misleading as indicators of quality (see Chapter 12) with citation measures being challenged with regard to their validity and reliability, while the true independence of peer reviewers may be doubted. More importantly neither track record alone nor a researcher's presumed authority in a field is an adequate guarantor of quality.

One aspect of researcher competence that may be overlooked is in the threats to quality arising from any subcontracted work and/or use of minimally trained fieldworkers. Most research managers will be well aware of fieldworker syndicates that form to take tea in a nearby café if the weather is inclement, while they take turns to role play for each other the respondents required to meet their daily quota. Any subcontracting over which the researcher loses control can undermine the value of an entire project and so is unethical. Ensuring commitment and motivation from freelance researchers or fieldworkers requires they are treated well financially and administratively and trained to the capacity needed for them to inculcate the culture of the research organisation on ethical matters as well as research quality – on understanding the sensitivities, vulnerabilities and capacities of research subjects that are covered throughout this book.

A quality proposal

A clearly written protocol is the first indicator of rigorous research. The stages in the research project will be clearly flagged together with the precise ways in which each of the elements in the research question will have been addressed. Such protocols contain clear justifications for the steps and actions, for the time taken to achieve each of the essential tasks, when the 'deliverables' might be expected and in what form they will appear. (A suggested protocol *Template for Research Proposals* is offered towards the end of the book.)

Some reviewers appear to be nitpicking about typographical errors, poor spelling and confusing syntax appearing in a proposal. This might seem trivial but their point is that the general public might see some of the products of this proposal and so the professional image might be contaminated: 'Can they not even spell correctly?' And rightly or wrongly reviewers might view carelessness in the presentation of a proposal as indicative of carelessness in other aspects of a researcher's work: 'If they can't take the trouble to proofread, can they be trusted to genuinely "care" properly for other people's personal data?' So taking care with the proposal may act as a more general indicator of being able to 'take care' with other aspects of the research.

In answering all the above questions raised in this chapter satisfactorily there may be some confidence that at least the design of the research has done all that is possible, within the limits of its methodology, to minimise harm to all participants – to have thought through the consequences of adopting each of the elements of the proposal. It sometimes means sacrificing methodological purity in order to minimise harm. For example, while covert participant observation may be theoretically justified in order to access the information essential to answering a research question, the potential disturbance to subjects' lives might be to such an extent that a compromise methodology must be selected.

In practice, the particular skills required in seeking qualitative data include balancing the control necessary for systematic and rigorous observation against allowing genuine attitudes to be revealed and the behaviour of interest to occur naturally. In this instance what is assumed within so-called qualitative theoretical perspectives neatly meets ethical requirements – it requires that researchers don't interfere too much. The problem is how to do that in practice and ensure that the required data are actually generated – we cannot wait around forever for people to authentically reveal their views and/or spontaneously engage in the behaviour of interest. Many research methods are precisely designed for the attitudes, knowledge and behaviour to be generated when the researcher is around to collect them.

On the face of it the nature of the data sought and generated for quantitative data analysis implies minimal interference in subjects' lives. But whether or not the collection, analysis and reporting of such data result in minimal interference can only be a retrospective judgement.

In all cases the researcher of quality is one that can judge the best balance between the data that are necessary to be generated in order to properly answer the research question against the prospect that the gathering and reporting of such data could result in 'measurable' harm to the research subjects. Justifiable design adjustments to minimise the potential for harm can still produce high quality research – but it takes a competent researcher to do that.

5
Minimising Harm, Maximising Benefit

(See pages 6, 7 and 8 of checklist.)

The heart of ethical scrutiny is the attempt to balance the risk of harm against the potential for benefits that can accrue to individuals, groups, communities, organisations and even societies from research participation. Consideration has to be given to the different kinds of harm, the likelihood of their occurrence and the ways in which they can be minimised. Concurrently ways of maximising both short and long-term benefits have to be explored (see Box 5.1).

Box 5.1   Milgram's experiments

Stanley Milgram's 'obedience to authority' experiments were conducted at Yale University commencing in 1963. Subjects were ostensibly recruited to participate in a study of memory. They were told they were to be 'teachers' and to administer a series of electric shocks of increasing strength to 'learners' whenever the latter made mistakes. The 'learners' were, in fact, actors who were instructed to emit audible signs of discomfort, extreme pain and agony according to the intensity of (mock) electric shock delivered by the 'teachers'. The 'teachers' who were the actual (duped) subjects were encouraged to continue increasing the punitive shocks by the experimenter who merely said: 'The experiment requires that you go on.' whenever the subject expressed concern for the degree of punishment being meted out. The surprising finding was the degree to which the subjects continued to obey the experimenter's instructions, despite the apparent signs of pain and distress evidenced by the 'learners'. And, in spite of the 'teachers' expressed concern given the 'learners' pleas to discontinue and their audible (mock) screams,

62 per cent of the instructors obeyed the experimenter's requests to the limit – sometimes delivering a size of electric shock that could have lead to the death of the 'learner'. Milgram wished to challenge the widely held view at the time that one could explain the mindless obedience which produced the atrocities of the Second World War by the socialisation processes which produced an 'authoritarian personality'. Instead he sought to demonstrate that such destructive obedience could be context-dependent and any rational human being could abandon their moral precepts and find themselves committing atrocities if the situation was persuasive enough. He felt these experiments vindicated his viewpoint. But the subjects' suffering (i.e. the 'teachers') was the main grounds for ethical concern, since the study revealed to them a capability they would never have thought of themselves. Even after considerable debriefing some of the subjects required extensive counselling and claimed that their lives had been damaged irreparably.

(see Milgram 1965, 1974; Slater 2004)

An extreme study such as Milgram's reveals the potential in all research to leave subjects with some long-term harm when the research brings out something in the subjects that they were not even aware of themselves. The offer of long-term Freudian psychoanalysis could not compensate for the damage that may be done.

Roger Sapsford (1999: 41) quotes the feminist scholar Shulamit Reinharz who likened researchers as engaged in the process of rape given their intrusion into their subject's privacy and when they 'disrupt their perceptions, utilise false pretences, manipulate the relationship and give little or nothing in return. When the needs of the researchers are satisfied they break off contact with the subject' (Reinharz 1979: 95). In part this may be due to an attitudinal problem with researchers and how they reveal that to their subjects. In brief encounters field researchers may have to collect a rapid response from many subjects – but they could still strive to adopt a demeanour that leaves the respondent feeling valued. In longer term encounters the researchers may wish to repair to their study to add the data and continue their analysis, while the subject may need some 'closure' time and some opportunity to come to terms with a relationship that appeared to have friendship at its core but was, in effect, highly instrumental.

Varieties of harm and distress

Researchers have to be aware of the range of ways in which their activities can cause distress to others – even in ways that might seem surprising to themselves. To seek someone's opinions merely because they fit a category of 'elderly person' could lead to their lowered self-esteem. One can never anticipate the emotional effects an apparently innocent question can have and which might even catch the respondent by surprise. Again questions which a researcher considers harmless or uncontroversial may cause embarrassment to a respondent – particularly so if they were not expecting such a question. It can be quite upsetting for people to have their ignorance publicly revealed simply by being asked a knowledge-testing question. The more so if it is the kind of question 'anyone should know the answer to'. Questions carelessly framed subtly show disrespect for respondents by placing them in such embarrassing situations.

Misperceiving the purpose of the research could raise false expectations about something being done, say, to 'solve' a problem facing a community. This might be connected to subjects failing to understand the nature of the commissioning and reporting process and how research evidence becomes the property of the commissioning and funding body – it might not be in the interests of such agencies to effect the change the respondents might have been hoping for. Hence there is a responsibility on the part of the researcher to make clear the limits on action that can be taken as a consequence of conducting the research.

Psychological distress might be more likely to be a consequence of social research than physical harm or illness, but the dangers of physical exertion in, for example, standing too long to answer a street survey or eye strain caused by a lengthy Internet questionnaire must be considered. (Simple things like attention to colour and font size can help alleviate the likelihood of the latter discomfort.) Evidently the physical harm is unlikely to be equivalent to any biomedical intervention and so may be harder to anticipate – it nonetheless needs to be guarded against.

Sometimes it is equally difficult to identify the social harm that might be consequent on participating in research. The time taken to invest, say, in attending a focus group or a citizens' panel or jury may lead to participants being unable to attend a regular social event in their community or family which is vital to their acceptance and/or status within that community. In such cases they would have to be assisted in recognising the consequences to them of their 'sacrifice' of time. Worse still some communities might ostracise an individual who had taken part in research which they might perceive to have put their own access to services and/or facilities at risk. Other social harms are much more diffuse. For example, merely by deciding to research some topics and subsequently reporting them brings them into public prominence and either encourages the 'spread' of the practices being investigated or produces an adverse societal reaction to a marginal group who wished to be quietly allowed to get on with their marginal or socially deviant activity since it was doing no harm to others. Thus studying and reporting drug users and their techniques endows them with some quasi legitimacy and may even encourage others to try drugs. Bringing glue-sniffing forward as a topic of attention gives it some notoriety and excitement that might be appealing to certain types of adolescents.

The most common economic deprivation to be suffered by research participants is their giving of 'free' time. This is frequently compensated for with cash gifts or vouchers – all of which may have consequences for the receipt of welfare benefits. Other unanticipated potential harms may come from employers who are unhappy about their employees taking part in a research study that may turn out to be critical of their employment practices. The participants' very livelihood could thereby be put at risk.

The legal consequences of research participation are likely to inhere in the respondents offering information that implicates them in illegal activity or discloses their involvement in criminality.

All of these harms can arise out of participation while others may be consequent on certain categories of people being excluded. If a research project fails to explore the situation of illegal immigrants in employment, for example, by excluding such subjects on the grounds of protecting their anonymity and fearing legal obligations to disclose their identity, the true facts of their situation may fail to be disclosed and the production of policies designed to resolve their situation thereby impeded.

Minimising harm

Having research subjects participate in the research design and in advising about the dissemination of findings may protect researchers from the charge of not adequately attempting to anticipate the harms that may come to them as a consequence of participation. That in itself is no guarantee of their subjects' protection since subjects may be no more able to anticipate some harms than researchers are able to do. (Moreover there are additional difficulties associated with encouraging subject participation that are addressed in Chapter 11.)

But risk of harm can be reduced by thinking through the consequences of the varieties of distress listed above. Psychological distress can be minimised by debriefing subjects after the research is completed to reassure them about the value of their contribution and also acquainting them with appropriate counselling support. For physical damages or discomfort the possibility of reparation via insurance indemnity schemes should be prepared for.

Ways of showing respect for research subjects can be subtly embedded in both the content of research questions and the manner in which they are delivered. The potential for social distress can be minimised by controlling the dissemination of research findings in ways that do not lead to community concerns about the contributions made by individual participants. Careful selection and use of language while conducting the research, ethnic and gender matching between researchers and subjects can all contribute to minimising communal consequences for individuals. Individuals might be just as culturally sensitive as they are personally, so similar care should be taken over cultural differences – this in itself requires considerable awareness for what such cultural sensitivities might be.

Material costs and economic disadvantage can be compensated by monetary incentivisation of some kind (see Bacon and Olsen 2003), while unwanted legal ramifications can be guarded against by seeking immunity from prosecution in collaboration with police authorities – something which is routinely arranged if conducting the research is in the interests of crime prevention and detection.

Maximising benefits

Tacit benefits cannot be assumed to be understood and accepted by all. They might have to be indicated anew with each project proposal and for each new scrutiny committee. Benefits from social research accrue differentially to individuals, groups, organisations and society. Currently there appears to be general cultural acceptance that enhanced scientific knowledge can contribute to the community and society if the accumulated evidence is sensibly applied (as discussed in Chapters 1 and 2). The breadth of the social gains is difficult to measure, may not be self-evident and so must be argued for. Social science has undergone fluctuations in its popularity being largely dependent upon government funding for its survival as a force behind policy formulation and, in turn, as a profession worth pursuing in higher education. Its popularity in North America has been due to continued recognition of the value of social science in both business and government circles since the 1940s.

The fortunes of the social research professions in the UK took a downturn with the Conservative Government from 1979 to 1997. The size of European Commission funding across the continent of Europe has boosted its recognition and the extent of the contribution that can be made to building an evidence base by virtue of improved comparative value. In a negative climate 'proving' the value of one's endeavours can be a daunting task. The generic pursuit of valued 'scientific progress' can be claimed and clarified to gain the support required and the understanding of the general public.

Such support and understanding also comes out of social science education being fully incorporated into all stages of the formal curriculum. For example, citizenship education requires an evidence base that draws extensively on social science. The research processes adopted in many professions is heavily derivative of social science research – such as in nursing, education and the whole range of allied health professions. Similarly business, advertising, media, marketing and so on all draw on the evidence generated by social science methods.

Many social research projects explicitly address government policy and service delivery needs benefiting both communities and individuals. From merely participating in a study community groups and individuals can receive benefits. Study participants often express their personal gains from the opportunity to air concerns. This may be the potential catharsis from sharing problems with independent observers, or from the feeling that by contributing to a project their interests may be more accurately represented to government or service agencies.

It is a researcher's responsibility to detail the steps taken to avoid or minimise harm and to maximise benefits. Some overall judgement will then have to be made about the anticipated benefits of the project outweighing the (unknowable) but *estimated* potential for harm. If ways of reducing the potential for harm and/or maximising the benefit cannot be identified, then doubts as to whether to continue the project have to be raised. Similarly if the balance of harms over benefits is seen to increase during the lifetime of the project, the ethical researcher should consider discontinuing the work. (This might not be inevitable since the discontinuance itself devalues the contributions already made by the research subjects. Discontinuing could be wasteful of resources, energy and commitment and so could be unethical.)

The only realistic way for researchers to conduct an assessment of this balance is to adopt a continual reflexive stance in order to conduct an ongoing estimate of harms and benefits and make both research and personal action judgements accordingly (Gokah 2006).

6
Selecting, Recruiting, Retaining and Releasing Participants

(See page 9 of checklist.)

The relationship with research subjects must be carefully managed and controlled at each stage of the research process. This means thinking about how subjects are chosen and encouraged to join a research project, how they are encouraged to remain in the project for the duration and how their withdrawal from a project is facilitated. The key questions include the equitable selection of subjects, resisting placing undue pressure on them to join and, equally, avoiding undue pressure in discouraging them from leaving. Awareness of systematic inclusion and exclusion of specific socio-demographic categories for reasons that are not linked to research design must be maintained and such systematic distortions avoided. The designed research focus may allow for the exclusion of certain categories of respondent – if so this must be achieved in as open and transparent a manner as possible. There may be explicit benefits accruing from being included in a research project, and these should be made clear at the outset – just as warning about disbenefits is essential.

Accessing participants and negotiating the research relationship

'Who' to access is largely a problem of choosing the most appropriate sample from the population and so is predominantly a methodological issue. All samples are, in fact, chosen more or less for convenience and/or purposively – even when randomised. But 'how' people are accessed for research purposes remains both a practical and an ethical problem. It is hard to separate issues associated with accessing participants in the first place, reaccessing them as part of a continuing study and remaining unimpeded in that access from 'gatekeepers' who may seek to control what participants may actually contribute to the study.

Attempts to conduct qualitative research on residents in older people's care homes offer telling examples of such difficulties. Older people might not fully understand what is required of them and the sustained nature of a commitment to participate. Those caring for them might be sensitive to the older people's comments and, as a consequence, being able to interview them alone and without the respondents' concern for what their carers might think they are saying could influence the honesty with which they participate and raise a myriad of connected ethical concerns (Fisk and Wigley 2000).

Awareness of the balance of power between researcher and researched is vital. This may be even less clear in qualitative research studies (Murphy and Dingwall 2001: 344). Making oneself available for study implies a loss of power in even allowing a researcher into one's life. The focus of the relationship is determined by the researcher's criteria, not by the research subject – otherwise the relationship would not exist. By their interpretation and representation of their subjects' lives, researchers are necessarily maintaining or challenging those subjects' location in the social hierarchy (Becker 1967).

To some extent exploitation of the subject is inevitable. People, opportunities, situations and meaningful spaces are all exploited to derive the 'rich, deep data' that are sought in qualitative research (Birch and Miller 2002). The establishment of rapport is an accomplished research skill and even friendship can be faked as part of the management of consent and the encouraging of continued participation. Even survey interviewers are trained to accomplish rapport in order to maintain response rates. And there is a danger that researchers may expose themselves to unwanted personal consequences if they disclose too much about themselves as a rapport-generating strategy (Duncombe and Jessop 2002: 118–19). However, while there is a sense in which friendship is necessarily implied in the establishment of rapport and the development of trust, it is important to remember that the relationship is one of 'formal informality'. In all likelihood the relationship would not have existed without the need for one party to secure a research goal. There is a danger in the researcher seeking to avoid exploiting the subject to such an extent that no research goals are accomplished – that would be a waste of everybody's time!

The negotiating of the research relationship particularly needs addressing by, say, health researchers who are also practitioners, or by researchers working for governmental or public agencies which also have service delivery/social policy duties. The disclosure of a practitioner status to participants is likely to have methodological consequences. Respondents may say and do different things for researchers they know to have other professional or legal obligations. Health and care workers conducting research might be perceived as having more power in the research relationship than if they had not been practitioners. Those conducting research on behalf of the police or welfare benefits agencies face even more problems if they are also police or welfare officers themselves. Ensuring participants have, and perceive themselves to have, adequate power to determine their role in the research is ethically necessary to the implementation of all the following considerations. This is a particular problem for children, old people and those with learning difficulties – all who may perceive themselves as possessing less power in ordinary relationships anyway.

As it is many respondents assume that researchers are necessarily agents of 'the authorities' and may only reveal such information as they wish those presumed authorities to know. So researchers who are, in fact, conducting projects on behalf of such authorities have a tricky balance to maintain: garnering such information as is required by the focus of the research without being 'duped' by the subject or by misleading the subject as to the potential value of the research in return.

Securing compliance

Finding and securing respondents, participants and interviewees for research projects raises the primary ethical concern of 'compliance'. Did subjects feel obliged to participate in any way? Were deceptive or unreasonable methods adopted to ensure a reasonable response rate? If subjects are reluctant to participate, what can legitimately be done to encourage their response? Many research ethics codes and guidelines warn against applying 'undue pressure' to recruit and to retain subjects. There is though an ethical judgement to be made about how much pressure is 'undue'. In some respects it might be best if the subjects could be the final arbiter of that; however, if they were able to be so, then the pressure can hardly be said to be excessive – one more dilemma in the moral minefield.

Researchers are often trained in appropriate language for securing compliance and certainly learn a lot when doorstepping about 'encouraging' people to respond in order to maintain a reasonable response rate. Such skills largely rely upon a combination of verbal/rhetorical techniques together with more subtle non-verbal communicative resources. Having an interviewer attempt to 'persuade' a subject to answer questions in a face-to-face or telephone interview setting cannot in itself be regarded as coercion – it happens all the time with cold-call marketing. Indeed standard interviewer instructions will offer guidance on how to convert the initially reluctant into respondents, plus the standard practice on reaccessing some refusals for possible conversion into a response. The legitimacy of such approaches can only be called into question when the subject 'feels' forced into compliance. So mechanisms need to be available for a subject to report such concerns. It might be a testimony to the compliance skills of a researcher more than active willingness to participate that secures a high response rate – and without excessive complaints being made we would never know.

Techniques for maintaining response rates and gaining access to respondents can raise some surprising ethical dilemmas.

If research subjects do not want to make themselves 'accessible' then – in accordance with the basic principles of research ethics – there is little a researcher can do about it. It may seem ironic that researchers do not like being researched – but that remains their privilege, as it is for any other member of the population.

The problem is that research subjects may not value a project as much as the researcher themselves does. In the case illustrated here (Box 6.1) the researcher could have 'shamed' the members of the research sites into compliance, or attempted various methods of gentle persuasion – by offering a range of good reasons for them being involved. One could demonstrate the specific gains to their organisation from involvement – which could range from payment, through the contributions to good practice the organisation might make or the good public relations image that comes out of being seen to be a helpful/concerned organisation.

Often people and institutions will allow access because they feel they 'have to' or that they 'ought to' . Thus the use of a 'name' – a respected individual or professional association – attached to the project can help.

Box 6.1   Reluctance to being researched

A researcher seeking to conduct a research project on change management in university departments met with considerable reluctance to permit access due to their concern over information disclosure and confidentiality. The researcher was surprised and disappointed that academics might seek to conduct research on others but shy away from being researched themselves.

Lone researchers have much bigger problems gaining access and/or reasonable response rates than familiar, well-known, well-respected and large research organisations do.

Targeting the right department and the right person in the department is the essential first step. A preliminary introductory phone call helps insure against wasting too much time. Researchers themselves can be reluctant subjects but one would expect a moral obligation to their professional colleagues to be more helpful about their research – unless they are concerned to conceal the very things that the research might disclose. The 'what have they got to hide?' question would be a distinct enticement to a journalist – social researchers are required to be more dispassionate and less sensation seeking.

After considerable persuasion access was grudgingly granted to the researcher in the above case (Box 6.1), but the respondents' reluctance delivered impoverished data, which undermined the value of continuing to conduct the research in that location. But what this example shows is that while some compliance techniques might be suitable for professionals and/or public institutions, they would certainly not be considered appropriate for the general public. It would not be considered legitimate to 'shame' an ordinary member of the public (or, worse, one considered to be especially vulnerable – see Chapter 10) into being recruited.

Equitable selection of participants

While elements of the research design may allow the systematic exclusion of certain categories of research subjects, it would be unethical for such groups to be left out simply because it would be inconvenient to include them. If there are genuine benefits to be sought for research participation, then it would be unfair if only those who were easily available were consistently chosen.

One legitimate ground for exclusion would be that participants should not be selected from groups unlikely to be among the beneficiaries of subsequent applications of the research. This is something not usually the case in pharmaceutical trials conducted in developing countries – the subjects testing out a new and expensive drug for developed countries are unlikely to be able to afford the drug once its benefits have been demonstrated. Such a practice would be roundly condemned in social research – however the benefits of many social research projects are rarely so easily measurable as to be able to suggest that the research participants will have been deprived of a valuable intervention in social service or social policy.

In the same way subjects ought not to be systematically selected from groups for reasons not directly related to the research focus of study – again that they are easily available, in some sort of compromised position (such as prisoners or other captive populations – again see Chapter 10) or that they are particularly manipulable.

In all cases 'convenience' and 'inconvenience' should neither count as a methodological or an ethical criterion. A challenging approach to the equitable selection of participants is put forward by Stephen Gorard who suggests we should give more consideration to the needs of non-participants in research even if at the expense of participants. He condemns the ethical obsessions with participants' rights at the expense of research design quality which sacrifices the benefits of the excluded participants – that is, the rest of the population or 'society' who might gain from the research findings. Meeting only the needs of research participants for 'short-term' ethical advantage sacrifices long-term ethical gain from the implementation of findings from well-designed research. Participant equity should recognise the true needs of the majority of the population (Gorard 2002).

Facilitating subjects' withdrawal from the research

The ultimate test of the enhanced power of research subjects lies in their knowing that they have the ability to withdraw from the study at any point. No matter how inconvenient this may be to the researcher, they have only fulfilled their ethical obligations if they not only permit such withdrawal when it is sought, but also facilitate it in terms of ensuring no harm comes to the subjects as a consequence of their withdrawal from the study. This may mean going out of one's way to ensure they receive the same treatment, attitudes and services they would have done had they not joined the study in the first place.

Rights to exclusion and/or inclusion

An ethical argument could be made that some groups/individuals ought to be intentionally excluded from study – that is, that some 'types' of people do not deserve the 'right' to be studied. If a researcher is interested in studying such subjects the problem of recruiting suitable subjects can additionally raise issues of accessibility but, as many research questions are complex, difficult topics generate difficulties in the attempt to address the many overlapping areas of ethical concern. A study of paedophilia illustrates precisely these difficulties (see Box 6.2).

Box 6.2   Research into sexual abuse

Richard Yuill was a PhD student at Glasgow University who was keen to question the assumption that all sexual relationships between adults and children are inherently abusive. Experts in child protection argue that such a view plays into the hands of abusers who justify their activity by claiming that the abused are willing participants. It was reported that in the course of his research (in 2001) Yuill had solicited interviews with paedophiles on the Internet, describing himself as a 'boy lover', and guaranteeing them anonymity. The University cleared him of all allegations of abusing his position as a researcher, his work had full ethical and governance approval, his examiners approved the work, the police had been informed of his work and took no action. Yuill explained that he used the phrase in an e-mail to help 'build trust' and ensure that he could access the subjects for interviewing purposes. He said the term ' did not describe his sexual identity'. He admitted some of the e-mails might have been 'too friendly' but he always identified himself as a researcher. He argued that if he had not protected his sources, despite their putative illegal activity, the research could not have been conducted and valuable knowledge about the attitudes and behaviour of such people would have been missed. Yuill has had to place his PhD thesis on restricted access [see Chapter 12 on dissemination] due to the abusive letters and e-mails he received and his concern for the motives of people who might want to view his results.

(*The Times Higher*, 3 December 2004, pp. 1 and 3)

Ironically the claim that viewing images of child pornography on the Internet 'for research purposes' is unlikely to stand as a defence against prosecution – although it has been attempted by some well-known offenders in recent years. But in general this case illustrates a range of challenging concerns. The researcher can certainly be regarded as having employed a degree of deception to gain and maintain access to respondents who, as a consequence of their potentially illegal activity, could understandably have been reluctant to be recruited. His guarantee of anonymity might be sustainable for the purposes of his PhD thesis and any other subsequent form of dissemination of his research since he might be assumed to be in control of it. That guarantee would be threatened if illegal activity had been disclosed and the researcher failed to declare it and/or the police determined to pursue the identities of the respondents. Some degree of protection of the researcher (and the subjects) is provided by the approval process of the University. Of course all of this challenges a broader public sensibility that might regard such subjects as 'beyond the pale' and so not deserving of such ethical treatment. On the other hand, if such work is not conducted, little of benefit to society can be explored about such behaviour and so little might be done to assist corrective policies and practices.

7
Giving Information and Seeking Consent

(See page 10 of checklist.)

Given all the variable influences upon ethical decision-making, keeping the issues separate for purposes of analysis or review is almost impossible. This is illustrated most forcefully when addressing the means and methods for seeking consent from subjects to participate in research. The frequently used phrase 'informed consent' alone illustrates the first combination of variables to take into consideration – there is a view that gaining consent cannot be separated from the giving of information. More often the phrase 'voluntary informed consent' is used which implies the subject was able to choose freely to give consent and to subsequently participate in the research.

Whether an individual chooses to engage in any activity in an entirely 'voluntary' manner is hard enough to judge in everyday life. Adding the decision to participate in a research activity merely complicates assessment of that choice. Assuming the research project was a researcher's mission and not that of the subject, this suggests a subject can reflect upon the implications of the research engagement for their interests and their life. It assumes the individual has the competence or mental capacity to make such a judgement. It also assumes they have been given adequate information about the research and that they are able to comprehend that information to the extent that it relates to the implications of their involvement.

Research ethics committees (RECs) often seek proof of consent having been properly sought and given by requiring the completion of a written, possibly signed and, in some cases, independently witnessed form. (They frequently ask to see the template for such forms prior to granting permission to proceed.) Such a highly formalised requirement seems sensible when a risk of harm to the participants may be anticipated. But it is also clear that such formality could alienate some potential participants who might fear the researcher is a representative of 'officialdom' and who might be wary of such engagements. While formal consenting may protect the researcher against any future charge of not giving adequate information, it is by no means legally binding and might not even guarantee the respondent's continued participation in a project.

As with all other ethical issues it is vital to remember that there is 'fluidity' in consenting. It is not a once-and-for-all act – it is not an event, it is a process. Consenting may have to be treated as ongoing throughout the research engagement. This has consequences both for the nature and flow of information as well as the potential for changes in the subject's capacity to consent. Both the amount of information provided in an ongoing research project and the relationship between researcher and researched are liable to fluctuate – and so too might the subject's view of their consenting.

There is an interesting parallel here with clinical work. Consent is required for all clinical contact, but it is mostly implicit and verbal. In the clinical relationship the clinician and client are 'trading' in consent. When a physician is presented with symptoms there is the assumption the client is compliant with measures necessary to seeking a diagnosis and recommended treatment. But the precise investigations and interventions to be conducted are then subject to subsequent and ongoing negotiation. The majority of cases deemed to be malpractice according to the Medical Protection Society are related to inadequate consenting, poor communication and, consequently, the giving of insufficient information. (As well as, incidentally, poor case notes or record keeping.)

The same criteria could apply to social research. Relationships between researcher and subject will vary in duration, intensity, tone and depth much as the doctor–patient relationship varies. In both cases a fundamental change in the relationship, and therefore the informed and voluntary nature of consent, occurs when some high-risk intervention is proposed and/or the subject's capacity to consent changes. In clinical situations the emergent intervention might be surgery or pharmaceutical recommendations, and in social research the questioning in an open-ended interview might begin to touch upon topics the interviewee did not expect, was not warned about and which they might regard as sensitive. When that happens the status of the consent given must be allowed to be amended or, even, removed. The ongoing consenting process may best be seen as episodic with distinctive 'markers' throughout – only one of which is the achievement, say, of a signed, witnessed, written consent form.

When the obstructive nature of RECs is commented on, addressing informed consent is the topic that occupies the critics most. Given the points raised above there is evident danger of expressing the problem in a manner that is far too crude and simple for the subtlety and sophistication that one requires for ethical review in the social sciences. Ethically problematised areas such as these have long been recognised as also methodologically problematic, so there is little that can be considered new about how one deals with them. Similarly there is considerable overlap between this issue and several others – addressing and solving one may compromise our ability to handle another. The problem of informed consent, for example, gives rise to challenges to our sensed vulnerability of research participants (see Chapter 10), to the use of deception, degrees of disclosure of information and methodological compromise (covered later in this chapter), to human rights (see Chapters 11, 13 and 14) and the nature of the relationship between researcher and researched (which recurs throughout this book).

What information could and should be supplied and why?

In some respects the information provided constitutes part of an informal contract between researcher and subject. In Rosenhan's case no consent from the subjects – psychiatrists and other staff in the mental health setting – was sought (see Box 7.1). The grounds that could be

Box 7.1   Rosenhan's pseudo-patient studies

D. L. Rosenhan's studies were reported in 'On being sane in insane places' (Rosenhan 1973) in which the hypothesis being tested was that distinguishing between sane and insane people is impossible in psychiatric hospitals. Eight co-investigators sought separate admission to a series of psychiatric hospitals by presenting with identical complaints about 'hearing voices' – they followed a script reporting the same sounds on admission. Immediately on admission they behaved as 'normal', and all but one were diagnosed as 'schizophrenic' and discharged, after varying lengths of stay, with 'schizophrenia in remission'. These and other pseudo-patient studies might be treated as service-evaluation studies with the only people duped being those whose job it is to diagnose and treat accurately and effectively. (It resembles a form of mystery shopping.) The added theoretical point to be made has to do with the potential for accuracy in the diagnosis of mental illness.

argued for such an omission being the value of the findings to the general public, future patients and, indeed, the staff themselves for future practice. Without the deception and the lack of consent the project would not have produced such significant findings. Retrospective consent to publish might have been sought to protect the professionals' standing or esteem in the eyes of the public – but their vested interests might have then led them to refuse consent on the same grounds.

This is why it is doubly important that the identity of the researcher, their research colleagues and the organisation they work for should be made clear so that the subjects and the public can make a judgement of their 'worthiness'. (This is the kind of information covered in Chapter 3.) In addition the subjects should be told where the money is coming from to fund the project. This allows them to judge whether they wish to be associated with the project given their views on the funding organisation. Of course the subjects may know little about such organisations so the researcher may have to inform them. The information leaflet given to participants should explain who the funder is and the name and the nature of the research organisation the researcher is employed by. In addition providing such information allows the subjects to check up independently on either organisation if they were inclined to.

It is vital to explain how and why a subject was selected. Any anxieties they may harbour over covert reasons for their selection can be alleviated by explaining the process of random selection or that they represent a category of persons the researchers are interested in – they fill a 'quota'. Depersonalising the criteria for selection will for many constitute some form of reassurance that there is nothing 'personal' in how and why they were chosen. When subjects are selected more purposively this has to be more fully explained and trust in the researcher's honesty and intentions incrementally established. The statement that only 'they' have the answers to the questions the researcher is interested in could be viewed with suspicion. In an early research of my own I interviewed a series of television and radio producers about religious broadcasting – each of them asked independently why I was interested in them since they 'only' made religious programmes.

My research was precisely concerned with the motives of religious broadcasters; hence, they were the only people who could help me. Consequently an appropriate explanation of the aims or purpose of study will justify the researcher's need to derive information from them. Similarly subjects are entitled to know just what will be expected of them if they agree to take part. The nature of the research process, what form it will take and how long it will last are all essential to informed consent. If any risk or potential harm or discomfort is anticipated, it is at this stage that the subjects should be informed. But this should also be balanced against the judgement of anticipated benefits. Subjects might be willing to take known risks if they too perceive the benefits to be worthwhile – even if not to them but to society or the general public. That is, after all, the basis of most clinical trials.

Given that all research contains some element of risk, no matter how minimal, subjects do need to know the conditions under which a study may be discontinued or how they may withdraw if anything concerns them or some untoward event occurs. This emphasises the voluntary nature of consent – they should be made aware of their ability to refuse to participate, that they can withdraw at any time and this will have no adverse consequences for how they will subsequently be treated by any-one involved in the commissioning and conduct of the study. If some form of counselling or other sources of advice might mitigate any harm or distress, these should be provided as standard within the information given at the outset. There is some danger that this could create a self-fulfilling prophecy – with people sensitised to extra concerns because they had been warned about the possibility that this might happen. So the relevant information should be couched carefully so as not to provoke the very outcome the researchers would seek to avoid.

If confidentiality and/or anonymity have been promised then the steps taken to ensure this should be outlined. If there are any limits to confidentiality/anonymity or threats to their maintenance, these should be disclosed. In particular subjects should be clearly informed about how the data will be reported and the study findings released. Targeted feed-back to participants is a way of demonstrating both the value of subjects and a concern for their well-being. But they should also be informed of the other avenues through which the research will be disseminated.

The provision of researcher and institutional contact names and numbers is another form of reassurance that ensures the subject has alternative routes through which to have questions answered, to make complaints, announce withdrawal or resolve a grievance.

It is interesting how different theoretical traditions appear to vary in the degree of attention they pay to gaining consent and supplying subjects with information – even those that stress the participatory involvement of subjects. Ethnography draws on extensive comparative anthropological experience across cultures and so tends to be highly ethically aware. Ethnomethodological researchers seem rarely concerned with seeking permission to conduct their studies – the employment of the Garfinkelian 'breaching experiment' for instance requires that the 'uninformed' participants remain ignorant of the purpose of the experiment. This involves 'creating artificial situations in which members have to do extra sense-making work in order to repair missing or contradicted background expectancies' (ten Have 2004: 53).

The most often cited example is having student researchers behave as strangers within their own family – observing and responding to normal household activities and practices as if they were alien to them. In this disrupting of the normal social order, the mundane tacit practices of routine social relations that remain unsaid are challenged, so that their purpose and significance might be revealed. Such ethnomethodological practices seem little concerned about debriefing subjects afterwards even though the subjects were evidently disturbed by the experiment (for example, see ten Have 2004: 39). Even ethnographers can appear a little resentful of the legitimate resistance of subjects to taking part in their cherished study: 'Further problems for ethnography can be related to the *illegitimate* and *private* character of observed activities and the possibilities for local members to *hide* such activities, or for gatekeepers to prevent or obstruct observations in various ways, especially by *denying access* to the field' (ten Have 2004: 132).

What is the most appropriate medium for supplying the information?

The giving of oral consent on the telephone or in a face-to-face situation does appear more natural and, consequently, more consistent with the ethos of qualitative enquiry; so, to ensure that as much information as necessary/possible can be demonstrated to have been given, researchers have taken to audiotape recording the consenting process. In the more formalised collection of quantitative data there may even be an expectation among participants of a formal consenting procedure.

With high-risk projects the signed and witnessed consent form may be the only way of establishing the correct contractual relationship between researcher and researched. The less separation between the giving of information, say in a leaflet, and the taking of consent then the more certain the researcher can be that consent was informed and voluntary. But key decisions have to be made about the design and content of consent forms and information leaflets to ensure the details are presented clearly and in a format suited to the subject's needs and abilities.

It is hard to be too prescriptive about both consenting and information giving since how they are done will depend upon the combination of the topic of the research, the nature of the subjects and the chosen research methods and instruments. Offering no absolute prescription does not mean that there is no 'right way' to do it – the correct procedure requires the provision of 'adequate' information and 'adequate' consent – what constitutes adequacy being very much dependent on the nature of the researcher–researched relationship.

The capacity to consent

Judging that a subject has the capacity to consent is to make an assessment of their cognitive and communicative competence. The researcher is being asked to assess that, assuming full and clear information has been given, the subject has the ability to understand, retain and analyse that information, come to an independent decision and express that decision clearly and effectively to the researcher seeking consent. It should be immediately evident how difficult a judgement that must be. While we generally assume such cognitive competence in adults, we tend to assume it to be diminished in the very young, the very old and those self-evidently disabled in mental function as judged, usually, by their behaviour.

Evidently the judging capacity to consent is a contentious area. There are two basic problems here – it assumes that only some (i.e. let's say mentally disabled) people lack the capacity to consent when more of us lack this capacity than we care to admit. I have certainly consented to participate in activities that I have later come to regret – and that does not only include research engagements. We cannot all know or anticipate what precisely we are consenting to – sometimes the researchers do not know either! Secondly it assumes that those with 'less capacity' do not wish to be free to choose themselves whether to participate in research – once again we patronise in making their decisions for them and assume that their disability limits their engagement with the world (in this case in research) that they may wish to be free to choose to engage in. We cannot and perhaps should not protect everyone 'from themselves'. The point is not that we should not judge the capacity to consent – we should only have to recognise that we have to make a judgement and that we could be wrong.

The recently implemented UK Mental Capacity Act's (2005) (Office of Public Sector Information 2007) prescriptions for consent in research illustrate how difficult this is to manage in practice. Researchers conducting long-term projects on healthy participants will have to withdraw participants, who might have subsequently lost their capacity to consent, from their study and to consult the individual's carers about the use of all previously collected data. In future all research with individuals who lack capacity must go through an 'approved body' which presently includes only certain identified RECs within the UK NHS (NRES 2007).

There is a section of this Act that deals explicitly with research, and many of its components are what one would consider normal safeguards for proper treatment of research subjects – whether they can be considered evidently vulnerable or not. But there are complications which, as yet, remain untested. For example, the determining principles of the Act allow that we must assume people have capacity unless they demonstrate that they don't – not including merely appearing not to have capacity or making 'unwise' decisions. Acts done relating to persons lacking capacity must be in their best interests and not restrictive of their rights and freedom of action.

So far so good, but the definition of a person who lacks capacity can set us a problem: 'For the purposes of this Act, a person lacks capacity in relation to a matter if at the material time he is unable to make a decision for himself in relation to the matter because of an impairment of, or a disturbance in the functioning of, the mind or the brain.' The problem is I am not sure how one would judge that during the research engagement – quite apart from the fact that some decisions people take or actions they make would make it appear they 'lack capacity'. Moreover an 'inability to make decisions' is defined as being 'unable ... to understand the information relevant to the decision'. Once again many of us who believe we have capacity may not fully understand the information provided.

One of my research interests entails interviewing people with epilepsy (Iphofen 1990). It is clear that they suffer from an 'impairment of the brain' (by definition that is what epilepsy is) but more often than not that impairment affects them intermittently; otherwise they are as likely to be as perfectly intelligent as other people, able to communicate clearly and so on. But what happens if they suffer a seizure while I am interviewing them – do I now assume that their capacity to consent has fundamentally altered, if only temporarily, and do I now discontinue the interview and seek a 'carer's' permission to proceed (as required by the Act)? I can guarantee that most, if not all, of my subjects would resent being so patronised and would wish to choose themselves whether to continue to participate in the research or not.

More complicatedly how many researchers conduct interviews with people with epilepsy but are not aware of it? It is not often a 'visible' condition and if that is not the focus of the interview, it is unlikely to present a problem – but what, again, if the interviewee suffers a seizure?

The Act later specifies conditions under which research can be carried out (but excluding clinical trials which are dealt with under other legislation) and indicates that 'intrusive' research is research carried out on a person who lacks capacity – and that would be unlawful. But it is also intrusive 'if it is of a kind that would be unlawful if it was carried out – (a) on or in relation to a person who had capacity to consent to it, but (b) without his consent'. Now that would rule out observational research of any kind if it was conducted without the prior permission of the subjects being studied. It fundamentally broadens the notion of what 'intrusion' actually is – legally at least.

There is, in addition, a *Catch 22* element to this Act. If a person lacking capacity feels aggrieved by a research engagement and decides to sue the researcher, that would seem to indicate that they do not lack mental capacity and so cannot be assumed to have been unlawfully consented into the research. (Presumably the charges would have to be brought by a carer – and so dependent upon the carer's perception of what harm might have come to the research subject.) Nonetheless it still disempowers the individual who is assumed to lack capacity.

The complications we face as researchers are compounded by the fact that such legislation remains fairly localised. This Act applies only to England and Wales, there is a different legislation for Scotland and none for Northern Ireland. And if one's research was even more international one would have to check the legislation in all the countries one was conducting research in. It is clear that while a researcher could be 'intrusive' in England and Wales, it is not the case when conducting research on people in public places in, say, the United States.

How should consent be gained and/or recorded – and by whom?

The general principles should be that consent should be gained in the most convenient, least disturbing manner for both researcher and researched. This also implies that it should be accomplished competently; which, in turn, suggests that researchers should be trained in (licensed for?) taking consent. In fact most survey organisations treat this as an important element in the training of field researchers/ interviewers – as do the pharmaceutical companies who offer workshops for clinical trial researchers in taking consent and 'securing compliance' – which means exploring ways to ensure that subjects stay in the study and do take the drug which has been assigned to them in the trial.

It is clearly important that consenting is done properly in the interests of the research professions, the commissioners and the subjects engaged in the specific study. Errors in consenting could account for a considerable degree of disenchantment with the research experience and thereby contaminate the field for future research.

Managing informed consent

(See page 11 of checklist.)

However consent is gained initially it must be managed and negotiated in an ongoing manner throughout the course of a research project. Gaining their consent to taking part is only one of the ways in which harm to participants can be avoided on the assumption that they too must participate in the anticipation and recognition of its potential. If they are to be able to consent they need to know fully what their participation entails. They will need information but here the ethical concern may conflict with a methodological one: How much information should they be given and in what form?

Too much information could act as a disincentive to participation by implying an excessive commitment of time or an inhibiting amount of emotional investment. Or it may be too 'leading' in revealing too much about the researcher's interests. Too little information could be construed as deceptive and result in participants' early withdrawal from the study when they find out more about it.

A greater difficulty with gathering qualitative data, in particular, is that while the participant might not fully know what they are agreeing to, the researchers may know only a little more since the research can be allowed, or even encouraged, to move in directions that only become appropriate when the research is under way. This means that consent has to be ongoing, and information giving conceived as dynamically integrated into the life of the project (see, for example, Miller and Bell 2002).

Ethical review committees, particularly in health research, often insist upon formal consent being achieved before the commencement of a project. This is clearly impossible if change is an expected and inherent part of the research process, and in such cases the methodological limitations on gaining 'fully informed' consent would have to be made clear at the outset. Indeed formal consent can be hard to achieve with some categories of groups and individuals who are, or who perceive themselves as, vulnerable and/or marginalised. There is a problem of how much some vulnerable participants understand what they are consenting to. This might be a problem for children or for the learning disabled and for older people. The use of proxies can help but this can sacrifice confidentiality. On the other hand reading and/or signing a formal consent form could appear to be establishing a more apparently 'official' relationship than the respondent had bargained for. The research relationship in such cases is inevitably tentative and gradualist.

Subjects should be given copies of both the initial information sheet and any consent form to keep – both to refer to and as proof for the researcher that information had, in fact, been given and consent taken. Even under clinical conditions consenting has to be seen as a dynamic process: 'Consent to treatment is a process that includes explanation and discussion about risks and benefits. The substance of these discussions should be documented, otherwise it would be difficult to prove that they took place' (Casey 2006: 11).

Managing the consenting process can become even more complicated if third parties or gatekeepers are involved. In some cases (e.g. when researching children under the legal age of consent) consent will need to be taken from both the child subject and the parent/guardian – a major problem arising if the former consents and the latter objects. The researcher will probably have little choice but to respect the parent's objection and there may be a reasonable assumption that the parent is acting in what they perceive to be the child's best interests. But there are real complications to sustaining consent throughout the project if matters of concern arise to either and not both of the consenting parties. Hence the need for a researcher to be a skilled diplomat and a negotiator in ensuring the fairest outcome to all stakeholders – and, in order to maintain transparency, able to record fully the rationale upon which the decision was based. Similar complications can befall gatekeepers acting on behalf of, say, subjects with learning difficulties or older people who are residents of care homes. In both the cases the agents responsible for their care might have their own reason for the discontinuation of a project which is not necessarily congruent with the interests of the subjects.

Chih Hoong Sin's (2005) work studying dementia across a range of different ethnic groups, with a mixed methods approach and a large team of researchers, illustrates the difficulties involved in the complex management of a multilevel and repeated consenting process. He challenges the formulaic requirements of ethical review committees: 'The fluidity of consent demands a more reflexive approach to its engagement' (Sin 2005: 277).

Exceptions to fully informed consent

(See page 12 of checklist.)

There may be times when information about the full nature of a study may have to be restricted in order to comply with a particular research design. This is particularly likely to occur with covert observational studies or ethnographic field research in which the researcher's role is not fully disclosed – also known as immersive fieldwork. To seek consent in such a situation would nullify the research method and the rationale for its adoption. But any exemptions to seeking consent must be detailed together with an explanation of why they have occurred. Thus there may be broad methodological justifications and more specific, strategic reasons to do with the safety of researchers and/or research subjects.

Incomplete disclosure may be justified if it can be demonstrated that participants should not be told too much – or anything – in order to accomplish the research goals. This could only be considered if it entailed minimal risks to the subjects, also if some way of debriefing them could be made available and, perhaps, if there were a way to provide for the appropriate dissemination of findings to subjects. In fact it may be the case that subjects could suffer from 'information overload' if they are told too much. After all they are not the professionals whose careers are dependent upon satisfactory outcomes. Giving too much information may impose a burden in that subjects may feel obliged to read everything provided. If the information were too technical, they may feel 'blinded by science', their ignorance revealed and their esteem damaged. If the information were excessively 'simplified', they may feel patronised and their esteem lowered for other reasons.

Observational studies in which the participants are not aware that they are being observed offer the best examples of exceptions to fully informed consent. There have been many such 'classic' ethnographic studies in the history of social research and they usually cover the fringe areas of society – criminality, social deviance, the sex industry, terrorist groups and religious cults. In fact Moser and Kalton describe observation as 'the classic method of scientific enquiry' (1971: 244). They express surprise at the relatively infrequent use of observational methods by social scientists when one reflects that 'they are literally surrounded by their subject matter'. However, in keeping with the rigour and systematicity that permeates the rest of this 'bible' of social research, they exhort that 'The method must be suitable for investigating the problem in which the social scientist is interested; it must be appropriate to the populations and samples he wishes to study; and it should be reasonably reliable and objective' (Moser and Kalton 1971: 244). Of course, observation entails the direct focus upon behaviour unmediated by the 'subject's' views on and potential distortions of that behaviour. Instead the potential for bias rests with the observer's recording skills and their interpretations of the meanings or intentions behind the behaviour. Thus it is not necessarily any more 'objective' than any other method of social enquiry in that

> observers are so much part of their subject matter that they may fail to see it objectively; ... their vision may be distorted by what they are used to seeing or what they expect to see; and ... they may find it hard to present a report in which observation is satisfactorily distinguished from inference and interpretation.
>
> (Moser and Kalton 1971: 253)

It is noteworthy that Moser and Kalton's massive (nearly 600 pages) tome which is such a classic in the annals of social research makes little reference to research ethics. The single, two-line, reference to ethical considerations is in the section on participant observation – and the subject index contains none of the 'key words' one looks for in research ethics. It is not that the work is unethical, but it does reveal how little importance empirical social scientists credited these as distinct issues in the late 1950s (when the work was first published) to the early 1960s. From then until the 1980s, however, appeared to be one of the most prolific periods of concern about ethics in social research with some major seminal works appearing (examples include Barnes 1980; Boruch and Cecil 1979; Bower and de Gasfaris 1978; Cassell 1982 Diener and Crandall 1978; Hoinville and Jowell 1978; Jowell 1983; Levine 1978; SCPR 1974). I do not cover the content and detail of these works in this book since they are summarised and discussed fully in the Social Research Association's (2003) guidelines – it is clear from a reading of the SRA guidelines just how much that early work has influenced thinking on ethical research and, indeed, foreshadowed most of the issues discussed here (see Box 7.2).

There is an interesting parallel with observational studies in two other areas of professional concern which have been the subject of considerable debate – the use of cameras in classrooms and in consulting rooms. Much as CCTV is employed routinely in shops, it has been proposed as a 'protective' measure in both educational and therapeutic settings. It has been proposed to protect both teachers and therapists against

Box 7.2   Venkatesh's immersive fieldwork

A recent example of dilemmas in observational study is the work of Sidhir Venkatesh who is unlikely to have been able to conduct his research on hustlers, prostitutes and drug dealers in any detail if they had been aware of his status as a researcher. His analysis of a drug dealing gang's accounts demonstrated how it adopted a business model successfully employed by many other modern businesses – such as McDonald's [see Levitt and Dubner 2005, Ch. 3]. What Venkatesh explains well is how inappropriate and ineffective conventional research instruments, such as questionnaires and interview schedules, can be in such an environment, in fact, how self-defeating they are in trying to learn about the lives of poor and marginalised communities. He came to see how just as his research subjects were 'hustling' for money, drugs, sexual favours etc., he was also hustling for the data that he saw as vital to his research goals. He had to become imaginative and devious in gaining information – otherwise he would be seen as an agent of the authorities and a threat to his respondents' access to services.

(Venkatesh 2008)

malicious allegations by students and clients of wrongdoing. It has even been suggested that cameras could be similarly employed in a protective way for researchers – an impartial recording and, therefore, evidence of their proper behaviour. In all cases fears have been expressed that the cameras might be exploited as a management tool to ensure researchers, therapists and educators were fulfilling their contractual requirements. The problem with this is that normal safeguards of confidentiality and anonymity could not be assured unless access to the video recordings was legally restricted or there had been a preliminary consensus established on how they could be accessed and for what purposes (Haigh 2008).

Covert research and deception

Occasionally RECs have accused researchers in the social sciences of adopting inherently immoral methodologies. These include covert observation – participant or otherwise – and research designs in which some form of deception is employed. Researchers can attempt to defend their position by offering examples of the forms of deception routinely employed in investigative journalism and mass entertainment. But these should not be seen as justification for poor deceptive practices in social science – the argument is almost: 'Well if they can get away with it why can't we? After all we are doing it for "better" reasons.' In fact, it is perhaps a consequence of the increased tolerance to deception in such spheres – and the publicly visible consequences – that there has been a reaction to the employment of deception for more 'legitimate' scientific purposes. But neither does that mean that the use of deception should be necessarily ruled out as inherently morally unacceptable. Bad practice in other spheres of activity can provide models for how not to do it in social research. Problems only arise when scrutiny committees see deception as inherently unacceptable – either in fear of litigation and/or for fear of being unable to estimate the degree of harm that 'may' be caused to participants.

The use of deception has been more than comprehensively debated throughout the social sciences for many years (see Bok 1979, Chapter XIII). And I would argue that there is nothing inherently 'wrong' with deception. In research terms deception is routinely employed in a mundane fashion in the blind randomised control trial in biomedicine now seen as almost 'ethically secure'. That is, participants are told of the form of deception to be employed beforehand. This is done regularly in market research when mystery shoppers are employed to test the service skills and systems of employees. More importantly various forms of deception are routinely, again mundanely, employed by several agencies with little public retribution and may even attract enthusiastic moral approbation – the police employ it for undercover operations and legalised 'entrapment' of suspects. Well-respected sociological research has shown how television news is inherently deceptive. News is presented by 'anchor' men and women and scripted to suit time slots of convenience to broadcasters – while looking at the camera to 'pretend' they are talking to the audience when they are actually reading the script from a cue monitor. All forms of drama (theatre, cinema, television, cgi) are deceptions with which we collude for our own recreation. There could be nothing more deceptive than most forms of advertising. But the public are not ignorant of this. Indeed it is culturally endemic to the human condition, embedded in folk tales and myths. The entertainment, fashion and art industries depend for their survival upon our collusion in the suspension of disbelief.

Once again the question facing an ethics committee should not be: 'Is deception wrong'? To answer that in the affirmative would be to deny practices that are central to human civilisation. Rather the committee should ask: 'Would the form of deception proposed here harm the research participants, the researchers and/or society in general in any way?' This is not an easy question to answer since that would have to be balanced against the benefits accruing to all of those constituent groups if the research was conducted successfully.

As Robert Rosenhal has pointed out: 'the ... researcher whose study might reduce violence or racism or sexism, but who refuses to do the study because it involves deception, has not solved an ethical problem but only traded it in for another' (cited in Bok 1979: 192). Thus a good case can be made for covert research not being seen merely as a 'last resort methodology' but as even recommended with certain topics, certain subjects and in certain settings (Calvey 2008).

The key question about deception has to do with whether or not it damages the trust the general public (and so future potential research participants) have in researchers. If deception leads to an undermining of trust, and so a reluctance to participate in research, there is then a risk to the success of future research projects (Bok 1979: 205 et seq.). The benefits to society of future research are thereby equally harmed.

> Thus, we are always confronted with a conflict of values. If we regard the acquisition of knowledge about human behaviour as a positive value, and if an experiment using deception constitutes a significant contribution to such knowledge which could not be very well achieved by other means, then we cannot unequivocally rule out this experiment. The question for us is not simply whether it does or does not use deception, but whether the amount and type of deception are justified by the significance of the study and the unavailability of alternative (that is, deception-free) procedures.
>
> (Kelman 1967 in Bynner and Stribley 1979: 190)

Another way of addressing this is to consider it alongside the issues of consent and vulnerability. Thus if the form of deception proposed in a research project minimises the research subjects' capacity to consent and makes them more vulnerable to harm without substantially contributing to societal benefit, then it becomes harder to ethically justify it going ahead. It is a complex question – but not simply dealt with by suggesting that deception in research is inherently wrong.

On the other hand Kelman posits the view that 'In institutionalising the use of deception in psychological experiments, we are, then, contributing to a historical trend that threatens values most of us cherish' (Kelman 1967 in Bynner and Stribley 1979: 195). Presumably by that he means honesty.

Finally, ethical review committees often ask whether a piece of research is likely to be excessively intrusive and so 'disturbing' the subjects' normal life routines. Again the Mental Capacity Act's attempts to define 'intrusive' (as discussed earlier) would rule out a considerable amount of existing research practice. Of course research is inevitably intrusive, but that intrusiveness is variable – dependent upon how much of the respondents' time, energy and so on it takes up. It also needs to be balanced against the concerns addressed above – thus, ironically, the more covert a piece of research, the less intrusive in ordinary lives it is likely to be but the more it is defined as intrusive by the Act. (It might become more intrusive depending upon how and where research findings are published – but that merely raises another set of ethical concerns.)

My point here is that the objection to unreasonable ethical scrutiny, conducted by those ignorant of social science methodology, is made on the grounds of the lack of sophisticated understanding of the balance of ethics with appropriate methodologies. That critique is certainly justified when review committees fail to think through the moral complexities that are routinely a part of human life in any case and charge social science with lacking moral awareness. In fact, they fail in their duties if they seem happy to mechanically insist upon the provision to research subjects only after acquiring an accessible information leaflet and a written, signed (possibly witnessed) consent form. That represents a complete failure to recognise that consent can never be simply given or 'gained'; it has to be managed and negotiated in a continuous fashion – whatever the research design. Thus anonymity may not be always required, and may not even be advisable for public figures with public accountability. And consenting and informing is necessarily compromised in some research designs. Formal/witnessed consenting may not always be ethically advisable. There may inevitably be consequences to disclosure in sensitive areas and with vulnerable subjects that challenge principles of confidentiality.

Seeking retrospective consent

Some of the concerns of ethics reviewers may be met if a promise is made that retrospective consent will be sought. But even this must be carefully considered. If subjects remain ignorant of the research having taken place, and no harm came to them during the process, then more harm than good could be done by subsequently informing them that they have been the subjects of research of which they had no knowledge. They may merely be upset at their activities having been 'secretly' observed, or disturbed by the researcher's findings about and reflections upon their actions. They may not like the idea that their ostensibly 'private' behaviour has been assumed to be 'public' and open to a stranger's gaze. (Of course it is true that any passer-by can be equally observing and thinking about our privately constructed public behaviour – the difference lies in the intent.) But if such work were excluded social science would lose the advantage of such classic insights gained from, say, the ethological studies of public life found in the work of Erving Goffman (e.g. Goffman 1971) or Jack Douglas (e.g. Douglas 1977) or the semiology of Roland Barthes (1972).

Useful comparisons with tapping phone calls can be made. For example, it is not illegal in the UK to audiotape record a phone call in which you are involved yourself. You could be sued for damages if the individual at the other end of the line found out and was unhappy about it, but they would have to prove a 'quantifiable loss'. In fact there are data protection implications depending upon how the recorded data were used. Disclosure to a third party is one such implication. Officials who attempt to do this are governed by the Regulation of Investigatory Powers Act (2000) and civil rights might also be protected under article 8 of the European Convention on Human Rights. (This issue was brought to light when Sir Ian Blair, the Commissioner of the Metropolitan Police in London, tape-recoded a conversation he had with the Attorney General, Lord Goldsmith. See *The Guardian*, 14 March 2006: 8.)

Another interesting parallel can be drawn with the work of journalists, novelists or documentary film makers who write or make films about an individual who may or may not have the capacity to consent but in whose case the work is treated as artistic, creative and reportage but not research. Some artists construct works based on members of their own family without asking them (e.g. Sue Bourne's film about her mother who was suffering from Alzheimer's *Mum and Me* screened on BBC1 UK on 20 May 2008). Charles Fernyhough (2008) meticulously studied his daughter's development from 0 to 3 years old and published the work when she was eight. I suspect that even if her retrospective permission had been sought, he should have waited until she was much older to seek it – or perhaps he had asked himself for permission as the child's parent and judged that she would come to no harm as a result.

New information and communications technology enhances the possibilities for the development of new observational methods with more opportunities for the undisclosed observation of quasi-public behaviour and the considerable difficulty of seeking any consent from those observed, let alone retrospective consent. Contemporary ethnographers have become increasingly interested in the forms of human behaviour displayed in the globalised culture enabled by new digital and electronic media.

Addressing these two issues areas together (consent and capacity) shows the extent to which they overlap. Thus we judge those lacking the capacity to consent as being more vulnerable. But that is only our perception – perhaps in light of pertinent legislation which is nationally specific – and our subjects certainly may not see it that way and we may be doing them more harm by making the assumption that they are made vulnerable by consenting to participate. The learning disabled, for example, are increasingly interested in self-advocacy. Our reasons for excluding them from a study or doubting their consenting capacity, is a direct challenge to their drive towards self-empowerment. A similar error is made when we speak of the disabled generally as 'suffering' from a condition – that is something that is seen as politically incorrect terminology for a self-empowering sector of the population keen to establish their social, political and economic rights.

Putting all the variables together that have been accumulated for ethical consideration up to this chapter illustrates the full complexity of the decisions to be taken. How much information should be given? How complex can/should it be? How can it be clarified without patronising the subject? Can the entire spectrum of risks be anticipated – if not, can a judgement of the degree of risk be made? That is, are the risks high or low? Can a proper assessment of the cognitive competence/mental capacity of subjects be made? Once again is the chance that they possess adequate mental capacity high or low?

Box 7.3 Using personal health information in research

The Medical Research Council commissioned MORI Social Research Institute to undertake work to gain insight into public attitudes towards the use of health information in medical research. This report suggests that confidentiality and consent feature highly in the debate over what information should be available, to whom, and in what circumstances. The importance of good communication with the general public about research was seen to be important in building attitudes of trust towards research activity.

See http://www.mrc.ac.uk/NewsViewsAndEvents/
InvolvingThePublic/Consultations/UseOfPersonal
HealthInformationInResearch/index.htm

8
Monitoring Safety

(See page 12 of checklist.)

The monitoring of physical safety should not be separated from ethical scrutiny – any potential risks to safety need to be assessed and if researchers feel unsafe or anticipate risk of harm to themselves, this concern must be addressed. The safety both of participants and field researchers has to be monitored since there may be some mutual dependence – in terms of environmental threats or changed local conditions.

Increased consideration has been given, more recently, to the safety of field researchers. An awareness of the risks (physical and emotional) to field researchers is both an ethical and a practical managerial concern to do with danger on the job (Lee 1995). Dangers in research may arise from interviewing or observing in potentially threatening locations such as hospital emergency units, or crowds of fans at sporting events or from the discussion of topics emerging which the researcher had not anticipated in interviewing in residential care homes, or in city centres or unfamiliar residential districts at night (Lee-Treweek and Linkogle 2000). There is now awareness that consideration for the safety of subjects should be matched by a consideration for those doing the 'subjecting'. An excellent 'code of practice' has been produced by Gary Craig, Anne Corden and Patricia Thornton and endorsed and distributed by the Social Research Association (Craig et al. 2001).

In certain types of research the risk of harm to the researcher is occasioned by the topic of study and the actions of the researchers themselves. This is the case for those carrying out covert participant observation in fields where the committal of criminal offences is the norm for the participants and might be expected of the researchers in order to protect their covert identity. It might be argued that the maintenance of 'normal appearances' requires the participation in criminal activity and if the researcher were not to comply, they might then be subjecting themselves to the risk of physical harm. On the other hand there is a risk of a distortion of the field in that the researcher has become so active in the activity being researched that they are, in part, only studying themselves. The study of football hooliganism offers a case in point. The difficulties in gaining and maintaining access in such spheres are used to excuse the researcher's participation in violent and potentially criminal conduct. It is hard to see how such research could ever be conducted without allowing the researcher to operate their own judgement about whether to engage in the research and to conduct their own assessment of the risk to permit judgement about its continuance (see, for example, Pearson 2007). It is difficult to see what formal protection could be offered for such research and institutions might have real difficulty in meeting their Health and Safety legislative requirements.

The nature of anthropological field research is such that it not only probably poses the greatest danger primarily to the researcher but also potentially to the subjects being studied. More often than not anthropologists are studying 'alien' or strange cultures – ones with value systems and moral orders vastly different to the anthropologist's. They are faced with moral dilemmas when, for example, marginalised members of the society they are studying are threatened with violence and/or death during their field observations. Their scientific objectivity is certainly compromised if they intervene and there is an assumption of moral superiority by doing so. Examples include the ways in which some societies treat females as inferior citizens, or societies in which AIDS is rampant blame certain individuals, for the spread of the disease – branding them sorcerers or witches. Intervention to prevent mistreatment of such individuals becomes a political and ethical act which cannot be methodologically justified and so the research project becomes undermined. Researchers expose themselves to danger if they record such maltreatment (for instance by photography) or attempt to bring it to some kind of formal/legal resolution. On the other hand to stand by and merely observe is to condone such actions and, by doing so, it may even increase the conviction of the perpetrators that it is justified. An anthropologist working with the US military in Iraq was killed 'incidentally' by a roadside bomb (Jacobsen 2008). Both action and inaction, as always, can have moral, even fatal, consequences.

One of the great advantages of the Internet and the world wide web is the ability to check on safety issues worldwide quite quickly and which tend to be fairly up-to-date. One of my Nigerian postgraduate students planned to conduct a study in the village in Nigeria where her family comes from – a quick check by her supervisor was made on the Internet only to discover there had been some recent localised violence in that region over oil rights. Prior to conducting the study she was able to ascertain how serious the situation was and whether or not it had subsided.

Researchers cannot always ascertain in advance where and what the risks might be – even when conducting research in their home country. Recent localised events can alter the character and ambience of a district and its attitudes to 'strangers'. So the first lesson is to be forewarned, the next is to be prepared.

Procedural safety checks

Research managers and the researchers themselves have a responsibility to anticipate risks and benefits to field researchers for participating in the activity, together with meeting any study-specific needs for researchers. Managers should establish and follow a set of safety checks or a full risk assessment in preparation for each project they conduct. Some concerns are generic and apply to all projects while others will be study specific.

Police checks (in the UK Criminal Records Bureau (CRB) checks are soon to be regulated under an Independent Safeguarding Authority (ISA) – see Chapter 10) are advisable to ensure in the first place that researchers pose no perceivable threat to their subjects. The fact that police checks are conducted may also offer respondents further reassurance about promises of privacy and data protection. In order to protect researchers, provision must be made for monitoring their safety throughout a project, together with awareness of any threats to subjects and researchers that might arise out of their specific research engagement. Reviewing some of the following issues might lead to advising that a project should not go ahead – not only should such consideration be seen to be an ethical one but it also ensures a degree of methodological rigour. One might have cause to doubt the validity and reliability of data secured from an insecure setting or relationship.

The Medical Protection Society's newsletter *Casebook* suggests that two key considerations can help minimise some of the potentially litigious respondents they deal with: communicate fully and clearly and keep careful notes of all engagements (if they can be audio recorded or video recorded then that is even more helpful), in order to record what happened and what was said by all parties. The practice of maintaining a reflective research journal or diary could be seen as a professional 'standard' which helps secure the researcher's integrity to some degree since it might include the researcher's perspective on a difficult situation or problematic respondent.

The safety of social researchers is of particular concern for those conducting research in the field on their own and in unfamiliar surroundings. But some of these concerns apply also in familiar surroundings where surprising things can happen. Professional bodies hold some responsibility for ensuring awareness of risks to researchers and do offer guidance to their members on their conduct in potentially unsafe surroundings. But research funders, employers, research managers and researchers themselves carrying out fieldwork should pay attention to these concerns.

There are many sorts of threats to the safety of social researchers when gathering data that require proximate social interaction. There is the straightforward risk of physical violence and/or verbal abuse. This might be linked to the characteristics of the subject or the nature of the topic of the research or the subject's perception of threat from a researcher. It may even be provoked by something unexpected emerging from the research. The researcher's safety may be threatened, not by actual violence but by the threat of it causing some psychological trauma.

What follows is a list of some straightforward procedures that can be adopted to establish minimal protection:

- ensure projects are adequately staffed (this might mean having another researcher accompany the primary researcher for safety);
- researchers could work in pairs or shadow each other;
- mobile phone systems are necessary to keep in touch with a responsible person at the research base monitoring the researchers' activities and whereabouts ('call-ins' being required at fixed time intervals and changes of itinerary being fully announced);
- mobile phones provided specifically for the project should be left turned on;
- if overnight accommodation away from the researchers' homes is required, it should be vetted for security and convenience to location;
- careful attention paid to the time allowed for interviews, etc. to ensure researchers are not overstressed and so remain alert to risks;
- conduct risk assessment of the fieldwork site – the nature of travel facilities (public and taxis), safe parking of private/rented cars, pedestrian environment (well-lit and 'defensible' spaces) including

routes in and out of densely populated areas, local escape rendezvous for researchers (comfortable cafés open at convenient times), check police authorities' and community groups' views of risks, check specific local tensions such as religious, cultural or racial divisions, any public health issues, possible language support needed, study maps of the area to enhance geographical familiarity and so on;

- formally notify police and community groups of the researchers' imminent presence in the area by letter and phone call;
- in general avoid cold-calling in areas where proper reconnoitring has not been accomplished;
- do not enter houses when the number and nature of residents is unknown;
- dress in an inconspicuous and culturally sensitive manner;
- keep valuable equipment out of sight – especially laptops, mobile phones and digital cameras;
- take particular care in multistorey buildings, lifts and car parks – where security staffing is minimal and/or unknown;
- carry a personal alarm;
- stay in public rooms in houses and avoid private locations to avoid the risk of being in a compromising situation, or in which there might be accusations of improper behaviour and/or where one's person could be at risk;
- carry authorised identification;
- researchers' employers have a 'duty of care' towards employees contained in relevant local legislation (in the UK it is the Health and Safety at Work Act and a European Union Framework Directive) but researchers too have to share in this collective responsibility for their own safety – or they could be seen to be negligent and so contributory to any untoward event;
- most practices for improved safety impose additional burdens on research budgets so these should be included as an element in budgetary proposals – some are infrastructural costs (specialist training, insurance cover, communication aids), others are more project specific (local knowledge, counselling in areas of specific sensitivity);
- inherently dangerous research methods/site/topics/times/respondents should not be imposed on researchers;
- risks in any of the latter areas need to be addressed in project proposals and by prior risk assessment of respondents and research sites;
- brief field researchers on local cultural and gender norms in behavioural interaction and forms of language use and appropriate dress;

- researcher preparation and training should include techniques for handling conflict, threats, abuse or compromising situations;
- debriefing after field research should include an assessment of fieldwork safety and any incidents recorded with violent incidents reported to the employer's health and safety officer and to the local police force.

Research organisations and researchers themselves should seek to remain up-to-date on emerging safety risks and be prepared to amend protocols accordingly (Kenyon and Hawker 1999, Paterson et al. 1999). Despite all of these precautions it will never be possible to fully predict where risk might arise for researchers, so it is vital to be alert to possible danger in all fieldwork encounters. And while a full background risk assessment can help, researchers should also avoid making stigmatising assumptions that could equally prejudice their fieldwork (Ritchie and Lewis 2003: 70). It is true that 'Dangers to fieldworkers come in all shapes and sizes. Probably more common than physical risk is the danger of emotional damage as one mingles – and empathises – with research participants in sometimes desperate and distressing circumstances. Researchers may find themselves victimised or harassed because of their gender or perhaps their ethnic status. The heavy demands of fieldwork can cause problems with partners and with family. Like any other work, fieldwork can damage your health if it's not conducted thoughtfully' (Fincham 2006: 19).

9
Strategies for Maintaining Privacy and Confidentiality

(See page 13 of checklist.)

As with all other elements in ethical decision-making there are tensions, conflicts and potential contradictions even in what appears at first sight to be an uncontentious area – that is, protecting the privacy of research subjects and keeping any information they provide as confidential. It is also here that the risks to a research organisation are heightened as a consequence of growing legal requirements to protect the data held on research subjects. A further complication is added in the tension between anonymity and confidentiality. They are neither mutually exclusive nor necessarily entirely congruent. In offering both anonymity and confidentiality the amount of useful data that can be disclosed might be severely limited. Moreover one might be able to retain anonymity while not treating information given as confidential; but breaches of confidentiality are also likely to undermine attempts at anonymity. This area of debate also challenges us to think more clearly about the ethical implications of the difference between the public and private spheres of social life and how concerns for privacy limit the critical insights that social research offers in democratic societies. This could mean that it might not always be in the public interest to maintain the privacy of research subjects when matters of public policy are being investigated.

One can think of confidentiality as a variable dimension: it can be 'high' or 'low' with some information being treated as a mundane matter while others so 'private' that the research subject might request it being treated highly confidentially. A researcher might choose to use and/or disclose only some of the information gained and this might be done in concert with research subjects. They might ask for certain parts of the data given to be ignored or kept secret. Of course, confidentiality could never be 'complete' since it would be hard to know what useful data could be collected from a subject if everything they say or do has to be kept secret.

Anonymity cannot be seen as a continuous variable, it is dichotomous – one either keeps an identity secret or one does not. It is true, of course, that controlling anonymity depends upon factors beyond the researcher's control. A determined enquirer could, usually by a process of elimination, guess at or even discover the identity of research subjects if enough geographical and/or biographical information is available in the published research report.

The researchers' responsibility is to bear all of these considerations in mind and do their best, in terms of their agreement with the research subjects, commissioners and other relevant stakeholders, not to compromise pre-agreed levels of confidentiality and anonymity. They have an obligation to remove, as far as possible, the opportunities for others to deduce identities from the compiled data. Confidentiality must be 'contracted' for in the initial encounter between researcher and subject(s). This contract could be verbal or contained within a signed consent form. They must also operate within the constraints of the law on how data on private individuals are to be held, managed and, if required by law, disclosed to the appropriate authorities.

Even here it is necessary to counsel caution. Signing a consent form immediately compromises anonymity and, possibly, confidentiality. In order to formalise the agreement to a research engagement and, theoretically, protect both parties signed consent forms set up a contradiction between consent and anonymity. What this means is, simply, that one cannot assume that signed consent is ethically both necessary and desirable.

Data protection

These issues also have to be considered in light of the current data protection legislation of the country in which the researcher is operating – that is, in the research site where the data are being collected and, if elsewhere, where the data are being analysed and stored. Since this is such a complex area most large-scale research organisations will have a data protection officer whose responsibility is to advise researchers on what is possible and what must be achieved within the law. They are also likely to have a data protection management policy which all researchers should be trained in and subscribe to. In the NHS in the UK a Data Protection Officer's advice will be sought prior to receiving either research governance or ethical approval. No claims for the maintenance of confidentiality and/or anonymity can be sustained if primary source data are not adequately protected and kept secure.

(Extensive information on data protection policies and regulations across Europe can be found on the RESPECT project website: www.respect.org. And the UK Medical Research Council have a thorough and comprehensive guidance document – Personal Information in Medical Research – which offers advice that can be of use to all researchers working with personal data of any kind. This document can be found at: http://www.mrc.ac.uk/ethics_a.html.)

How can generic data be protected?

The first question to be addressed here is the storage of data. Identifying information has to be kept in a secure locked file with restricted users, in a specific location and with access restricted to named, accountable members of the research group. If held in a computer the same criteria should apply – the key file must be password protected. Preferably the data must be encrypted restricting access to only those with the requisite codes.

An immediate problem is revealed here in the 'portability' of computerised data files. They can be emailed, transferred to disc or flash drive or, even, left on the hard drive of a laptop computer. Either way their physical nature enables them to be lost, mislaid or stolen and the information contained accessible to others (see Box 9.1).

Box 9.1   Personal data in the UK

The irony in these comments will be immediately obvious to anyone aware of the breaches to the security of personal data held by various UK government departments in 2007 and 2008. First HM Customs and Revenue lost child benefit details for 25M people, the Driver and Vehicle Licensing Authority lost records on car drivers and the Ministry of Defence (MoD) lost data on 600,000 potential recruits when a laptop was stolen from a naval officer's car. The subsequent MoD enquiry revealed that a total of 69 laptops and 7 PCs had been reported missing. They also claimed they did not have the technology for encryption so the data could be accessible to anyone without the need for any particular technological sophistication. Only following this did the British Government implement a regulation to prevent data holders in the civil service from taking their laptops home/out of their office.

The first principle of anonymity and confidentiality with generic data is the need to separate identifiers from responses – the identity of the respondents being separated from the information they have provided. So the data in itself must not reveal the link to whoever provided it. Thus cases are often assigned numbers and the numbers linked to the originating individuals are stored separately and securely. The temporary suspension of this requirement may be allowed for the identification of responses for subject matching in the short term and for the necessary reliability checks from the generalised analysis to the raw data – thus it may be necessary to keep the data linked to the 'case' (i.e. individual) to which it applies for the sake of the integrity of the data. This would also be necessary, again in the short term, in order to track response rates. But this is a precarious period of the data gathering process during which data could be linked to specific individuals and both anonymity and confidentiality compromised. Consequently data security measures must be tightened during this period. Moreover it is necessary to have a policy about how identifiers are to be destroyed if confidentiality is under threat.

Given the growth of collaborative international research it is possible that identifying information could be further separated from raw data by being kept in a foreign country. (One would have to bear in mind the vulnerability of such data in different countries where different legislations might apply.)

Of course another way of separating identifiers from responses, useful for both qualitative and quantitative data analysis, is the application of pseudonyms or aliases to link data from the same source. With large datasets this may be impractical but for the small datasets typical of qualitative research, the assignment of a pseudonym sustains the humanising nature of this research style. (Throughout literature there is a worthy tradition of the employment of pseudonyms to protect authors from legal and political reproof or, even, unwanted publicity – Dodgson, Defoe, Bronte, Pope and so on.) There may be a temptation to select pseudonyms that appear particularly well suited to some of the characteristics of the research participant in, say, ethnographic studies. But if anonymity is to be successfully retained, no matter how appealing, this temptation should be resisted as it may offer subtle and latent clues to a respondent's identity.

In ethnographic studies, as long as there is some preagreement, the disclosure of the identities of the research participants in their cultural contexts might not only be seen as apt but also as vital to the insights gained from the research. This might not be free from risks (see Box 9.2).

Box 9.2   Anthropology in Indonesia

After being released after five months imprisonment in Indonesia for violating her tourist visa and conspiring with separatists, Lesley McCulloch, an anthropologist, admitted she lied during her trial to protect her contacts in the Aceh separatist movement in Sumatra. At her trial she claimed she had been ambushed by separatists and forced at gunpoint to go with them. She later admitted that she had gone to South Aceh to do research and collect information for her studies of the Indonesian military, their human rights abuses and illegal businesses in Aceh. 'The story we gave [during the trial] was to protect our sources, not so much ourselves, but those who'd set up the trip for us and arranged the meetings.' Although her fellow prisoners regularly bribed the guards to be allowed home for the night, neither she nor her lawyers ever handed over any money in return for favours. McCulloch was not banned from returning to Indonesia.

(Aglionby 2003)

This case raises several issues. The researcher did not respect the laws of the country nor the system of justice in operation. She even lied – claiming to be a tourist – to gain entry to the country. However without such deception it is unlikely she could have gathered the material necessary to investigate injustices, corruption, violence, bribery and so on. Ironically it appears she is not even banned from returning to Sumatra – one wonders whether or not, no matter how vital the data, the researcher would be wise to take a chance on returning.

More importantly the researcher has contravened some basic ethical principles that were discussed in Chapter 1. By lying to achieve her research goals she has 'contaminated the field'. Thus, if she can lie to gain access to her research subjects, why should we assume she would not lie about her research findings or in her concluding report? If she is capable of lying once, might she not be capable of lying again in order to 'colour' her research in a direction favourable to her perspectives, opinions and research career? So who can trust her now? Her anthropological colleagues, the Sumatran authorities or, even, her research subjects – the people she claims to be wishing to help? The problem with such deception is that outside observers cannot know the moral limits the researcher has set herself – whatever her claimed intentions, doubt has been cast on her real motives. Even if we share her view of the corruption of the Sumatran authorities, can we trust anyone who has chosen to be corrupt to achieve her research goals? The claim that there was no attempt to bribe the prison guards to achieve special favours might either be disbelieved or even suspected to be a deliberate ruse to persuade external observers of her moral integrity. It is a classic ethical and logical dilemma – once the lie has been told, and the observer knows that, nothing the liar says can be treated as truth.

Of course, one could argue that the only mistake she made was to admit to the lie – a really good and seasoned liar without honourable intentions would know not to do that and could continue in their deceptions while claiming good intent (see Bok's (1979) *Principle of Veracity* as discussed in Chapter 1). Thus supporting the view that good liars succeed and honourable people are condemned for their moral naivety. Once again, though, we must take care not to rush to judgement in condemning the lie and liars. As was touched upon in Chapter 7 deception is neither an artificial, deviant nor even dispensable feature of social life. It holds a key place in history and can even be seen as a productive element in human success and intellectual enlightenment (Campbell 2001).

The research report itself may be designed in such a way as to deflect anyone seeking to identify participants. Thus key information in reports (such as precise geographical locations or detailed descriptions of buildings or people) may be changed to avoid inadvertent identification. While it is a challenge to accuracy, such information might not be vital to the report's conclusions but preserves the privacy of respondents. Similarly the reporting of research information in an aggregate form helps minimise the chances of unwanted identification.

It is well known that journalists have refused to reveal their sources even if criminal and/or immoral activities have been disclosed. They protect their sources largely not to gain some higher moral ground but to protect their commercial interests – akin to the researchers' problems of contaminating the field. News depends upon inside information for its sensational and immediate quality. That is what sells newspapers. If they routinely disclosed sources no one would ever tell them the things that make their product saleable.

The added problem for social science is the combined methodological and ethical pressure for research accounts to be somehow 'sanitised'. Blackman (2007) illustrates this in his discussion of 'hidden ethnography': 'empirical data that are not released because it may be considered too controversial' (Blackman 2007: 700). Researchers often share anecdotes about the emotional borders that may have been crossed in private with each other, but rarely would these emerge in research reports. He expresses the fear that 'ethics committees and the desire for clean research will hamper ethnographic studies from getting 'up close' and result in a failure to gain insight into the lives, motives and experiences of people on the margins, or in situations involving risk' (Blackman 2007: 711).

Maintaining assurances

A major problem is that neither researchers nor their subjects are always in a position to know what the threats to the maintenance of anonymity and confidentiality may be and, therefore, how they could be anticipated. Whatever precautions they take themselves could be circumvented by the actions of determined others. Researchers certainly need the continued backing of their managers, supervisors and any regulatory committees to be able to fulfil their promises of confidentiality (see Box 9.3).

There might be a question about the University's own ethical stance in first giving permission for a study to proceed and then withdrawing it or, fearing litigation, refusing to support a researcher's promise to retain confidentiality. It raises many questions about what protection researchers can expect from the organisation within which and/or for which they are conducting the research. It also makes it clear how

Box 9.3   Confidentiality issues

Russel Ogden conducted interviews for research into assisted suicides/euthanasia for a PhD at Exeter University in the UK between 1995 and 1998. After first granting permission for the study via his departmental ethics committee, the University subsequently withdrew support by making it clear they would not recognise his promise of confidentiality and anonymity to his interviewees. Thus although he had to promise anonymity in order to secure respondents, since the acts he was studying were illegal, the University felt it could not support him in protecting their identities. He could not complete his studies or his PhD and the University was forced to pay him financial compensation. Subsequently the University's policy is to refuse to support research that has problems associated with the maintenance of confidentiality.

(Ogden 2003: 14; Farrar and Baty 2003: 60)

difficult research into illegal acts may be to conduct in any meaningful way – such as by interviewing the people responsible for them.

Thus researchers can only *strive* to protect their respondent's identity and do their best to hold the information given 'in confidence'. To take another example, if a subject subsequently, accidentally or intentionally, chooses to reveal their participation in a research study to their friends, family or the general public, there is little the researcher can do about it and so they cannot be held responsible for such action. If a subject wishes their identity to be disclosed as part of the research report, the researcher then has some dilemmas – principally the effect this might have on other subjects of their research (knowing the identity of one participant might help identify others who desire continued anonymity). Some subjects may wish their identities to be disclosed in order to maintain some link to or 'ownership' of the data while gatekeepers to more vulnerable subjects might seek identification to 'charismatise' the data donors (Grinyer 2002). The researcher should resist requests for the identity disclosure of any subject when such disclosure could lead to the failure to preserve the anonymity of other subjects who had requested that their identities not be disclosed. Either way the researcher still has a responsibility to anticipate the potential disadvantages of removing anonymity and may warn the subjects of such pitfalls.

It is interesting that subjects may not be as concerned as researchers have to be about these issues. Recent studies have suggested that most subjects are not fully aware of what they are consenting to when they agree to participate in research (Graham et al. 2007). One might argue that often researchers cannot anticipate all the things that could go wrong so they too are not in a position to warn subjects of all the dangers of participation. To help in making their decision to consent we need more insight into what subjects' understanding is of their participation – do they understand what it means to give consent? Do they fully understand what is being promised when confidentiality and/or anonymity is offered?

The Graham et al. (2007) study demonstrated the centrality of the relationship between 'interviewer' (the field researcher) and 'interviewee' (research subject). This is the key to participants' motivation to comply with researcher requests, to see the project through to completion and to sustain a commitment to providing accurate responses. This vindicates a point made at the outset of this book about the vital role of the researcher in the field in sustaining ethical research engagements. It shows how important the interviewer's skills are and, consequently, the vital need for good interviewer training. The same is true for less face-to-face encounters. A 'relationship' with the researchers and the project is sustained indirectly by, say, a trustworthy, clear and well laid out self-completion questionnaire. This might be achieved by an accompanying letter that not only introduces the project but also personalises the researcher(s).

These sorts of gatekeeping issues become even more important when dealing with subjects who are assumed to have less 'capacity to consent' such as children. That seems to mean that they might not fully understand what they are consenting to – much as adults don't but perhaps to a different degree. The main tension here is between the rights of children to decide for themselves and the parental right of control. This is usually legally enshrined but the UK law for one is not entirely clear in helping resolve this tension for the purposes of research. (Chapter 10 deals with children as subjects more fully and with their capacity to consent.)

We could do with more studies about how subjects make their decisions to participate in research and that would certainly enhance our ethical awareness. However by enhancing subjects' understanding of these issues we may be inevitably posing more of a problem for researchers. (See Chapter 11 on involving the public.) In any case the personalisation of reported data may affect its theoretical value by being seen to be excessively unique and not usefully generalisable.

While confidentiality is also a matter of obeying the law on data protection, the information given by those being researched is, by definition, introduced into a more 'public' domain by virtue of its disclosure to the researcher. The researcher has to try to make clear to the respondent precisely what this sharing of confidences might imply for the respondent. After all these *data* are 'given things' or 'donations' – given to the researcher. In a qualitative research interview for example, the apparent friendship established between interviewer and interviewee might lead to the disclosure of more information than the interviewee first intended and there may be regret that so much has been disclosed and a need to address the social and emotional consequences of that.

The duty of confidentiality is owed on the basis of a contractual (formal or informal) understanding between researcher and researched. But that duty can be breached by either party to the contract if, say, police authorities request data which are relevant to a case they are investigating or a court issues a *subpoena* which demands the data be disclosed. If criminal activity is disclosed by a respondent the researcher has to choose between obedience to the law and a breach of any confidentiality and anonymity originally promised. The researcher's moral integrity only remains intact if this is clearly understood by the respondent prior to the commencement of the research. Yet making that clear may have methodological consequences in producing a tendency to minimal disclosure by the respondent as a safety precaution. Once more though, it takes a cautious respondent to always bear in mind the sensitivity of their own information once released into a more public domain.

One device is to randomise responses in order to disguise potentially incriminating information. In that way researchers could not subsequently be *required* to disclose identities.

Problems with anonymity and pseudonymity

It should not be assumed necessarily that the assurance and guarantee of anonymity is an ethical prerequisite. Nor should it be assumed that the allocation of pseudonyms offers ethical reassurance to participants. Anne Grinyer's research experiences and consequent reflections suggest that these are more complex issues than they first appear (Grinyer 2001, 2002). Standard data protection concerns and legal requirements imply the maintenance of anonymity whenever possible. But Grinyer's respondents held varying opinions on this and many changed their views after reflections on the consequences of their sensed relationship to the data and their dissemination. Her work was a study of the effects of the experiences of young cancer patients on parents and families. At first participants agreed with formal requests for and offers of anonymity, but after initial reports of findings they experienced a sense of a loss of 'ownership of the data' and desired an authentic reflection of their experiences by retention and reporting of the true identity of the patients and their families. Unsuitable pseudonyms offered no solution since the choice of an 'inappropriate' name could even cause further distress.

Grinyer and Thomas (2001) advise collecting sensitive data in a sensitive manner with any information to be imparted by their respondents about their own experiences '... on their own terms and in their own time' (2001: 162). The method they adopted was via narrative correspondence. They made a public appeal through a variety of different media to seek people willing to 'tell their story' – either by writing or tape-recording an account 'of their own' – according to their own dimensions of relevance and not to answer particular questions set by the researcher(s). In fact two thirds of their respondents refused anonymity; however it was decided only to use subjects' Christian names in order to preserve some degree of anonymity – thereby protecting the subjects from unanticipated risks as a consequence of identity disclosure.

Evidently how important this is seen to be will vary according to the topic of the research – it might be more problematic for research in emotionally sensitive and personal areas. But the lesson is not to assume the necessity for anonymity, and not to assume that all forms of identity disguise are acceptable and that participants will not change their minds.

The public and the private

To minimise potential risks to the research organisation all research staff may be required to sign a confidentiality agreement. Indeed to establish mutual rights and obligations and reduce the consequences of shock or unpredicted revelations there could be a requirement for all partici- pants to the research to sign such agreements – research managers, field researchers, subjects, funders/commissioners and so on. Such contracts would then contain and clarify the conditions under which breaches of confidentiality could occur – such as with legal requirements to disclose information about criminal activity (according to the Children's Act, the Mental Health Act, etc.). Once again Data Protection Officers should hold expertise on these matters and their advice regularly sought.

Some organisations (e.g. the UK National Centre for Social Research (NatCen)) have established disclosure panels which researchers can consult if they find themselves party to information they suspect they might have to disclose for legal reasons. Such a panel advises the researcher and helps to protect both researcher and research organi- sation. The legal situation is clear that any disclosure of criminal or reportable illicit activity breaks the confidentiality bond, and strictly the researcher should make that clear to respondents beforehand.

As with all other such situations the researcher in the field might find themselves balancing morality with the law in attempting to make the right decisions about disclosures. The prime dilemma is to balance the moral stance of confidentiality, with the legal position, while also judg- ing the 'seriousness' of any reported offence and balancing that against the potential danger to 'as yet unknown' others who could be harmed by non-reporting.

Researchers' main concern here has to do with what might be consid- ered to constitute 'public space'. When in a Post Office recently, I was asked: 'Are you paying interest on your credit card?' – clearly with the intent of selling a Post Office financial product – their credit card – on more favourable terms than the one I currently held. To ask such a question as part of a research project would meet severe challenges under ethical review. When cashing in some premium bonds on the phone, I was asked 'Would you be looking for a high interest savings account?' – again it is my business why I was cashing in the bonds but a sales pitch relating to my personal financial details appears deemed more acceptable than a similar research question. Perhaps even more concerning since at least a spontaneous street researcher presumably doesn't know me and so may be better able to maintain anonymity – my bank, post office or national savings 'tellers' might not.

More obvious challenges to our understanding of what constitutes 'public space' occur in direct (participant or non-participant) observation studies. Where social and/or individual behaviour is being observed without the subjects' knowledge, researchers must take care not to infringe what may be referred to as the 'private space' of an individual or group. The problem is that this varies between cultures and subcultures. Some societies and subcultures establish very clear demarcations between what is considered personal and, therefore, private space, and what is made more generally visible for others. The most notorious transgressors of such rules are the paparazzi who follow the rich and the famous hoping to catch evidence of some private indiscretion which they decide should be made available for public consumption. The only check on their behaviour is litigation. Researchers cannot afford such contamination of their field so, where it is practicable, they should attempt to obtain consent after the event. At the very least they could interpret behaviour patterns that appear deliberately to make observation difficult as a tacit refusal of permission to be observed. (Those very actions might themselves be of social scientific interest, but there would have to be very good justification for disobeying the tacit refusal of consent in order, for example, to better understand how people manage their public/private space and so enable the continuing development of even more ethical observational research.)

This tradition of observation studies have been covered previously in Chapter 7 (such as Erving Goffman's ethologically inspired works) that are essentially spontaneous or opportunistic research engagements.

The social scientist as an intuitively interested observer of human social interaction observes some noteworthy pattern of behaviour and writes about it. It is perhaps different only in depth of analysis and theoretical background from the kind of human-interest writing that columnists for newspapers and magazines publish. It would not be expected that retrospective consent for such commentary should (or even could) be sought. Other examples are vox pops or vignettes – one overhears a comment by a passer-by and uses it, or one finds oneself engaged in really insightful discussion that highlights a particular phenomenon of interest. To neglect to report it might mean the loss of a valuable insight into the human condition from which we all might learn. But it must be employed with care and sensitivity to the individual's awareness that their accounts and behaviour might be 'collectable' and reportable in a research study. J. Michael Bailey, a psychology professor at Northwestern University, Illinois, found this to his cost when complaints were received after he used unconsented stories told to him by two transsexuals in casual conversation in a bar and at a wedding (Bailey 2003; Marcus 2003).

Once again what lies behind all these reflections are ideas for accomplishing the best way of respecting the rights of others – even in unconsented observational studies.

Archiving and data retention

A major threat to confidentiality and anonymity lies in data retained after the completion of a project and/or preserved in a data archive for some future analytical purpose (secondary research). In the UK there is a legal obligation implicit in case law which prohibits researchers from passing on information to a third party without the explicit consent of the research subject – and only the research subject can decide which of their data can be considered confidential. The general principle is that consent should be given for all uses of data for secondary purposes – thus if data have even only the potential to be passed on or made available for further analysis, this should be clarified to respondents. It again illustrates the importance of a clear consenting process and the provision of adequate information. If the data are required to be retained and archived for subsequent study, the subject's permission must be gained in advance (Backhouse 2002). But this should not prove a disincentive for seeking to archive data or else valuable opportunities for further analysis will be lost. (Links to the relevant UK Data Archives can be found in the websites listed at the end of the book.)

There are added data protection problems associated with the secondary analysis of qualitative data collected for some other purpose. It is essential that the archiving principles adopted are declared and understood by both participants and researchers.

The policies for qualitative research can be found at the major archive sites:

http://www.qualidata.essex.ac.uk and http://www.dipex.org.uk.

Principles for managing archived quantitative data are also well recognised.

On preserving and sharing statistical data:
http://www.data-archive.ac.uk/home/PreservingSharing.pdf.

Information about the UK Data Archive licence with depositors, plus a download option for the form can be found at:
http://www.data-archive.ac.uk/depositingData/LicenceAgreement.asp.

Associated user forms can be viewed at:
http://www.data-archive.ac.uk/orderingData/linkAccessAgreement.asp.

A particular area of sensitivity and enhanced need for care with data is the secondary access to and use of patient or health records. In the UK the Care Record Development Board has published the report of a working group on the secondary uses of patient information, including research. The report explains the existing arrangements for use of patient information in research and recommendations for future action to support the appropriate use of patient information for research (see Box 9.4).

Box 9.4   Integrated Household Survey and privacy

A 2,000-item survey from the Office for National Statistics, the *Integrated Household Survey* has raised concerns about privacy. They plan to randomly select 200,000 homes, questioning each occupant, so producing about 500,000 individual respondents. The questions concern sexual behaviour, intimate relationships, private money matters and health-related behaviour such as alcohol consumption. There are questions on contraception, whether men have had vasectomies, the brands of contraceptive pill women take, and whether they have ever used a 'morning after' pill. There are questions on the dates when previous relationships ended, the precise amount of take-home pay, and whether people earn extra money from second jobs or from bonuses. A major concern is that the data will not be anonymised at the point of collection – only after collection at a central Government agency – hence concerns about the potential vulnerability to loss of the data or potential for sharing with other agencies.

(Harper 2008)

(The Report is available from the Connecting for Health website: http://www.connectingforhealth.nhs.uk/crdb/workstreams/secusesreport.pdf.)

In late 2008 there were proposals in the UK to enhance researchers' ability to directly access NHS data in the form of primary health care records – with a view to improving access to patients' inclusion criteria when recruiting for research trials. While one is beguiled by the research opportunities, the proposals would mean a fundamental change in the uses to which the data would be put that was not originally agreed to or understood by those who 'donated' it to the health service when in an intimate relationship with a health professional in the first place. The plea that researchers' integrity matches that assumed of those responsible for health service data collection and storage is ironic in an era of highly mobile (therefore vulnerable) data technology when no one, least of all government agencies, can guarantee its security. It is a step further in allowing agencies (that may not even be state agencies) access to and control over personal data which is part of how people structure and control their identity in the modern world. As such it is a human rights issue. Moreover this reflects an astonishing naivety about how robust that data source can be. The assumption is that quasi-census data are less prone to error – as if people always tell the truth to health professionals, that they tell the 'whole' truth and that data collectors never make data entry mistakes. The danger lies in assuming that such data can be highly valid; thus the inferences drawn for whole populations may be more prone to unknown error than a sample-based study when more cautious conclusions and recommendations are routinely made.

In general, good practice suggests that research should be conducted in accordance with the principles of the applicable country-specific national data protection legislation. But care should be taken not to confuse the 'protection' of the data with privacy/confidentiality. Protected data may still be made publicly available – its protection may relate to its integrity (i.e. its link to context and to subject).

In business, management and public policy research it is quite common to reveal the identity of organisations involved in research and to identify individual key informants – at least those assumed to be less vulnerable at the more elite hierarchical levels. That would best be accomplished as part of a preliminary agreement ideally with the problem being addressed in open discussion with research subjects with the aim of obtaining some degree of informed consent to a potential disclosure. In cases where disclosure of the identity of a subject (whether an individual or an organisation) is central and relevant to the research neither confidentiality nor anonymity can be guaranteed.

Indeed the disclosure of unanticipated but serious public accountability issues is ethically justified. There is more of an expectation that not preserving anonymity is both methodologically essential and in the public interest – enhancing the presumed public benefits to research. The full value of such research may depend upon researchers' skills in report writing and the medium chosen for dissemination and the quality of its content. Seeking a deliberately salacious outlet may boost a researcher's notoriety and their short-term public visibility but it might not help in securing further commissioned projects for management or public organisations.

It has to be acknowledged that some risk of unintended disclosure is always present in any project. Researchers should be able to demonstrate that, where agreed, they have taken all reasonable steps to prevent the disclosure of identities and, where not agreed, they have very good reasons for allowing the disclosure.

10
Dealing with Vulnerability

(See page 14 of checklist.)

The notion that some subjects are deemed to be more vulnerable than others is, again, likely to be influenced by diverse cultural preconceptions and so regulated differentially by localised legislation. It is likely to be one of the areas where researchers need extra vigilance to ensure compliance with the local law.

The discussion contained in the previous chapters should demonstrate that all members of the population and so all research subjects can be seen as vulnerable in some respects. Indeed we may not know our vulnerabilities until the 'intervention' of a social researcher exposes us to them or until a research engagement 'tests' or challenges us. This means that we all have the potential to become vulnerable and so the distribution of vulnerability in the subject population is, necessarily, unknown. In some respects it is impossible to build the full potential for vulnerability into research designs and proposals. There is no reason to assume that a research ethics committee can anticipate vulnerability any better than the researchers themselves – unless they are more attuned to seek it out. What matters is that both researchers and reviewers anticipate the potential for its emergence and make available procedures for dealing with it. (Remembering always that vulnerabilities might not be made explicit or disclosed and that, though latent, it was the research engagement that prompted them.)

So some of the points considered in this chapter might apply to us all – but some categories of the population are generally expected to be more vulnerable than others. There may be a popular consensus that some members of society are visibly (or understood to be) more vulnerable than others. This means that, according to our judgement, are there ways in which these people are more exposed to risk and harm than the 'normal' population by virtue of their assumed vulnerabilities?

Clearly that is a social judgement and we may be in danger of pat-ronising some individuals or sectors of society who wish to be seen as 'strong enough' to make their own decisions about their presumed vulnerability. Evident/visible physical disability leads to presumed vulnerability, but to be 'precious' about the disabled may lead to their social exclusion and the lack of adequate representation of their views and experiences in research studies. Even this should not be simply assumed – children can be very wise, mentally disabled people astute on some specific matters and the physically disabled extremely wary of repetitive research engagements. The main message of this chapter might be to encourage researchers to be sensitive to emergent vulner-abilities and manage undue stress to participants by employing the strategies discussed earlier.

To illustrate, just how vulnerable is someone who is recognisably obese? What if they consider their 'fatness' to be unproblematic or they have grown politically active in terms of 'fat rights'? Alternatively what if someone asks me an apparently innocuous question about parents and I become upset because of my relationship with my parents or my grief at having lost them and so on? As active participants in social life we all have the potential to be vulnerable to something – all of these responses could equally have been generated by something we read in the newspapers, saw on the television or was done or said in the street. Researchers cannot predict that vulnerability, nor can they cater for it comprehensively – but researchers can attempt to minimise the more obvious vulnerabilities by careful phrasing of questions and considering what to do if there is an evident emotional response. That response may even be anger at the 'effrontery' of a question – even ethics committees cannot protect members of the public from being offended, their role is only to minimise the chances of that happening *as a consequence of* the research taking place.

So when we are reviewing the potential for enhanced subject vulner-ability, we should not be asking: 'Are these subjects vulnerable?' Instead the question is: 'Are these subjects made any more vulnerable than they might ordinarily be in their daily lives as a result of their participation in this research?'

Protecting participants: Vulnerability and marginalisation

Researchers have a duty to attempt to protect all participants in a study from any harmful consequences that may arise out of their participa-tion. This is even more the case when those groups or individuals are less able to protect themselves. Children are seen as particularly vulnerable, while older people may be both vulnerable and marginalised. Children may lack the sophistication to perceive when a study is not in their interests or when disclosure is damaging to them (Alderson 1995). Older people may be excluded from most studies due to their lessened economic and political importance in contemporary society. The ethical researcher has to guard against all these 'disprivileging' possibilities.

It is unsurprising that increased awareness of the ethical problems associated with the study of marginal and/or vulnerable groups or individuals should come from feminist researchers. Gender biases in research arise from the assumption of homogeneity in participants and this can lead to the dominance of masculine perspectives. Feminist research has succeeded in highlighting and making more visible the traditionally private worlds of females, families and households (Cotterill 1992). That, in itself, is not without ethical concern – how those worlds are made public and the consequences for the people in the study may then lie outside of their control. Barron (1999) shows how intellectually disabled women are doubly disadvantaged (i.e. made more vulnerable) research subjects both in their status loss from cognitive impairment and from their gender. A self-appointed alliance with such groups may mask the effectively superior position of the researcher. This is also methodologically problematic in that data might be interpreted poorly and the informants further 'objectified' in the process. This is another reason for ensuring ongoing/continuous review of ethical conduct in research with marginalised groups.

More recently researchers have become concerned about the potential for harm to groups or individuals who may be typically 'excluded' from studies as a consequence of their sociocultural location. Such exclusion might mean that their interests are inadequately represented in a study and the researcher's (necessarily) limited perspective on the world cannot guarantee the inclusion of all groups. Typically this relates to lesser-abled individuals routinely being missed by all types of social surveys – individuals with learning disability may be excluded from street interviews, those with vision impairments missed by postal questionnaires and so on. Researchers may even fail to pay enough attention to sectors of the population more liable to drop out of studies of any longitudinal nature – older people may be more likely to contribute to a study's 'mortality' (technically and literally) than other vulnerable groups (Bhamra et al. 2008). While 'who' to include is primarily a methodological problem, ethical concerns arise when routine exclusion perpetuates or exacerbates an individual's or a group's lowered status in society.

Some threats to vulnerability are so subtle that they may be hard to recognise. Researchers are ever more accustomed to being cautious about communication across cultures and to avoiding gendered or racist language. But some of the ways in which offence can be caused are so deeply embedded in our language use they may not be easily recognised (Karpf 2006: Chapter 12). If it is the case that men and women have fundamentally different linguistic schemata that reflect different dimensions of relevance and cognitive structures, then the choice of phrasing in interviews and in questionnaires is anything but methodologically and ethically trivial (Tannen 1994, 1995). This is not just a question of gender differentiation in language; there are subtle metacommunicative 'frames' that hide implicit assumptions about relationships and similarly tacit mechanisms for checking and asserting hierarchical relationships that can seriously impair the validity and reliability of research interactions – quite apart from the unintended 'offence' they might cause. Sometimes these may be no more than the inappropriate employment of terms of endearment – such as calling someone 'dear' or 'sweetheart' (see Tannen 1992: Chapters 5, 6). All we can do is seek to improve our knowledge about how such mechanisms operate and to gain skills in the more sensitive employment of language.

The key to how participants are ethically accessed and then protected lies in attending to the concerns already considered in previous chapters – seeking informed consent, care with data generation, ensuring anonymity and confidentiality when appropriate and allowing – even making it easy for – participants to withdraw from their involvement.

Some of the detailed specific features of each of these potentially vulnerable groups are considered next.

Children (minors)

Children are frequently assumed to be one of the most vulnerable groups in the population, so extra care has to be taken when they are the subjects of a research project. The seeking of both the child's and parental consent and the screening of interviewees – including a police check (a CRB check under the new ISA in the UK) – are often advised. But the extent to which this has to be accomplished appears dependent upon the age of the child, the location or site of questioning/ interviewing, the presence of a parent as chaperone and the length of time spent with an interviewer. All of these factors have to be balanced against methodological accuracy and the guaranteeing of confidentiality and/or anonymity, if requested, for the child's response (Alderson and Morrow 2004).

The ISA has been established as a result of the Safeguarding Vulnerable Groups Act 2006 and will assess every person who wants to work or volunteer with vulnerable people. An ISA registration permits work with vulnerable categories of people and is transferable between employment – with lists of 'barred' individuals being retained for employers to check online. So researchers once 'licensed' can carry their registration to different research sites.

The problem of research with children has increasingly become one of protecting their rights, ensuring their participation is free and informed and that the protections guaranteed by the law are routinely observed. One can see a problem immediately in that parents or guardians have legal rights and duties to protect children at least until they are 16 in most matters (with formal educational institutions acting *in loco parentis* when the children are in their care). The question becomes of how does one protect the rights of a child to choose freely to participate in a research activity while still observing the parents' rights to decide, on their child's behalf, whether or not it is in their interests to participate?

Physicians find themselves having similar problems with confidentiality in the care of children and researchers can gain much from considering how they are advised to resolve such dilemmas (see *0-18 years: Guidance for all doctors* (2007)). The General Medical Council (GMC) in the UK advises careful communication to ascertain the needs and wants of both parents/primary caregivers and children. This means balancing the principle that young people deserve the same respect that one should guarantee to adults at the same time as recognising their relative immaturity. In a survey of under 18s the GMC found that children felt that doctors were not easy to gain access to, did not listen to them, spoke over their heads and did not keep confidences (Anthony 2008). There is a danger that children may perceive social researchers in the same way and so adjust their response in any research engagement accordingly. Doctors are advised to share information with other agencies responsible for the care of children if they have any suspicions of neglect or abuse. However, just like doctors, researchers have to balance the maintenance of confidentiality with care for the rights of the child. Once again, in the last analysis, it is the researcher – perhaps in consultation with the child and perhaps also the caregiver/parent – who must judge the balance of responsibilities (see Box 10.1).

Box 10.1   Child neglect and abuse

To explore the links between child neglect and any subsequent abuse, children's case records were studied. It was a case control study comparing children who had been neglected but with no record of abuse against those who had been neglected and apparently subsequently abused. What became clear was the lack of coherence/integrity in the formal records held by different agencies. Their trigger for action in terms of placing children on an 'at risk' register, and more thorough monitoring by relevant agencies, was a paediatrician's opinion – usually contained within a letter that frequently imposed the appearance of a seamless case upon evidently disparate documentation.

(Cody et al. 2000)

Such a study confirms the point made in Chapter 2 that even secondary research (documentary analysis, archival or case studies) might raise considerable ethical concerns. One might ask whether or not such studies ought to be conducted if subsequent recommendations to changes in policy and practice do not follow. It also exposes agencies faced with difficult childcare decisions to critical review which might undermine their confidence to act effectively.

The problems posed by researching 'sensitive' issues with potentially 'vulnerable' subjects is addressed in their work by Hester et al. (2008, see also Hester 2006) researching obese children who attended a residential weight loss camp. This research raised questions of balancing potential benefits and risks for participants compounded by a desire to tap untold experiences in order to inform practice in ways that might benefit obese children in the future. They adopted a progressively focused interview methodology together with an established counselling technique as a research tool allowing both researcher and participant to profit from the research experience.

While a great deal of energy has been expended on the ethics of research with children, very little has been done to find out children's own perspectives on ethical issues associated with their participation in research. Using fairly innovative, 'user-friendly' techniques for accessing children's views a NatCen team found that the interviewer has such a key role to play in ensuring that children understand their participation rights in research that it is vital they are well trained, and that they are accorded some flexibility – using their own judgement – in both information giving and in the consenting process. What counted as 'sensitive' or personal topics varied considerably between the children interviewed – making it difficult to predict which areas of discussion required more careful approaches. But ultimately they were unable to conclusively answer a key question: Just how much do children comprehend what is being asked of them and what the research may be for? Hence it remains difficult to assess just what 'capacity' for consent children do actually possess (Reeves et al. 2007).

People with disabilities

Research can contribute towards the achievement of human rights and social justice for people with disabilities; but, equally, if not conducted properly it can obstruct those very aspirations (United Nations 1993). Useful guidance on the ethics of research with people with disabilities is offered by the National Disability Authority (Ireland) (2004). They first outline a set of overarching 'core values' which should apply to all disability research. In fact these values summarise the central principles of all ethical codes on human participant research. They require respect for human rights, dignity, equality and diversity of all involved in research. They promote social justice, well-being and the avoidance of harm, together with facilitating participation so that no groups – the disabled in particular – are systematically excluded from research for reasons of ignorance or avoidance. They advocate the maintenance of high professional research standards and the fulfilment of legal responsibilities.

These core values are then operationalised in a set of guidelines for 'good practice' which make recommendations summarised as follows:

- *Plan for inclusion*: researchers need to examine the ways in which disabled people might be ignored or avoided systematically in research designs intended to cover a 'general' population. Do field researchers conducting face-to-face interviews have materials prepared to meet the needs of the disabled and/or do they physically locate themselves in sites where the disabled might not be accessible? (For example, are the information sheets and/or the consent forms reproduced in enlarged font or Braille for people with vision impairments or sight loss?) If participatory research is appropriate, the active participation of people with disabilities might help to ensure the representation of their interests. Different forms of participation at different stages of the research process may have to be considered, as well as the implications of the appropriateness of different research methodologies to people with different forms of disability (see National Disability Authority 2002).

- *Anticipate diversity*: people with disabilities are not a homogeneous group. They display as much cultural heterogeneity and variety in resource needs as the rest of the population. Varied appropriate methods of communication, access and participation will be required to cater for, say, diversity in sexual orientation, ethnicity and other social situational factors. There needs to be recognition that 'the lived experience of disablement is shaped by the impact of other social characteristics' (Zappone 2003).
- *Minimise harm*: ensure the research will not damage the established rights or limit the legitimate entitlements of disabled people. It may be necessary to consider ways in which people with disability can be empowered to participate in research, and the ways in which they can become disempowered (M. Oliver 2003).
- *Provide disability awareness training*: researchers should be specifically trained in the needs of disabled people and appropriate national and international legislation. This should include promoting sensitivity to the history of exclusion of people with disabilities and the abuse of people with disabilities by some forms of research.
- *Avoid 'over-researching'*: some groups and some individuals are researched more frequently on the grounds of their ability to articulate their condition (assumed to be representative of a particular category of disability). Alternatively some disabled groups or their representatives might be more politically active and so make themselves more accessible than others. To over-research is both methodologically unsound as a 'sampling' strategy and may be harmful in terms of making excessive demands on the time and physical energy of the disabled group or individual (Mitchell 2003).
- *Collaborate with people with disabilities*: both research on disability and the avoidance of systematic exclusion will be enhanced by considering including people with disabilities in research planning and design, as active participants/researchers themselves and/or as members of advisory groups. Opportunities for people with disabilities to become trained professional researchers should be made available.
- *Make use of 'disability consultants'*: consider ways in which the expertise of people with disabilities or their active and informed representatives can be used in an advisory capacity before and during research projects. Recognise the value of accumulated knowledge and experience of people with disabilities, voluntary disability

group members or even the peers and/or family members of disabled persons.

- *Facilitate research accessibility*: use accessible and appropriate language and be sensitive to its use. This not only means employing the standard 'intelligent layperson' forms of language in interviews, questionnaires, proposals and reports but also avoiding insensitive uses of terminology. For example, most disabled people do not like to be viewed as 'suffering' from their condition – their disability is a part of their identity, so it is 'lived', neither merely nor necessarily 'suffered'. In addition research reports should be available to and readable by disabled members of the population – in particular when such research has direct implications for their lives.

- *Examine membership of research ethics committees*: review bodies should consider ways of including people with disabilities in the process of ethical scrutiny. Many of the other concerns in this list can be addressed by such effective representation.

- *Ensure that disability is not an obstruction to fully informed consent*: all the previous points made here cumulatively build to facilitating informed consent. With the proper representation, consultation and participation of people with disability, together with accessible research materials, and the employment of an ongoing, dynamic, negotiated consenting process (as discussed in Chapter 7) then that consent can be considered to be fully informed and properly managed.

- *Exercise caution with the use of gatekeepers and proxies*: if research on and/or with disabled people is to be meaningful, then it is vital to ensure their voice is heard and their perspective revealed as much as possible. Gatekeepers by definition control access to people with disability (whether they be formal and or informal carers, or care managers/providers, family and friends) while proxies are presumed to speak on their behalf. In all cases this must be treated as 'indirect' evidence and it might be hard to avoid. People with disability may be unable to speak for themselves and may need the services of an advocate and/or interpreter. But the researcher must be aware that this necessarily changes the dynamic of the relationship between researcher and researched if the subject is disabled. In some cases the person with disability may be unable to prevent the intervention of a gatekeeper since they may be dependent upon them for their care. Use of proxies, gatekeepers and so on may be the only way to ensure the interests and rights of certain categories of disability and, consequently, by no means invalidates the research, but it certainly has implications for the status of the evidence produced by such means. Particular care over the consenting process is required when any form of proxy is involved.

• *Take extra care with anonymity, privacy and confidentiality*: people with disabilities may be more accustomed than the rest of us to threats to their privacy. Their relationships with health and social care agencies necessitate more public considerations of their status and needs. But the research process should not exacerbate that situation nor assume it is not a concern for them. The same regard for their dignity and privacy that is accorded to all human participants should be granted to people with disabilities and the threats to these principles watched out for.

• *Consider budgetary implications and project timeframes*: specialist research materials, translation facilities, production of additional reports and discussion papers all have cost implications for research budgets. In addition the extra time that physically disabled people might require for research participation and/or attendance at review and advisory committees or planning teams will need to be taken into account. If people with disabilities are excluded from research for budgetary reasons this should be clearly stated.

All of the above considerations also apply to people lacking mental capacity – and they raise additional concerns which have already been touched on in Chapter 7. Striving to empower and include persons considered vulnerable by disability raises many challenges (see Box 10.2).

Box 10.2   Research with learning disabled people

My colleague John conducted a study of the transition from an institutional care environment to sheltered housing in the community. His attempt to seek 'inclusion' – ensure the voices of learning disabled people themselves were heard – was challenged by his supervisors. They believed proxies would be better (their closest carers) since more information would be gained from them. John strove to keep including the learning disabled people themselves, but it turned out to be a daunting task – since they varied so much both in what they could say, how they said it and how they chose to opt out and discontinue their participation. Should John have followed his supervisors' advice from the outset and not striven to be so inclusive?

Pregnant women

Women are considered particularly vulnerable when pregnant for a combination of sound physiological, social and psychological reasons. The profound physiological changes they are undergoing while 'natural' are not 'normal' in the sense that they are not usually being frequently experienced within the lifetime of any one woman. Moreover the fact they are carrying an unborn child enhances research risk on the grounds that at least two potentially vulnerable categories of individuals are involved. However to exclude them from research during their pregnancy due to heightened risk assessment might mean losing valuable insights by which knowledge, policy and practice can develop. Their vulnerability is also enhanced by the multitude of social pressures on them at this time – from family, friends, welfare and health agencies. Consequently they may experience some confusion arising out of multiple advice sources and a reluctance to refuse consent to participate in research with apparently authoritative sources in case it affects the care they receive (Jones and McGee 2007). Once again none of us can be considered 'immune' to such multiple influences, it is merely that the likelihood of such being the case for pregnant women is enhanced.

Older people

Just because people are visibly old, it does not mean they should be considered vulnerable – especially if they do not want to be seen as such and regard such a view to be 'ageist'.

The main problem with older people as vulnerable subjects is their assumed physical and mental deterioration. Such assumptions lead to stereotypical attitudes towards them and expectations about them. Since they form such a large and growing sector of the population in advanced industrial societies they should rarely be excluded from studies making claims about the whole population and research targeted at them should consider and address the consequences of such stereotypical behaviour. It might be advisable with older people and other distinct population categories that researchers add some extra ethical principles that take account of systematic variations in the older sector of the population, while allowing that they should be accorded at least the same rights as all members of the population. Such guiding principles have been suggested by Tom Kitwood under the umbrella notion of 'personhood' (Kitwood 1997). They include recognition, respect and trust. More recently the guiding principle of 'dignity' has also been proposed in a major EU study (Tad 2005). If all the subjects were accorded consideration under these principles, then no special positive discriminatory action need be taken for older people per se.

In practical terms then, to maintain the dignity and personhood of older research subjects one would have to anticipate the potential limitations to their participation in research and adjust methodologies accordingly. Most of the good practice recommendations listed above for people with disability could equally be applied to older people. (Taking care never to suggest that being old is, in itself, a 'disability'.)

Research into dementia offers another challenge to catering for a range of potential vulnerabilities – ageing and mental capacity. The problem of how to access the 'authentic voice' of older people made less able by cognitive decline is one confronted in different ways by many researchers (Williams 2007). Keady and Williams (2007), for example, have developed a 'co-constructed inquiry' approach in their opposition to 'a research process that "took for granted" researcher control over data collection and analysis'. Their search is for a way of facilitating the integration of 'the expertise of those who live with a long-term condition into the research process. ... (by sharing) ... a common language, a common set of beliefs and a common purpose' (Keady and Williams 2007: 35).

There is also an issue of studying older people in residential or care homes when, in addition to the generic concerns of research with older people, there is an element of them being constrained by their institutionalised status and so not entirely free to choose to participate or not and in what they might wish to say. Again the challenge is to find a way to facilitate their genuine participation in the research in the face of 'gatekeeping' activities and/or the older research subjects' fear of such (Fisk and Wigley 2000).

In some respects older people in institutionalised settings have some of the characteristics of a 'captive' population. So, perhaps paradoxically, given the condemnation of covert research in some circles, it could be argued that observation could be the least intrusive way of researching aspects of the lives of older people since it is less likely to challenge them emotionally and physically. A range of naturalistic observation methods could be employed for which in some cases they need not be made aware of and, in others, might be positively enjoyed (Clark 2007).

Captive populations: Prisoners, students and armed services personnel

Ironically students and prisoners share the fate of all potentially 'captive' research populations. Prisoners have found their privileges withdrawn for refusing to take part in research, and students find that being on the receiving end of research studies is taken for granted as a requirement of their course of study. Members of the armed forces can feel similarly 'required' to participate in research. In all cases there is a danger that such subjects may not be as fully informed as is required in studies of 'normal' populations.

Although Allen Hornblum's (1998) account of research on prisoners does relate to medical experimentation, the principles that emerge are generalisable to most research with captive populations. The medical researchers' attitudes displayed total disrespect for the moral status of their human subjects by their delight with the easy availability of 'acres of skin' upon which their allergy tests could be conducted. It is worrying that we seemed to have not moved far from Nuremburg if such views were still being held. The problem revealed in Hornblum's account is that the prisoners made their own ill-advised estimates of risk of harm within the context of their imprisoned status.

The prisoners' need to prove complicit with the authorities while in detention alongside the extra remuneration they received was enough for them to counter fears of the potentially physically damaging nature of the studies that were conducted. It was not that they couldn't refuse, rather they were sufficiently disempowered to hold the view that they couldn't; and the lack of adequate information about the studies further impaired their ability to make self-protective decisions (Hornblum 1998). This suggests that any social researcher conducting research with 'captive' populations must explore more comprehensively than usual the status of the subjects' capacity to give fully informed consent. And it is not that a more subject-oriented approach – such as participant observation – can necessarily assume a more ethical treatment of captive populations if they are, again, less favourably positioned to be offered fully informed consent (see, for example, O'Connor 1976).

Between 1939 and 1989 UK Government scientists conducted a range of life-threatening trials on service personnel at the Porton Down Ministry of Defence research establishment with inadequate ethical review or fully informed consent (Press Association 2006). The enquiry documents can be viewed at:

http://www.mod.uk/DefenceInternet/AboutDefence/Corporate Publications/HealthandSafetyPublications/PortonDownVolunteers/.

In a similar vein while it might be considered unethical to 'require' social and behavioural sciences students to participate as subjects in research, there remain subtle pressures upon them to do so. Psychology undergraduates at Manchester University (UK) who refused to participate in the required 15 hours of research in their first year were instead assigned an extended essay on ethics. Psychology students at Stirling University were expected to participate in eight experiments during their first two undergraduate years and if they did not, they could be refused entry to the Honours programme (Farrar 2003). On the other hand where would the discipline of psychology be without the thousands of studies that have been conducted on students and that have substantially contributed to its development?

Developing and maintaining rapport and involvement

Being there, being interested, listening and hearing remains a sine qua non of qualitative research. Research subjects often have a way of knowing – as we all do as ordinary human beings – if this is being accomplished authentically. More than that there is an inherently long-term expectation of involvement between researcher and researched that is implied in any relationship of trust (Duncombe and Jessop 2002). Honest and immediate responses to potential breaches of trust have to be made. This can be as apparently trivial as requiring more time and energy investment of the participant than was originally implied. And this can happen in qualitative research when repeat visits are deemed necessary to enhance validity or as a check on the reliability of data gathered. It can happen in a social survey when, for example, a questionnaire takes much longer to complete than the researcher promised. In both cases the ongoing development of the research relationship provides insight into the potential for increasing a participant's vulnerability.

By consenting to participation the respondent has already to some degree allowed the researcher into their life. The degree to which that involvement is to be continued or deepened has to be continuously negotiated. Thus a participant who agreed originally only to receive a final report might be expected or expect to read, review, critically comment on and/or contribute to that report. The precise nature of the mutual expectations of researcher and researched will have to be continuously clarified for methodological as well as for ethical reasons. It is vital that, given their presumed vulnerable status at the outset of the research, the process and outcomes of the project do nothing to exacerbate that vulnerability.

There may be a limit to the degree to which participants can remain truly involved which depends upon the conceptual level or the detailed technical language adopted within research reports. The researcher comes from a professional and disciplinary tradition which the participants may not share. To ensure participants' continued understanding of how their contribution extends theoretical knowledge, it might be necessary to 'translate' the research products for their benefit. There is clearly a danger of either demeaning the participants or of limiting the nature of their contribution by the inaccessibility of the terminology.

Here, again, the potential for conflict between researcher and professional (carer, civil servant, welfare officer, etc.) roles can emerge. 'Being listened to' is something many clients often plead for. Ironically, more time may be spent with and listening to a 'patient as a subject' within the context of a research project than in routine therapeutic engagements; or in interviews with a young offender than they might spend in their encounters with the police. While the researcher who is also, say, a health professional may cope with that personally, a problem of appropriate disengagement from a research relationship which has therapeutic implications can arise. Preparations for that disengagement could be made both with researched clients and health or social service colleagues.

Categories at risk of 'exclusion'

When considering so-called vulnerable categories of persons, to ensure non-intentional exclusion, researchers will have to be attentive to some 'risks' that would not or could not ordinarily have been anticipated. While they might not be deemed directly relevant to the focus and aims of the research, to unintentionally exclude such categories would mean producing non-representative samples. Thus standard demographic variables are unlikely to be ignored by most competent researchers: age, sex, educational attainment level, employment status, occupation, marital status and so on. But consider the following potential categories:

- Disability (physical and/or mental and/or intellectual) Degree of visibility of disability (from high to low)
- Abuse (experience of: physical, sexual, emotional)

- Violence (personal experience of: physical, sexual, emotional)
- 'Safety' measures available (access to phone, transport, social networks, etc.).

Giving consideration to this additional range of categories shows the extra needs of respondents who fit these criteria and the need for researchers to consider ways in which such respondents could be included. The heightened need to preserve anonymity to enable such respondents to participate implies thinking about greater use of computer-assisted personal/self-interviewing techniques. This might require the use of hand-held devices or the provision of a private cubicle in 'not-too-public' an arena. In both cases researchers would need to be on hand to guide and/or offer debriefing opportunities while still maintaining the privacy of the individual respondents. The provocation of action by respondents as a consequence of the act of responding might require the easy availability of speed-dialling phones with access to emergency services and/or advice and counselling agencies.

11
Involving Subjects in Research: The Public, Participants, Service Users and Carer Groups

(In checklist see page 8 on potential benefits, page 9 on equitable selection and page 15 on dissemination.)

Although the focus of much of ethical scrutiny and ethical decision-making relates to the minimisation of harm to research subjects, we sometimes do not think enough about how, by their more effective inclusion in research design, planning, data gathering, analysis and dissemination, they can participate more in the process and so contribute to their own minimisation of harm. We pay token allegiance to this when we label them 'stakeholders' or 'participants' but not if they are not allowed effective opportunities to contribute. In some research traditions they can become full collaborators or co-researchers.

This area of concern certainly points up a tension between methodology and ethics that runs throughout social research. Do we need passive, compliant subjects who merely accept the things we do *to* them or say *about* them? Or should we only do research *with* them and show that we prefer knowledgeable participants who can be constructively and actively involved – but who may at times be recalcitrant when the researchers' primary focus is on, say, the completion of the research in good time?

Clearly it is not always possible or methodologically desirable to allow subjects too much of a role. Indeed it should by no means be seen as ethically 'compulsory'. Public and participant involvement very much depends upon the substance of the research, its aims, the proposed design and the methods to be employed. However it may be the case that such involvement can improve the way that research is prioritised, commissioned, undertaken, disseminated and even implemented in policy and action – in other words, it can enhance the research benefits. Moreover public, participant and/or service user involvement can offer insights into problems and anticipate harms that external researchers might not have thought of. Researchers should then raise their awareness of what it means to involve the public and/or research subjects and to help anticipate problems that may arise and how to overcome them.

The value of participation

Evidently the public and those being studied are capable of making judgements about the benefits of social research to themselves and/or to society. They are as capable as the rest of us of understanding the importance of enhanced scientific knowledge. They certainly seek this out from popular news media and enjoy sharing collective comments on events of the day. They can be aware of how societies and communities gain from knowledge about a problem, how scientific progress is made and the contribution that 'evidence' can make to policies. Research adds to the sum total of educational knowledge and so the public gains indirectly from the experience of better-educated social science graduates. By participating in research individuals gain knowledge and experience that they might otherwise have missed or information and insights that could enhance their life style and opportunities. Or they may gain personally and more directly from having opportunity to air their concerns; or even the potential catharsis that comes from sharing problems with an independent observer.

More actively oriented research participants will value the opportunity that research affords for improving service delivery. If a research study enhances the provision of services to the community, then study participants may gain both directly and indirectly. Service users who become research participants will have had direct experience of the policy consequences of previous research outcomes and so might perceive any threats to research success in advance. Research which reflects the needs and perspectives of service users may even be more likely to produce successful policy and practice recommendations – that is, ones which actually work.

There is a notion that ethics review procedures should 'protect' service users. This could be seen as patronising and excluding; service users should be able to decide for themselves, with advocacy support if needed, if they wish to be involved. If, for example, they communicate in different ways than those conventionally employed, this should not be a reason for excluding them; rather, support and appropriate facilitation is required to enable them to take part. However one way of ensuring that ethical review acts in the interest of service users is to centrally involve them in any systems that are established to advise or promote research ethics in health and social care research.

Effective participation

A key question is how to ensure the most effective contribution to research from the public and/or specific service users. It is important to remember that the public cannot be assumed to be passive and/or acquiescent, nor that they may not be knowledgeable about how they wish to participate in the research (see also Chapter 9 on confidentiality and consent). This is particularly the case for service users and disabled people. The growing political awareness/astuteness of such groups has major consequences for researchers. This means they are likely to be articulate and vociferous and researchers need to be prepared for their empowerment.

If the decision is taken to include public/user representation, then it also has to be decided within which of the stages in the research cycle they can be best employed – and that may mean they should be considered to be engaged in all stages of the research process. They can, of course, be involved in selecting and prioritising the topics to be studied, in the tendering and commissioning process, in helping to design and manage the research, as active researchers themselves (in data collection and analysis), and finally in the writing of reports and the dissemination and evaluation of the research.

Research ethics committees (RECs) already incorporate lay members who act as representatives of the public interest. But lay members are not necessarily representative of any particular community nor are they necessarily experienced service users – although serving on a REC is the least contribution service users can make. It also highlights the issue of how 'representative' such individuals can be. After all what is the nature of 'the public' they represent? They can only draw upon their own specific experiences and observations and may not even be users of the service being researched. But there are practical limitations to effective representation since it is likely to be unpaid and dependent on voluntary service, availability and their willingness and ability to articulate public concerns.

More importantly such intensive public involvement fundamentally alters the professional status of social research and the methodological consequences for this need to be fully explored. Not all research designs are suited to such involvement. The most subject-inclusive research method is participant action research (PAR) which suggests a variety of strategies for incorporating subjects effectively (see, for example, Whyte 1991, Reason 1994). But the 'objectivity' of some research designs would be seriously compromised by excessive contribution from the subject population.

A major concern is the selection of the primary goals of the research. Any research which establishes alliances with participants may find that the research goals may have to compete with the action-oriented aims of the subjects. Researchers will carry theoretical as well as potentially ideological assumptions into the field. Thus methodological and policy/practice ideologies may lie in tension with each other, with the danger that one set of concerns dominates the other (Ruano 1991). If the social scientist's perspective dominates, then any emancipatory impulse could be seen as merely patronising the participant. The participant's commitment may be more to social reform than to methodological purity – in which case the researcher's pursuit of objectivity is tainted (Ruano 1991: 216). So while 'this means that the researcher must be willing to relinquish the unilateral control that the professional researcher has traditionally maintained over the research process. This does not mean that the professional researcher must accept every idea put forward by key practitioner collaborators' (Whyte 1991: 241). But Whyte does go on to suggest that researchers have to use 'rational discourse and powers of persuasion in planning and implementing PAR'. In which case I wonder what that suggests about the true balance of power in the relationship.

In some cases the need to access participants, the nature of the topic under study and the chosen methodology can 'impel' researchers towards a participatory approach. The personal concerns of the participants can compromise the professional concerns of the researcher – to say nothing of the danger that the nature of such personal relationships could directly affect the personal concerns of the researcher. Compromises with funding and commissioning agencies can impede the full pursuit of participants' interests and concerns. And, ethically, perhaps it could be argued that should be the case since they are paying!

Moreover the initiating methodology and design might have elements of the professional researcher's vested interests, while the data to be collected might have been directed by the commissioner's information needs and not those of the co-researchers. Budgets for participatory research can be difficult to estimate given the variable time that may need to be spent on addressing group dynamics, interpersonal relationships and any specific research skills training that participants might need. Roles have to be established and the balance between 'leadership' and 'facilitation' remains uneasy in participatory research. Collaboration, cooperation and partnership each imply different models of group research engagement, and different implications for the balance of power between co-researchers. Given all of these complex and variable influences, Peter Reason suggests that there is no one method of collaborative inquiry and that 'those who want to use collaborative methods ... should study what others have done, explore the range of methods that is available, and then invent their own form which is suitable for the project they wish to undertake' (Reason 1994: 201). While this is sound advice it is clear that it does not help resolve the potential for even more complex ethical decision-taking than is required for experimental designs.

The effectiveness of subject or public participation in research can be enhanced if the experience of interest groups operating in this field is drawn upon. The UK national advisory group that promotes public involvement in health and social care research is called INVOLVE: http://www.invo.org.uk/index.asp.

INVOLVE's focus is on health research so its 'public' includes patients and potential patients, informal carers, users of health and social services, people targeted for health promotion programmes and health and social services interest groups as well as organisations representing those who have been affected by exposure to harmful products or substances – pretty well all of us then! Their wealth of experience of user involvement can help guide researchers on the best ways of incorporating the public in their research projects.

The James Lind Alliance supports the idea of patients and clinicians shaping research together: www.lindalliance.org.

Once again the balance of power between researcher and researched still requires attention since specific interest or pressure groups will have accumulated a range of political skills and persuasive powers from their lobbying activities to such an extent that the researchers may find themselves, and the methodology, dominated by participants with 'too much' experience.

Effective selection of research participants

Some of the above concerns can be met if research participants are selected from groups likely to be among the beneficiaries of subsequent applications of the research. For some commentators on participation the starting point is the principle that ethical research is research that is of benefit to service users. The principles I am repeatedly espousing here relate to the 'balance' of harm and benefit and that benefit may be indirect – of use to society at large and future service users. Care must still be taken to ensure participants are not systematically selected from groups for reasons not directly related to the research focus of study such as the fact that they may be easily available and so accessible, or that they have little choice but to participate, or might be considered relatively easy to manipulate (prisoners, students, etc. as discussed in Chapter 9). Correspondingly participants must not be systematically excluded for reasons of inconvenience that are not related to the research focus of study.

The extra time needed to include user groups and/or members of the public will be increased if the subject participants are incapacitated in some way. Otherwise, as suggested in the previous chapter, there is no reason to suppose service users or carer groups any more vulnerable than the rest of us other than the potential compounding of their vulnerabilities as a consequence of either being included or excluded from research.

Researcher as subject and subject as researcher

There is a whole field of study devoted to investigating the researcher *qua* researcher. Some of it is reflective and aids understanding of research products as outcomes of the researcher's particular concerns (made evident in reflective journals and diaries). Others are more reflexive in focusing on the ways in which the researcher's individual characteristics – attitudes and behaviour – have a direct consequence on the direction the research takes. (The origins of these approaches are contained in Schon 1983 and Gouldner 1970 and developed and broadened to a concern with risk in late modernity in Bordieu et al. 1992 and Giddens 1991.)

Often, as a consequence of the spread of research practice and research awareness, practitioners (in health, social care, government) become researchers in order to gain a fuller understanding of the attitudes and behaviour, and the policies and practices which directly affect how they do their work, as much care has to be adopted here as with other participatory research. Since the researcher adopts multiple roles – researcher, practitioner, subject and principal disseminator – there is a great deal of tension about which one of the roles takes primacy at any one time.

Investigating a practice-related problem does not necessarily lead to its solution. By problematising a situation the researcher may undermine the practitioner's (i.e. their own) ability to continue doing the job.

If others (professional colleagues) are involved, decisions have to be taken about how transparent one can be, both in engaging with the research activity and its findings – particularly if those findings lead to changes in practice. Research into one's own practice can lead to serious ethical conflict which might be difficult to resolve – examples include: a police officer researching into policing organisations, prison officers investigating the prisoner's experiences and teachers exploring the educational system (Sapsford 1999: 41). Similar problems face the increasing number of clinicians – nurses, midwives and other allied health professionals facing conducting research on the patient category they most frequently deal with (Iphofen 2005).

In similar vein the nature of the subjects' involvement in dissemination needs to be considered. The challenge is to disseminate research in ways that benefit the general public and/or users of specific services might be considered as part of the process of securing ethics approval. So the involvement of those directly in receipt of policy outcomes or with the consequences of the more public discussion of issues that might normally have been confined to their own circles poses a problem of the potential for research reports to be 'coloured' in the direction of such interests. It might be difficult to identify or even resist if the subjects have actually acted as full collaborators or co-researchers (Petit-Zeman 2005). This is discussed more fully in the next chapter.

Cautionary notes

If ethical decision-making is generally a dynamic process, as argued throughout this book, it is even more so when subjects are extensively and intensively involved – hence it will be more demanding of consideration on the part of researchers and subjects alike. Once again while some ethical consequences can be anticipated, not all can be and the subjects become even more implicated in those decisions than if the study was being conducted *on* and not *with* them: it will be even more necessary 'to negotiate in practice the ethics discussed in principle when the group was forming' (Treleaven 1994: 158).

More importantly there is an implicit assumption that public and/or service user involvement is of benefit to the participant and empowering. But this is not necessarily the case and researchers need to be aware that their desire to incorporate the public into their cherished project might not be matched by any sensed need in the public they seek to include. The public do not have a 'right' to be included so the view that they ought to be granted such a right is a political act that endows participation with a form of democratic 'value'. To feel obliged or per-suaded to participate is coercive and so cannot be regarded as necessar-ily empowering or emancipatory. To put such pressure on potentially vulnerable service users may even exacerbate their vulnerability – and they might not be the best judge of that happening. Even by allowing the subjects a 'taste' of empowerment while collaborating on a project could prove frustrating when they find themselves back in their own culture – their sensed relative deprivation could even be exacerbated by the experience.

In the research setting – whether that be in the most well-intentioned action research or merely collaborative – since it is a research project the balance of power (in skills, knowledge, experience and resources) still lies with the researcher. There are many devices for attempting to even out this power differential but it is difficult to demonstrate clearly that a redistribution of power has been accomplished, that the participant had freely chosen to join the project and that no additional distress or harm was suffered. There may indeed be a subtle tyranny to participa-tory research that requires careful examination and reflection (see, for example, Cooke and Kothari 2001).

12
Disseminating Findings

(See page 15 of checklist.)

There is a surprising range of ethical issues associated with the dissemination and reporting of project findings. It helps to think of this as a problem of how knowledge is managed and shared. The phrase currently employed for this is 'knowledge transfer'. What new knowledge has been gained and what is the form and focus of dissemination – who is the 'audience' for our findings and how best should it be shared with them? The series of questions that need to be addressed about publication include those contained in the classic mass communication formula: What is communicated, to whom, how, when and why? These are of necessity interrelated questions and it is quite difficult to separate them.

It need not be seen as ethically inevitable to publish. We may publish all, a part or nothing of our findings (i.e. embargoing them), largely depending on judgements about the harm and benefits that might accrue from our knowledge transfer. Once we have decided upon the constituencies considered to be an appropriate audience for our work, we can decide the form in which the information might best be released for maximum benefit. We must then try to identify or anticipate any potential harm arising out of dissemination, we must take care to assign intellectual property rights where they are due and acknowledge all the recognisable sources of information employed by referencing them.

Once again it is impossible to anticipate all problems associated with new knowledge in advance. In the early stages of a project proposal it helps to air potential problems and this can attune the research team to issues that could arise later. In fact it might not be a bad idea to consider dissemination issues at the outset, even though these might change during the life of the project.

Disseminate to whom?

Our audience constituencies are likely to be at least as wide ranging as the original stakeholders in the project – and more, such as those who may be considered to be 'users' of the research. It could include: the general public, the research participants who donated their time, insights and information, the academic/professional audience of other researchers in similar and/or related fields, the government and policy makers at all levels, service users, those who might be affected by policy changes consequent on the research, voluntary/interest groups, practitioners in related fields, journalists and others involved in mass media who rely upon research for interesting/challenging news stories and so on.

Our first ethical concern to these constituencies is to judge whether or not the information released will benefit them or contains the potential for harm. For example, if a control group was involved and the results of a trial intervention shows the intervention to have benefitted the experimental group, it might not always be in the interests of the control group to let them know what they may have missed out on. It would take fairly altruistic research subjects for them not to be upset at their disbenefits.

The greatest loss of disseminatory control is to journalists who pick up research outputs and 'interpret' them according to their news values – seeking conflict and controversy since that makes for more exciting and, therefore, more saleable newspapers. That is why learning to prepare press releases and to be interviewed for radio and television is one of the skills contemporary researchers are often now trained in. They have to become quite skilled in resisting a news reporter's 'drive' towards the opposing view. This becomes especially difficult if the interpretation of findings is complex and subtle – especially so if there is no 'opposing view', since they may feel the need to create one!

On the other hand researchers' major complaint is when their findings are not so broadly disseminated and their publications infrequently cited. The greatest dissatisfaction is with reports that merely 'sit on a shelf' or articles in journals read by only a few people and do nothing to justify the researchers' and/or funders' efforts. Hence articles in more 'intellectually-oriented' but more broadly read periodicals are often sought to explain the findings more fully and, hopefully, help to ensure that key policy recommendations are not merely ignored.

Why disseminate?

Without publishing findings the charge could be made that all stake-holders' time had been wasted – that is clearly an ethical concern. To produce 'results' and then keep them to oneself might seem a scholarly indulgence not to be tolerated in modern society (see Box 12.1).

In some respects many of the issues raised in a case such as this are the kinds of things considered in Chapter 4. One could debate in detail the nature of the peer review process. Who were the 'peers' and how were they chosen? What precise influence did they have on the project proposal? What sort of role does the funding body have in terms of supporting government policy that makes a study such as this worth funding? Why was such a large grant necessary to interview 30 people and so on? And quality/standards issues such as these *were* addressed in the public debate on this case.

But just as important is the researchers' and Research Council's responsibility (as funder) for what happens to the information deriving from the findings. It is disingenuous for modern, media-aware research-ers to claim no ability to control the dissemination of their work in the popular media – especially with such a topic of contemporary public

Box 12.1   GM crops and research dissemination

'UK farmers want to grow GM crops' was a headline in a British Sunday newspaper reporting a study conducted by Andy Lane of the Open University. This was a £131,000, ESRC-funded project into *Farmers' understanding of GM crops as new technology*. The ESRC press release began with the statement: 'Farmers are upbeat about geneti-cally modified crops, according to new research.' And one of the key findings reported in the researchers' own project summary leaflet was that farmers 'believed that GM crops offer clear and economic envi-ronmental benefits to themselves and the wider public'. These results were based on interviews with 30 farmers selected on the advice of a GM industry pressure group which also advised on the project. The farmers were all large scale farmers who had been involved in GM tri-als. The ESRC and the researchers defended the study on the grounds that the study's focus was on farmers with experience of GM crops and was never intended to be representative of all UK farmers, and that the proposal had been fully peer reviewed.

(Corbyn 2008)

concern. However sophisticated the technical report – knowing the consequences of such a simplistic interpretation of the findings and how such things get buried in complex reports – the funders and researchers cannot have been unaware of the care needed in interpreting their findings for popular consumption. In reporting findings that will be distributed to the general public researchers must take great care that the more subtle elements of their work are disseminated in such a way that they will not be easily misinterpreted. Of course there is little they can do if newspapers or other popular media choose to wilfully misinterpret, but even in such cases they should be alert to any reports about their work and be prepared to attempt to counter misinformation.

This is a generic problem for all research – few researchers have easy access to popular commercial outlets and fewer still will find they can control how their work is treated in such media. However it is also the case that researchers should not assume the general public to lack the ability to read and discern with some degree of technical sophistication a fuller account of the work done. Given the easier availability of the Internet and cheap costs of publishing information on the World Wide Web, there is really little excuse for researchers not offering a more careful, detailed account in such a form. They may have to encounter dialogue with an informed and intelligent public – but that is something that increasingly researchers should consider as part of the justification for continued public support of their work.

Was any harm done as a consequence of this interpretation of findings? One might imagine that the many thousands of farmers who were not interviewed would not be too pleased that the public might now think that they hold such views. The public perception of GM crops and their potential might be swayed by this view apparently being held by UK farmers in general – thereby altering public opinion – so this is unlikely to go down well with the anti-GM lobby and could be said to undermine their cause on the basis of misleading information.

It could be assumed that researchers will have much more control over their formal reports to funders and commissioners and in their outlets in scholarly journals.

Peer review

The main method of 'quality control' for the dissemination of research findings remains the peer review process. But this is a highly flawed procedure which is heavily reliant upon trust and so raises many ethical concerns. It is a 'subjective and therefore inconsistent process' (Smith 2006a: 179). There are plenty of examples of fraud and misconduct in peer review with plagiarism occurring in some cases and rejection due to prejudice against particular authors' work and/or their favoured methodologies.

The central problem is focussed on who can be legitimately counted as an authoritative yet independent peer. Such an individual would need at least an equivalent, if not more knowledge of the field and background of profession, discipline and methodology than the author. It is hard to come to an objective judgement that peer review is effective in actually accomplishing what it claims to do – filter the dissemination of knowledge and information so that only the best gets through and the 'truth' emerges. Systematic review of the process suggests that there is only a belief that this is the case – no good evidence – and that peer review is no better at detecting fraud and error than could be achieved by chance (Jefferson et al. 2002).

Despite its flaws it looks likely to remain operative since there is a consensus that generally accepts it and there appears to be no good alternative: 'How odd that science should be rooted in belief' (Smith 2006a: 182). The best that researchers and authors can do is to hold the peer review process itself under review, participate in it (be willing to review others' work) and when it is being applied to one's own work, ensure that the system operating within the chosen journal outlet is as fair and transparent as possible. Despite the plea for 'evidence-based policy making' in modern government, there is still a concern to control research that might report 'negative' findings – that is not consistent with previously declared government policy programmes. Tombs and Whyte (2003) reported how four papers were withdrawn from a British Society of Criminology conference since the Home Office, who had funded the projects, were unhappy that the projects reported 'mixed success' from Government crime initiatives. This raises questions about the effective role of research sponsors and their rights in the dissemination of research findings (see Chapter 3 on commissioners/funders).

It also raises questions about who owns this information. When researchers collect data it is assumed they have been 'given' to them and so treated as a gift. It might not mean that they fully 'own' it since the data donor might claim rights to it in retrospect. Once analysed, however, the data become 'findings' and if the research subject had no part to play in the analysis it is hard to see how they can claim ownership of the knowledge thereby produced (see Box 12.2).

Box 12.2   Poverty and research dissemination

Researchers might be stealing from the poor by holding on to data about poverty captured from many data sources over a series of years. In so doing they slow the understanding of poverty and hamper poverty-reduction efforts. Leading analysts in research institutes in Europe and the US hold the monopoly over some quantitative datasets for extended periods, making them available to policy makers in advanced countries while limiting access to poverty researchers in developing nations. In some South Asian countries official statistical agencies refuse to place officially collected data in the public domain until they have secured enough income from private companies willing to pay for access to it. Even qualitative researchers hold on to vital life history and experiential accounts in order to enhance their own career prospects by publishing first and delay archiving or making the accounts publicly available for analysis. Good practice would require datasets to be made more publicly available on research organisations' websites once they had been 'cleaned' for purposes of anonymity/confidentiality.

(Hulme 2003a, 2003b)

Harm in dissemination and non-dissemination

A survey for Cancer Research UK conducted by National Opinion Polls in 2004 showed that only 29 of 1000 people questioned knew of the higher risk of developing cancer from being overweight despite the existence of extensive evidence to this effect (Meikle 2004). This relatively poor knowledge suggests that many people are at risk to their health for simply not controlling their diet and taking more exercise. Ensuring that more people know this should be a responsibility of health researchers in general, but spreading such knowledge without care and consideration for the anxiety that may be caused among not only overweight people, but also among people who perceive themselves to be overweight, poses a danger to their emotional and psychological state.

Poorly controlled dissemination can even cause harm to the reputation of researchers (see Box 12.3).

When research participants or service users are involved in the dissemination of research findings, their criteria of relevance may differ from those of the researcher. In such cases researchers have to guard against influences of that kind compromising their impartiality, otherwise the

Box 12.3   Researchers' reputations

Whatever the merits or demerits of the work of B. F. Skinner, his findings on operant conditioning and his views on the potential of behavioural science for social order and control, his real notoriety came with the poorly reported 'application' of his research to the socialisation of one of his daughters and the supposed deleterious effects this had on her life ('The baby in a box'). It was reported that she was kept in a temperature controlled 'box' and treated much like one of his laboratory pigeons in an attempt to prove the validity of his child development theories. Of course the story was greatly exaggerated on first report and subsequently lead to many false rumours about what had happened to his daughter – who, in fact, has lead a full, rewarding life as an artist and who has made it clear that she loved and highly respected her father.

(Skinner Buzan 2004; Slater 2004: Chapter 1)

primary claim to be acting in society's interests would be jeopardised. This does not mean that researchers cannot 'take sides' – but that if they do they should make this clear and they should clarify the grounds on which they believe it reasonable to do so.

The same rationale should apply to policy makers, government departments and/or professionals who may be concerned that they may be expected to become committed to implementing the 'best options' emerging from the project. They are perfectly entitled to disagree with research findings – again they will need good reasons for doing so – but the criteria for their own continued survival are political, not scientific. So we should be clear about their motives and intentions in comparison to our own.

Howard Becker's overview of this problem some years ago offers a useful set of grounds for judging how researchers should assess the consequences of reporting their work:

[I]t is that one should refrain from publishing items of fact or conclusions that are not necessary to one's argument or that would cause suffering out of proportion to the scientific gain of making them public. ... Even though the statement as it stands cannot determine a clear line of action for any given situation ... it suggests ... that the scientist must be able to give himself good reasons for including potentially harmful material ... (and) ... it guards him against either an overly formal or an overly sentimental view of the harm those he studies may suffer ... (and) ... it insists that he know enough about the situation he has studied to know whether the suffering will in any sense be proportional to gains science may expect from publication of his findings.

(Becker 1964)

Becker's conclusions were drawn after an overview of studies that chose to report socially damaging information about a community whose members could be fairly easily identified, a decision to report confidential information about an interest group whose members were deemed 'unlikely to read' the outlet in which the information about them was reported and studies of proscribed organisations who, as a consequence of their activities, had placed themselves so far beyond the moral community that any research reporting their 'secret' activities could be deemed legitimate (Becker 1964).

Eliciting 'data' and knowledge production

The source material for qualitative research is unlikely to be anonymous data. It is more usually a person's account, story, imagery, considered responses and, in that sense at least, is primarily owned by them and given by them. Since data are literally 'given things', the subjects' agreement to participation in research entails 'gifting' their experiences to the researcher as data. It is likely in the first instance to be their 're-presentation' of a personal experience and has, therefore, a precious, human quality. If a respondent talks about their experience of pain in their illness or disease, for example, they will be disclosing an intimacy – something that reveals a quality associated with the nature of their existence as a human being.

In the same way all data generated from human responses are, in essence, 'gifted' even if it is nothing more than a superficial counting procedure.

But then, as a necessary part of the process, the researcher manipulates this data in some way by coding, classifying, reinterpreting it and, ultimately, by disseminating it in a form accessible to interested others. The researcher's ethical responsibility is then associated with how that shared gift is cared for (whether or not the data continue to be treated as 'precious' as they are analysed, transformed and reproduced as new knowledge) and how the person who shared the data is cared for as a consequence of that data being delivered – albeit in a different form – to a larger audience.

Part of the problem here is that an essential element of the research-er's task is inevitably to select from those data enough of them to permit the description, understanding, explanation and so on that are part of the purposes of the research – the production of this 'new' knowledge. Conventionally this is known as 'data reduction' and is inevitable since the full richness of the person's unique and individual original experi-ence can never be captured. Nor can it be fully reproduced. One of the researcher's tasks is to help convey that experience authentically and in a way that might be useful for purposes of explanation, policy making or practice. So there is always something of the researchers themselves that must be included in the re-presentation since they were party to the mediated reproduction of the experience. The researchers have to maintain a reflexive position, gauge how much of what emerges is dependent on or independent of them and consistently hold themselves accountable for the knowledge produced (Holland 1999).

A more worrying trend is the growth in favour of meta-analyses which relies on a 'data-expansion' approach. The assumption is made that by accumulating quantitative data the evidence for or against a particular view is somehow enhanced (see discussion in Chapter 4). Unfortunately in addition to all the limitations on the 'validity' of reported findings discussed here, there is the added problem of 'credibility' – whatever the 'p-value', how each study was conducted and the data analysed can be disguised or hidden within the cumulative view. And yet many journals are happy to publish such findings securing them a potentially unde-served credibility. In a highly controversial paper John Ioannadis has made a convincing case for why most cumulative published research findings using quantitative data are 'false' (Ioannadis 2005).

Intellectual property and sharing knowledge

Acknowledging all sources and careful and comprehensive referencing is essential to giving credit where it is due. It is a first principle in estab-lishing rights to intellectual property. But the current pressure to pub-lish and to claim the ownership of knowledge can lead to dishonourable behaviour and, even, to scientific fraud (see Box 12.4).

The temptations to cheat are many and varied, and more effort must be put into understanding the causes and consequences of scientific fraud (see Box 12.5).

Several problems emerge from such an exercise. First there is the eth-ics of subjecting busy people with serious intent to the time wasting and the consequent indignity of a fraudulent submission – this includes the

Box 12.4   A typical multifaceted ethical dilemma

Here is an ethical dilemma about how knowledge is shared and the worth of that to society and other professionals.

'I have been asked to referee an article that cites ten of my papers, but that (in my professional opinion) does not merit publication. In view of the promised use of metrics in determining the future funding of my department, should I (a) put my institution first and accept the paper, (b) put my subject first and reject it or (c) claim a conflict of interest and decline to act as a referee?'

(Robert A. Wilson, Professor of Pure Mathematics,
Queen Mary College, University of London,
Times Higher Education, 10 January 2008: 22)

Box 12.5   The Sokal hoax

In 1996 Alan Sokal published a paper entitled 'Transgressing the Boundaries: Toward a Transformative Hermeneutics of Quantum Gravity' in the journal *Social Text*.

Apparently the paper claimed to be about assessing the philosophical and political implications of unifying quantum theory with Einstein's theory of gravity and general relativity. As is now well-known it was a 'spoof' article intended to undermine the 'subjectivist and relativist philosophies' Sokal claims that Leftist critiques of society and science employ too often and to their disadvantage. Of course, it also raises issues about peer review and the ability of reviewers to make critical judgements of the worth of a paper that is not strictly within their field of competence.

(Sokal 2008)

referees for the paper, the journal's editor and, by no means least, the readers of the journal. Who is being fooled or fooling themselves when attempting to make intellectual sense of a complex paper delivered by an authoritative expert in the field? The unethical intent might be mitigated by an ethical consequence – if such a consequence is great enough to be balanced against the harm caused. So, for pragmatic reasons, such as lack of time to adequately review and check the paper, such papers can creep through the vetting system. One outcome could be to improve the vetting system – making it harder and more time consuming subsequently for others to publish with serious intent. Another might be to so discredit the journal, the field of study and related authors in the field that their work is discontinued, thereby depriving society of the potential benefits that may have accrued from such work in the future. That perspective might be counterbalanced by the view that, if such a field was so easily discredited, its value in contributing to knowledge would be similarly challenged. However, can such a view be sustained in consequence of the publishing of one hoax paper? If a field of study is genuinely weak and failing to contribute to society and the growth of knowledge, then surely it is better if the processes of 'normal science' are allowed to determine the survival of the field of study and, perhaps, the journal. All our time would be much better spent in ensuring that deliberately fraudulent papers (at least ones without a claim to larger political aims) are identified and the authors sanctioned.

The problem with Sokal's exercise is that it exploits a major flaw in the main method of research dissemination – the scholarly journal. Genuine research misconduct is difficult enough to identify let alone control, although some commentators do believe that a significant contribution to this can be made by journal editors and their peer reviewers/referees (Smith 2006 a & b). In this regard an organisation called the Committee on Publication Ethics (COPE) was founded in the UK in 1997 to address breaches of research and publication ethics (see the COPE website: http://www.publicationethics.org.uk/).

It is a voluntary body providing a discussion forum and advice for scientific editors and aims to find practical ways of dealing with the issues, and to develop good practice. It represents an attempt to define best practice in the ethics of scientific publishing. Its origin and primary focus have been with misconduct in biomedical research. COPE offers a set of advisory guidelines on: study design and ethical approval, data analysis, authorship, conflict of interests, the peer review process, redundant publication, plagiarism, duties of editors, media relations, advertising and how to deal with misconduct. An insightful and alarmingly lengthy array of cases of fraud and attempted fraud can be found on the website. Admittedly these are in the field of health and medical research but social research cannot be regarded to be immune, and more so since few cases are reported or investigated for their fraudulent potential.

In the complex interrelationship between ethical review, publication and intellectual property, even governmental research councils have been found to 'misbehave' (see Box 12.6).

Box 12.6   Funding councils and unethical behaviour

A student who had participated in a field trial on a small municipality's drinking water found his name appearing on two academic journal articles of which he had no knowledge. Both papers neglected to report any negative results from the trials which in fact had been terminated prematurely when residents complained of laundry being bleached, the water smelling of chlorine and small pets dying during the trials. The Canadian Natural Sciences and Engineering Research Council (NSERC) had sponsored the trial which was part-funded by the company that had patented the alternative water-purifying technique being tested. The student was threatened with an action for defamation when he complained to the journal editors (one of which later retracted the article), but the NSERC failed to respond to the accusation that it had failed to maintain research standards.

(Fine 2006)

Since commissioning/funding councils are equally capable of engaging in unethical behaviour, it is even more vital that both individual researchers, with the support of their professional associations, disclose actions of this nature and work together to maintain and espouse professional standards that can help expose and remove corrupt research practices.

13
Systems of Ethical Approval and Formal Ethical Scrutiny

(See page 2 of checklist.)

> The trouble with you health people is that you're always thinking that these review committees are about ethics ... this has nothing to do with ethics – it's about management.
>
> > (An overheard comment made by the Vice Chancellor of a UK University to a Dean of a Faculty of Health)

In many respects the substance of this chapter represents the inspiration for this book. But it is only possible to fully address the issues associated with formal ethical review when all of the issues contained in the previous chapters have been covered. The steady growth of ethical scrutiny in social research became the motive for a fuller discussion of the issues upon which such scrutiny is based and which so occupies the concern of social researchers in its potential to obstruct and disrupt their main goal – their mission to research the social world. I made my position clear in Chapter 1 that good research can only be done by good researchers who are ethically aware. This does not mean that I uncritically condone the growth of formal ethical scrutiny, but neither do I crudely condemn it. My argument is that we need to understand and manage it for the benefit of productive social science.

It is the case that the moral threats arising out of developments in biomedicine and health science have spread into the social sciences alongside a commensurate concern that health science review processes have tended to dominate in judgements about the appropriateness of methodological procedures in social research. Institutionalised ethical scrutiny has grown in sectors which formerly allowed professional control to judge the moral worth of a research activity and the risk of harm to research subjects. This has been seen by many commentators as evidence of further restrictions upon academic and research freedom. At best ethical review has been charged with obstructing or inhibiting research and, at worst, with being profoundly anti-democratic.

The argument of this chapter is that given the difficulty of reversing the growth of ethical scrutiny, we need to enhance professional involvement in it and find ways to ensure it becomes facilitative of research and in the raising of ethical awareness among researchers. There is a role for the social science professional associations to act as mentors, provide training and advice and hence to promote their own ethical codes and/or guidelines. However critics have even charged the professions with simply furthering the restrictions on practice by the applications of generic ethical codes.

Some of the criticism of ethical scrutiny is misguided and arises out of confusion between research governance and independent ethical review – the former being more concerned with institutional risk aversion (i.e. management), the latter genuinely with the protection of research subjects and researchers. An enhanced professional involvement with scrutiny procedures can challenge the dominance of governance over ethics and a proactive engagement with ethical review can restore researchers' rights to conduct research.

The growth of formalised ethical scrutiny

Historical evidence overwhelmingly demonstrates that the growth of concern for ethical conduct in scientific research originally grew out of the revelation of the inhumane nature of research conducted by Nazi medical doctors on prisoners, ethnically maligned groups (not only Jews, but Slavs, gypsies and black people) and the mentally disabled. The disclosure of these abuses occurred during the Nuremburg Trials of Nazi war criminals – but the historical record also shows that abuses of research subjects had taken place by scientists worldwide in the pre-war period and, indeed, continued long after the Nuremburg trials and in spite of the dissemination of the Nuremberg Code on medical research ethics.

In 1963 a team of New York researchers deliberately infected mentally handicapped inmates at Willowbrook asylum with hepatitis to test experimental vaccines. Between 1932 and 1972 Tuskegee investigators withheld penicillin therapy from poor black Alabama farm workers with syphilis in order to fully understand the natural history of the disease. In the early 1960s researchers at the Jewish Chronic Disease

Hospital in Brooklyn injected live cancer cells into elderly cancer patients without their permission. The catalogue of similar abuses globally in both the pre-Second World War period and well into the 1970s is extensive and well documented (see Dingwall 2006; Gaw 2006 for additional references).

The 'ethical rationale' for such conduct required the belief that the work was of benefit to science and humanity, in general, and that the research subjects were somehow 'not fully human' or at least inferior beings who could be treated in 'less than human' ways – not that much different from the logic applied by some Nazi doctors. Indeed prisoners and enemies in war have been seen in many societies to have forfeited their rights to fair treatment by their illegal acts and/or by their assaults on the persons and territory of those judged to be defending themselves. In fact, the principle that prisoners should not be subject to scientific research against their will, implicit to the Nuremburg Code, was not fully adopted by the USA until 1976 (see Gaw 2006: 177).

Campaigns for greater regulatory control to prevent similar abuses occurred throughout the twentieth century and culminated in the Declaration of Helsinki and the European Union Good Clinical Trials legislation.

Ethical scrutiny can also be seen as an element in a systematic attempt to prevent or minimise fraudulent scientific research. Real damage can be done to the whole field of social science from even just a few highly publicised cases of research misconduct. Research subjects will be cautious about participation and institutions wary of commissioning in fields for which there is public distrust. Again while most of the more damaging cases are in biomedical research, it would be unsafe to assume that the same pressures do not exist in social science (see Chapters 3, 12 and Smith 2006b), and there are enough cases of ethically suspect social science practice in the past to counsel caution – as can be seen from the issues covered throughout this book.

So, perhaps, ethical scrutiny has grown for good reasons. Ethical decisions must be reached in a transparent manner – researchers must be seen to behave ethically for the sake of the goals of the discipline and of the profession of social research. Formalised ethical scrutiny is intended to assist researchers in estimating and balancing risks of harm to participants, researchers and organisations and considering what benefits might accrue to society, groups, individuals, organisations and so on. For example, ethical review should include the requirement that a full risk assessment has been conducted to ensure the safety of researchers (see Chapter 8). It has become a means for clarifying lines of accountability – about who takes decisions, on what grounds and who is responsible for errors and misjudgements. It offers external, independent and collegial mentorship/advice. And, to aid transparency, it provides the means for retaining a systematic record of what decisions were taken and the reasoning behind them. It should also offer or assess procedures for handling complaints and the redress of grievances against researchers and research organisations.

Current systems of ethical review

To refer to the procedures of ethical scrutiny in the UK and Europe as 'systems' is to some extent an administrative conceit. There is little that is 'systematic' about the range and variety of guidelines, codes and formal scrutiny procedures to which social scientists may have to be subjected in order to conduct research. However the responsible researcher will have to be aware of the process of ethical scrutiny that is required for certain topics, in certain organisations, with certain categories of people and/or in certain geographic locations.

In fact, it is perhaps the only area of ethical decision-making where a straightforward decision-tree can be established and operated to facilitate the scrutiny process (as on page 2 of the checklist). It also helps to adopt such a decision-tree or action flowchart in order to avoid unnecessary duplication of effort when seeking ethical scrutiny. If scrutiny external to the researcher's organisation is required to gain access to certain classes of respondents, then there may be little point in seeking full internal scrutiny from a research organisation's own review procedure – unless, of course, there is a view that projects ought to be 'quality-assessed' in this way prior to leaving the organisation and prior to being viewed in a more public arena.

Any outline of contemporary scrutiny procedures is fated to become redundant possibly even prior to the publication of this book. Hence some summary observations will be made here, while links to the appropriate regulatory systems in the UK and internationally can be found in the Recommended Websites towards the end of the book (and will be updated regularly on the book's website).

Globally the review systems remain many and varied with considerable range in the levels of scrutiny required – dependent on issue, topic and research site. Some are long established and settled – the USA, Canada and Scandinavia offering examples of the most stable of such systems. Some cover all research with human participants, others subdivide between topics (such as biomedicine, social science, anthropology).

Some countries have established genuinely systematic procedural operations through which all researchers must go to gain public funding.

Professional research associations in the social sciences offer an array of codes or guidelines which vary in the degree of prescription they embody and the nature and amount of sanctions available to members who transgress them. Many are educative and advisory in an attempt to encourage researchers to take responsibility for their own moral actions without the fear of some punitive application. Growing international concern for the conduct of ethical research has led to a European Commission-funded project on the maintenance of standards in socioeconomic research. This project is called the RESPECT project and information about it can be found at: www.respectproject.org.

As a result of increasing pressure to establish a parallel to the US system of Institutional Review Boards (IRBs) in universities, British universities have more recently collaborated to establish a Universities Research Ethics Committee (UREC) that has established a place for itself in the Association of Research Ethics Committees (ARECs) which was previously dominated by biomedical health research interests. One of the drivers for this development was the increasing insistence from the major UK funding councils that all human subjects research be ethically reviewed if funding was to be given, and this was subsequent to a review by Tinker and Coomber (2004) that pointed out how few universities actually possessed RECs.

For social researchers it was the requirement by the Economic and Social Research Council (ESRC) that receipt of all funding from them was dependent upon compliance with their Research Ethics Framework (REF) that has led to the increasing concern with the potentially obstructive nature of ethical review. The ESRC claimed that their 'framework' was to be treated as complementary to existing guidelines, not an 'add-on' or another hurdle to be overcome. However if compliance with it is mandatory to receive ESRC funding, its mere existence must represent another hurdle – researchers have to ensure they meet all the other guidelines they must follow along with this REF. So it does, in effect, duplicate existing systems and codes.

The claim was also made that this framework sets standards to be followed by all UK social research. With no disrespect to the team that produced it (some excellent papers emerged – see Brown et al. 2004; Boulton et al. 2004; Lewis et al. 2004; Webster et al. 2004) – quite apart from the massive presumption of such a vital project being completed in an alarmingly short period of time, at a meagre price by a, necessarily, small team of researchers without the full collaboration with the appropriate professional associations – there is a frightening arrogance behind such a claim. Research councils have a specific institutional/ public policy brief which is linked to their funding source and the criteria by which they exist and survive. It is fundamentally a governmental agency which has become increasingly *dirigeist*, linked to economic outcomes and central government policy directives. The threat to academic freedom and professional integrity is evident when an agency with such a defined and centralist purpose dictates how a science should proceed to establish its dimensions of relevance. Fortunately the work funded by the ESRC does not, and should not, encompass all that is done in the name of social science research.

However this approach marks a continuing trend since all the other major research councils that did not already possess extensive ethical guidance (unlike the Medical Research Council), subsequently felt the need to develop their own ethical research frameworks. Ironically the UK governmental social research units have only recently set up systems of internal ethical review for the projects they conduct and/or fund (Government Social Research Unit 2005).

Knowing the law

The ethically responsible researcher has a duty to the subjects of their study, to society, to the funders of their research and to their profession(s), to remain *aware* of their legal obligations. After that obedience to the law then becomes an individual moral choice. 'If a Law is unjust, and if the Judge judges according to the Law, that is justice, even if it is not just' (Alan Paton in *Cry the Beloved Country*). Most researchers are not so naïve as to assume a necessary congruence between the law and morality. The ethical way to behave is to be informed of the law and then to decide whether or not the law should be obeyed.

Participant research such as that conducted by Pearson (2007) on football crowd violence illustrates the dilemmas to be confronted by ethics and governance committees. Assuming such research is considered worth engaging in, the governance perspective must be upon the 'quality' of the science (i.e. is this the best/only way of properly investigating this problem?) and the institutional risk (what threats to the research organisation and/or its employee – the researcher – are implied by this technique?). If involvement in criminal activity by the researcher is deemed methodologically necessary, it is unlikely it could be condoned for managerial reasons by the governance review process – unless police permission had been granted. That would be akin to complicity in the crime and it is unlikely any research organisation could be publicly seen to condone it. Ironically the ethical review process could lead to the view that such a decision is the researcher's own – if they choose to risk harm to themselves for the sake of their work, then it is their choice, as long as that does not result in associate harm coming to the research subjects. My suspicion is that, once again, no research ethics committee would risk the public condemnation if their permission to proceed became known.

Neither research governance nor ethical review should regulate against the possibility of research of this nature being carried out. But neither should researchers expect the committees to condone actions of which they reprove or which they cannot condone as a consequence of their public responsibilities. It is not simply a case of necessarily and unquestioningly obeying the law, but of where the consequences of not doing so are considered to fall.

As the law is established by the state, it may not always suit the agencies of any particular state to act ethically. Thus laws may be established to maintain the authority and status of those already in power (legitimately or not) at the expense of human rights and/or other aspects of natural justice.

Hopefully this should be less the case with developing internationalism in legal matters and effective non-governmental agencies keeping a watch on the actions of states (such as the Red Cross, the Red Crescent, Oxfam and Amnesty International). But the UN Declaration of Human Rights – the best example of international standards in ethics – to which most countries are signatories is not even supported by the legal system in many of those signatory countries. Women's rights in particular are violated in many countries which have signed up for the UN Declaration – they are discriminated against in access to land and employment, education, justice and health care (*Amnesty Magazine* 2008).

Views of the universality of human rights should not however be accepted uncritically, nor should it be assumed that such universal ideas about rights are those based on an essentially westernised view of morality (Parekh 2004). Adopting caution about the universality of rights should not lead us to assume general ethical principles to have merely local relevance. Ethical guidelines in research can and perhaps should be applied internationally; the broadening of ethical concerns suggests we cannot consider ourselves to be operating in splendid isolation. To take a recent topical example, questions have been asked about the appropriateness of conducting trials for AIDS drugs in the developing world – with individuals and in societies that could never afford to purchase the developed drugs when their efficacy is proven. Ethical standards in social research must be so generalisable that work of a similar nature would be inconceivable in social science.

The major UK legislation that could affect consent, participation and the protection of research subjects' interests includes the Data Protection Act (1998), the Human Rights Act (1998), the law on Intellectual Property Rights, Freedom of Information and, of course, the full panoply of criminal law. For example, the Human Rights Act came into force in October 2000 and incorporates into UK law rights and freedoms guaranteed by the European Convention on Human Rights. Strictly it applies to action by 'public authorities' so it should not directly affect research conducted by private and independent research organisations – unless such work is being carried out on behalf of a government department. (Further information can be gained directly from the Human Rights Unit on: http://www.homeoffice.gov.uk/hract/.)

Following procedure

In recent years a uniform procedure for ethical review of research proposals concerned with human health has been established across the UK. This is supported and implemented by the National Research Ethics Service (NRES), which coordinates the development of operational systems for Local and Multi-Centre Research Ethics Committees (LRECs and MRECs), on behalf of the NHS and the Department of Health (DH) in England. It maintains an overview of the operation of the research ethics system in England, and alerts the DH and other responsible authorities if the need arises for them to review policy and operational guidance relating to RECs. It also manages a national training programme for Research Ethics Committee members and administrators. It liaises with similar bodies having responsibilities for other regions within the UK.

(Their website address is: www.nres.org.uk.)

There is a single online standardised approval form for all such committees, which must be completed by all applicants proposing research on NHS patients and/or staff, and recommended standard procedures for seeking informed consent and producing patient information about the research.

The DH have also established a Research Governance Framework for Health and Social Care that defines the broad principles of good research governance and attempts to ensure that health and social care research is conducted to high scientific and ethical standards. Research governance is concerned with proper accountability throughout the research process and the establishment of such a framework is a formalised, administrative procedure intended to reduce unacceptable variations in research practice across health and social care. It is also intended to enhance the contribution of research to the partnership between services and science since it documents standards, details the responsibilities of the key people involved in research, outlines delivery systems and describes local and national monitoring systems. This can be found at: http://www.doh.gov.uk/research/rd3/nhsrandd/researchgovernance.htm.

This system only strictly covers access for research purposes to patients and staff in DH and NHS institutions. The boundaries of the framework for social care research are still far from clear; there is ambiguity about whether it should include research involving statutory social services, all social care-related research or non-clinical health services research. In fact, there is no equivalent national system covering the 'general public', so researchers not operating within an institutionalised framework are still in a position to police their own ethical decisions. If people choose to participate as subjects without being accessed as patients or employees of the NHS, they are free to do so. The researcher's problem then only pertains to how the formal organisation of the NHS chooses to relate to them if they sidestep institutional review. Few modern researchers operate independently and as indicated above, systems of governance based on the NHS model are growing up elsewhere. Thus university-based researchers are increasingly expected to submit proposals to their own internal institutional ethical review committees operating at Faculty and/or Departmental levels.

Some of the problems that researchers face from these committees have already been hinted at. Difficulties were experienced by qualitative research-oriented social researchers in the past because many members of LRECs and MRECs knew little about such research and often critically scrutinised these research designs and methodologies as they are seen to affect research ethics. They continue to justify asking methodological questions on the grounds that an intervention in people's lives is unwarranted if a research design is flawed and unlikely to meet its intended objectives. The most common reasons for proposals in the social care field being refused ethics committee approval seem to be criticisms of the proposed methodology. In addition, encounters between social researchers and LRECs often reveal a lack of consensus between the LRECs covering different geographical areas – and more than one researcher, whose project was declined, has merely taken the same proposal to another ('easier') committee where it was approved. There is also seen to be an emphasis on protecting staff and institutions against the potential threat of litigation rather than promoting the rights of research subjects although the NHS system now formally separates governance from ethical review. Research governance committees operate within each of the NHS Trust bodies as reviewers of the 'scientific rigour' of a research proposal and the risks to the Trust of permitting the research to be conducted on their site(s). This is intended to remove any confusion over the 'independent' status of RECs – leaving them only to consider the ethics of proposals and removing a charge of conflict of interests if they appear to be seeking to 'protect' the organisations or groups from which they have been drawn.

Sometimes research managers inherit someone else's failure to comply with correct approval procedures (see Box 13.1).

It is clear that approval to conduct research via governance and ethics committees in health and social care is a complex process within the UK NHS and it has been subject to constant change over the last ten to 15 years. Even now some local and regional variations apply even though the system has been steadily rationalised as described

Box 13.1   Inheriting someone else's error

My advice was sought on the following:

'Before I took up a post as research manager for a national charity a researcher had been appointed for a commissioned qualitative research project to find out the experiences of a group of disabled people who were users of health and social care services. I can find no evidence that she sought the necessary ethical approval.

What should the researcher have done and what can be done about interviewing users of "joined up" services (health and social care)? The researcher is arguing that she didn't recruit "patients" as such but rather social services clients and asked them about NHS services in the same interview.

There seem to be so many different ethical approval processes, committees and organisations that researchers have to go through it is no wonder they make mistakes, and get frustrated about the delays.'

above making it easier for multisite approval to be gained from one source.

In the case outlined above ethical and research governance approval should have been gained from all the appropriate authorities in order to interview users about services. In the future this manager will clearly ensure correct procedures are followed. In fact there need be no legal concern here since the NHS/DH has no sanctions against 'unapproved' studies. But there can be a loss of goodwill and a reluctance to assist any organisation or individual researcher not following procedure in the future – quite apart from any ethical concerns the researchers might have about the findings of the particular study. The cultivation of good relations with the Chairs and administrative support officers for such committees will ease procedures in the future and, indeed, it might have even been worth seeking permission retrospectively and admitting that an honest error had occurred.

Vigilance and joining scrutiny committees

If members of RECs in the past knew a little about some key social research methodologies, then social scientists could have done much more to inform and educate them as opposed to merely resenting them and distancing themselves from the process. If social scientists voluntarily joined these scrutiny committees, they could begin to take responsibility for judgement calls and collaborate with others in making decisions transparent. In the inevitable airing of views that is required to make such judgement calls, I have every faith in the ability and skills of social scientists to argue their case. In this way committee members from other disciplines and professions might broaden their knowledge and understanding of some of the intricacies and necessities of social research – making it less likely for social research projects to be rejected on the grounds of methodological ignorance or methodological prejudice.

So the culture of ethical review via such committees needs to change for social scientists to have more faith in them and for them to begin to 'add value' to the project planning element of social research. A peer supportive collegial dialogue between the social science community and ethics committees is necessary. The potential contribution of social science researchers in education, training and mentoring ethical research processes in a range of settings and in multidisciplinary teams should be promoted. To help committees make informed judgements about qualitative health research projects, the Medical Sociology Group of the British Sociological Association agreed upon a short guidance document in 1996 on the criteria for the evaluation of qualitative research. (This has been reproduced in many sources – most recently as Appendix 1 in Alderson 2001.)

Seeking transparency in research governance has increased the importance of ethical review committees which, in turn, has raised the dilemmas involved in ensuring that the quality and independence, essential for good research, are balanced against the rights of, and obligations to, those being studied. It has been argued that the growing power of ethics committees is more a consequence of an institutionalised fear of litigation than of higher moral concern and their 'gate keeping' poses a threat to research freedom. Since committees err on the side of caution, any innovative research or research which might be regarded as sensitive is unlikely to be sanctioned. Indeed some traditional social research methods – such as covert observation – are still viewed with such suspicion that social researchers will be disprivileged in comparison with journalists who have no such qualms about engaging in covert observation when there is a chance of a 'good story'. The eminent sociologist Howard Becker, renowned for his innovative approaches to observational research, has suggested calling himself a 'conceptual artist' in order to evade ethical review.

Experience of the IRBs in the United States does suggest a cause for concern in all human subjects research, and highlights the difficulties and delays involved in gaining permission to engage in what have been conventionally understood as legitimate forms of enquiry. Similarly research governance committees in the UK are caught between the protection of the organisation they are 'acting for', the disparate interests (lay and professional) that they represent and the maintenance of general principles which are protective of human rights. These issues may sometimes be too subtle for the committees to deal with, as they are currently constituted.

And, of course, social science professional codes or guidelines cannot legislate for all possibilities in the field. The SRA ethical guidelines lay stress on the balancing of obligations – to subjects, funding agencies, colleagues and society. Balancing such potentially diverse interests goes to the essence of ethical decision-making.

It is vital to encourage discussion and debate about the promotion and conduct of high quality ethical research since the development of formal governance and accountability structures is likely to increase. Janet Lewis, former Research Director of the Joseph Rowntree Foundation, has proposed that the bodies that fund social care research should be responsible for ensuring that proposed research designs are

Box 13.2   Public attitudes to research governance

So little is know about the public's attitude to ethical review and research governance that the Wellcome Trust commissioned a team from the University of Surrey to conduct an in-depth study of the role governance plays in shaping attitudes to biomedical research, to explore public responses to the principles and processes associated with different models of governance and to investigate the processes that function to reassure the public and which instil confidence in the way biomedical research is governed.

The concluding report indicated that, from the perspective of members of the public, the ways in which personal data were handled, the care that was afforded to guarantees of anonymisation, the handling of sensitive material and the security of databases were diagnostic of whether research governance was working well and could be trusted.

Public Attitudes to Research Governance: A qualitative study in a deliberative context can be accessed at: *http://www.wellcome.ac.uk/ doc_WTX038446.html*

ethical – thereby suggesting that independent funding agencies should be more concerned with the judgement of ethical standards. Those involved in social care research have been concerned to establish an ethical framework and accountability system that is not dominated by biomedical researchers who may be less likely to understand the special concerns of qualitative health research.

It is clear, however, that the language of codes and the heavy bureaucratic procedures involved could distance the public from an understanding of research governance and, even, alienate the researcher into adopting a 'tick box' mentality towards meeting administrative requirements at the expense of careful and continuing reflection into the moral consequences of their work (see Box 13.2).

The 'ethics police' critique

The critique of codes, guidelines and ethical scrutiny systems covers a range of topics and concerns. Alongside the growth of ethical scrutiny there has been concern expressed by social scientists for the consequences of freedom of speech, academic freedom to choose on what and how to conduct research and democratic decision-making during the research process. In essence the charges made are that formalised ethical scrutiny and research governance have been spreading unwarrantedly beyond the life sciences. And, as a consequence of its temporal precedence in the field, there has been a biomedical hegemony – RECs being dominated by reviewers with biomedical interests, expertise and backgrounds. They are seen to be familiar with and so favour certain methodological paradigms over others – the RCT attaining gold standard status, followed closely by meta-analysis and systematic review. The worth of all other methodological approaches being judged in relation to one (idealised) experimental design and two forms of systematised summary protocols (one statistical the other narrative/procedural). This means that researchers from other disciplines and professions find themselves subjected to ill-informed methodological judgements posing as ethical concern. Weighty administrative protocols inhibit and even obstruct potentially valuable research resulting in restrictions to academic/research freedom. This process has been seen to hamper the work of social scientists and is charged with being fundamentally anti-democratic.

Although the concern is widespread throughout the social and behavioural sciences, it is not exclusive to them. Health and biomedical researchers too have found research governance and ethical scrutiny to be obstructive and a disincentive to engaging in research – so much so that committees have noticed a marked reduction in the number of proposals they have to review and a concern has been expressed for the development of research skills at this fundamental level. Novice health researchers are being put off by the apparent minefield of review processes and protocols that confront them. (This is less so in pharmacological research where the pharmaceutical companies have the resources to employ research proposal writers whose sole concern is to ease the burden on researchers of the scrutiny procedures their projects must go through.)

There is a lengthy history to this debate with criticism of the ethical scrutiny of social science beginning with the growth of IRBs in the United States in the late 1970s and concerns being articulated throughout the 1980s. More recently one of the most prominent critics, Dingwall (2006), has argued that the rise of ethical regulation in social science is an outgrowth of ethical regulation in the biomedical sciences, which he views as threatening the proper role of social science in a democratic society. He challenges 'the illegitimate generalisation of a model of research governance based on the particular risks and challenges confronting biomedical researchers'. A bureaucracy has been generated to service a demand for ceremonial conformity in the interests of a combination of vested interests (managers, physicians and lawyers) which promotes further regulatory procedures in a drive towards what he calls 'ethical governance'. Endorsing Haggerty's (2004) view he regards 'regulatory creep' as colonising institutions and intensifying the regulation of organisational practices (Dingwall 2006: 51). Moreover, he suggests that biomedical researchers can do considerable harm since they have more authority to secure compliance and their research 'techniques' can cause physical harm, even death, while: 'At no point are we going to forcibly inject dependent patients with irreversibly toxic green stuff. Why are we treated as if we were going to?' (Dingwall 2006: 52).

The roots of concern for ethical human subjects research can be located in the biomedical field where, building on the Nuremburg Code (1947), major contributions in establishing central principles can be found in the World Medical Association's Declaration of Helsinki (first published in 1964 and updated in 2008). But Dingwall is equally exercised by the imposition of the ESRC's research ethics framework upon universities. By seeking this formalisation the ESRC has intervened in a fundamental methodological element of the research process. He sees this as a

> creeping tyranny (that) feeds on our reasonableness. We must stop colluding and call it by its proper name, a process of censorship that is disabling to the democratic values by which we seek to live. Ethical governance and professional ethics should not be confused. Ethical governance is about censorship and the exercise of power. Whatever the motives for which it is advanced, it is profoundly anti-democratic. Professional ethics is about respect for our common humanity and the mutual obligations that this creates. It is about integrity and virtue in our scholarship. Those are real values, values of liberty that always challenge those who dislike democracy and prefer to sustain a world where their views and assumptions will go unexamined and unquestioned.
>
> (Dingwall 2006: 57)

While Dingwall's focus is on the inhibitory practices of RECs he sees professional ethics as distinct and protective of research values. Spicker (2007) on the other hand focuses on the moral coercion of professional ethical codes, although he is equally concerned about restrictions on research freedom and, therefore, on democratic practice specifically in the area of public policy research. He charges professional ethical codes with a tendency to emphasise the rights of participants which is too narrow for ethical policy research. His view is that there are necessarily conflicts between the rights of participants and the rights of others in the spheres of organisation research and public policy. Policy research needs to be guided by standards related to public accountability and the promotion of welfare. The ethical codes drawn on to advise policy researchers tend to be too general to address the prime concerns of this field of research which is the critical analysis of public policy and practice.

Spicker (2007) illustrates by focussing on what is regarded as one of the main areas of moral behaviour in the treatment of subjects (one given greatest attention in ethical codes and ethical review) – that of informed consent where 'Organisational research is an obvious and necessary exception. Organisations cannot speak or write letters, put up a website or even silently leave their records on the desk; officials have to do it on their behalf' (2007: 105). For this to be achieved particular officers of the organisation are invited or nominated to respond on behalf of the organisation in so far as their participation is determined by their role in the organisation, it is neither fully voluntary nor free from coercion – and neither can it be.

> Constraint, pressure and restriction of people's freedom of action are part of the normal context of public policy. Identifying and responding to such pressures is a normal and unavoidable part of the research process. An ethical position requires these issues to be balanced with other considerations, but they are not an obstacle to research in their own right.
>
> (Spicker 2007: 105)

So, he argues, most ethical codes overgeneralise when promoting a right to participate and a right to refuse to participate. Politicians, public officials and people in positions of public trust should be publicly accountable. Public institutions cannot be assumed to possess the rights to confidentiality that might be accorded to private individuals. There exists an issue of differentiating between public and private spheres in research terms.

> Research in public policy is far more commonly undertaken in the public domain, it relates to social and public roles, and the primary

duty of the researcher is to other people. The kinds of issue that should be considered in policy research are respect for persons, the need for public accountability and the potential for benefit or harm which the research may have. The principles that are actually being applied are more likely to relate to voluntary participation, consent, confidentiality and the protection of participants. The problem for policy research, then, is not just that generalised guidance is being elevated to the status of rules. It is that these are the wrong generalisations, and the wrong rules.

(Spicker 2007: 117)

Murphy and Dingwall (2001: 340) in turn have counselled caution in the application of codes in that they may not be adequately 'method-specific'. Their generalised prescriptions may unnecessarily constrain valuable qualitative research or blunt researchers to the particular sensitivities of those currently under study. General principles may have to be operationalised in different ways that are directly linked to the methods and topics of study.

Similarly Mauthner et al. (2002: 18–19) criticised the UK's SRA ethical guidelines for not including feminist sources. When the guidelines were originally being written in the 1980s, there were few feminist sources that raised generic ethical decision-making problems. The two references they cite to support their criticism are both specific to the problem of interviewing women. The same omission could be levied at many distinct categories of 'excluded' or marginalised participants and would have more than doubled the annotated bibliography that was provided with the guidelines. But they also claim that 'awkward tensions in the aims of professional associations' ethical statements would be cured if they were explicitly informed and guided by a theoretical and feminist approach to ethical dilemmas' (Mauthner et al. 2002: 21–22). Such 'awkward tensions' are the stuff of the paradoxes in moral philosophy that have been discussed throughout this book – and countless more in ethics and moral philosophy. I seriously doubt that they can be legitimately resolved merely by the adoption of a specific theoretical paradigm. They then propose a series of alternative guidelines which can all be subsumed within the generic principles of the SRA guidelines. Although some of their additional points could have helped articulate the specifics of those principles – especially, say, their plea for increased context awareness and reflexivity. (It seems as though guidelines aren't such a bad thing as long as they are informed by one's favoured theoretical perspective.)

To reassert the general point I am making here. Some social researchers appear to reject and denounce any form of externalised regulatory measures intended to secure standards, protect the public and help guide researchers in the inevitable ethical decision-making they have to confront. In my view they could instead be actively contributing to the collective revision and amendment of complex codes and guidelines to facilitate their inclusiveness, at the same time as volunteering to participate in ethical review committees, and thereby raise the standards of critical scrutiny.

It is evident from other contents in Mauthner et al. (2002) that they referred to the SRA website during the process of writing their book. The updating of the guidelines was going on for over a year and requests for contributions to the debate frequently sought and incorporated where relevant. It would have been more collegial if these critics had 'shared' the gift of their insights and perspectives with the group of experienced professionals who were attempting to get the guidelines right and hopefully to cover as many approaches to social research as possible. The same charge could be levelled at Dingwall and Spicker – by contributing more actively, it may be that we can improve the systems of ethical scrutiny to ensure good research continues to be supported.

Analysing the scrutiny process

Addressing the concerns of these critics requires a more thorough exploration of the range of theoretical and empirical questions that lie behind them. We need to ask:

- Is social science research being obstructed by people who have 'no right' to do so?
- Are ethical scrutiny committees undemocratic in their practices and processes?
- Can social research do as much harm to people as biomedical research?
- Are there some spheres of research where the participants cannot be assumed to have as many rights as in others? (That is, can we be 'selective' about the application of rights to research subjects?)
- Are we so concerned about gaining consent from participants that it inhibits methodologically robust research?

- Can ethical guidelines for research be so comprehensive as to preserve the integrity and direction of all major theoretical perspectives?
- What sort of stance should we expect from the professional associations operating within the social science field?

The dilemmas inherent in research practice revolve around the problem that being good as a researcher and as a human being necessitates making choices between alternative courses of action and, therefore, is often a form of compromise. Given the nature of social research, whereby researchers are frequently in face-to-face contact with their respondents/participants, and/or handle personal data about them, it is vital that each researcher takes full responsibility for the management of their own ethical practice. 'Ethical awareness' among researchers, managers and commissioners depends on constant reflection on the ethical implications of their work, continuous professional development with regard to ethical practice and the existence of peer mentors able to advise and guide when difficult situations arise.

When we argue that social science cannot do as much harm as biomedical research, we are trading the 'effects' of physical illness and mortality against psychological, emotional, political and economic disturbance. I certainly would not want to attempt to measure someone's emotional trauma against their physical pain. Nor would I wish to measure the opportunity cost of gains to medical knowledge from the deaths of research subjects, as against the consequences of failing to adequately develop studies of the politics, culture and social infrastructure of, for example, Islamist societies. Of course we can do harm by doing (and not doing) social research, and harm has been done. That alone is adequate reason for independent scrutiny of our research intentions.

How do ethics committees operate?

There are a series of supplementary questions entailed here: How extensive and all pervading is the regulation of social science research? What precisely is its regulatory nature? Who is doing the scrutiny and how are they doing it?

To assess if social science research is being obstructed by people who have 'no right' to do so, we would need to examine the constituents of ethics committees, and we would need some evidence of their operating procedures to assess the degree to which their decision-making could be considered democratic. The problem here is a classic methodological one – we may have some institutional guidelines (constitutions, standard operating procedures and such like) that outline how they should operate, but we lack sufficient empirical studies on how they do actually operate in practice.

The grievances expressed are largely against two sets of bodies – NHS RECs, which oversee social research with patients, and university RECs, which regulate research conducted by academics employed by those universities. It is worth reasserting that there remain plenty of researchers in social science who are neither employed by universities nor seeking to research within the NHS and so do not necessarily have to face these committees. They include market researchers, government researchers, researchers working for private research organisations and individual/own account researchers. More importantly there exists no comprehensive 'system' that attempts to regulate all our research activity. This means there are many gaps in the regulatory process and it cannot be nearly as comprehensive and restrictive as critics often suggest. In essence there is little other than the law to prevent researchers from conducting research which may be seen as unethical by others, as long as they are not dependent upon research councils for funding and as long as they care little about the sanctions that may be imposed upon them by professional associations. Of course few researchers are quite so independent of financial sources that they can ignore the prescriptions of funding agencies and few operate without the membership of one or the other of the professional associations. In both cases this serves to legitimise their activities.

Throughout the debate the confusion between research governance and ethical scrutiny has continued and the ESRC framework has only served to compound this confusion. Indeed we should not really be talking about 'ethical governance' – as pointed out earlier in this chapter, systems for ethical review must be seen as independent of the need for research governance. The latter is concerned with risk assessment, risk aversion and institutional accountability. Ethical review on the other hand requires combined independent and expert judgements on the balance of harm and benefit to all participants and stakeholders in the act of engaging in research.

The critics tend to conflate institutional risk assessment and damage limitation with the balancing of harm and benefit. There are overlaps but anticipatory governance procedures are about making a judgement as to the potential for 'successful' outcomes of the research – that is the chances that it will be completed without adverse events that could result in actions for liability or grievance claims of some kind. But successful outcomes also depend upon the quality of the research design and process – this means asking if the research was well planned in that its successful completion could be anticipated and of sufficient methodological 'quality' in that its stated goals could be predicted to be achieved. Ethics is about balancing harms and benefits and so the probability estimate should have to do with the chances of harm coming to individuals balanced against the chances of such harm outweighing the potential benefits. This represents an attempt to ensure harm is minimised or avoided and that benefit is maximised.

Of course, the critics are right to complain if institutional procedures fail to make this distinction. If research governance is not separated from ethical scrutiny, then it is hard to see how RECs can truly operate in a detached and independent manner. To judge the ethics of a research project primarily in terms of the harm that might come to the sponsoring institution that 'houses' the researcher is to judge science in terms of damage limitation. Little valuable science would ever have been accomplished on such a criterion. Dingwall argues that this represents a form of censorship and restriction on the freedom of speech. There is no denying that institutional governance certainly does that, but such is the restriction on the freedom of speech of most university academics in the UK and the US – who can be charged with bringing their university into disrepute. That is the true force of the IRB system in the States and will be a consequence of its operation in universities in the UK as the UREC system spreads. To challenge that is a matter of academic freedom, which must remain separate from the 'advisory' role that should be adopted by RECs. Indeed there are plenty of other forces that intervene in the full and free dissemination of research – editorial and peer review, and the concerns of publishers' lawyers. Other than that one is perfectly 'free' to publish – and maybe 'perish' – and there is little difference from the state of affairs prior to the growth of ethical scrutiny.

Process

Assuming that such a distinction can be maintained (and there is argument both that it cannot and should not), RECs are frequently charged with processual obstructions to research. Complaints are made that they are time consuming, subject to frequent delays and not easy to use, and that scrutiny procedures are frequently unnecessarily duplicated. There is a temptation to align this criticism with a counter-managerialist perspective and condemn the growth of RECs as a further symptom of audit culture, quality management and the irrationalities of the flawed but imposed performative measures of research assessment one finds throughout higher education worldwide (see, for example, Darbyshire 2008). It may be that management seeks to highjack ethical review into the service of other goals and, again, such managerial exploitation is something that must be guarded against – hence the virtue of ensuring ethical review maintains a formal 'independence' from the organisational structure.

Any objections relating to administrative complexity can be addressed by establishing appropriate procedural mechanisms. There is no reason that administrative mechanisms should not be made more facilitative by, say, the adoption of self-completed, online review application forms (such as the NRES system); proformas for consent letters; standardised participant information sheets; decision-trees or checklists to assist the decision-making process and consistency in the routes taken to reach certain decisions and so on. It goes without saying that these should not restrict the flexibility of researchers in adopting and introducing novel procedures for giving information and/or gaining consent that might be more appropriate to their particular study.

Whatever system is adopted should also recognise that ethical decision-making is not a static, one-off exercise. Only the field researcher truly confronts the unanticipated aspects of ethical research as it occurs in a dynamic, spontaneous manner. Ethnography, for example, is all about building relationships in the field with people and so it is hard to anticipate what ethical issues might arise at the commencement of a study – they can crop up continually and, surprisingly, throughout the project. So to be inclusive, ethical scrutiny needs to allow for such variations in a methodological approach.

Proper ethical review requires addressing ethical issues at all stages of the research process – from specification, through tender, the ongoing monitoring of a project in action and its final dissemination. Once again the responsibility for ethical review need not be constantly maintained by a full REC review – it can be delegated, to the Committee Chair or to the researchers themselves with the request that difficult decisions be referred to the full REC for advice. As the repository of knowledge held by ethics committees grows, so too grows the awareness of minimally problematic methods and techniques – in such cases 'expedited' reviews would be advised and fuller consideration reserved for evidently, more ethically complex projects.

At times it is the very constituency of RECs that is criticised due to their attempts to balance expertise, independence and 'lay' representation. As voluntary members they can only be said to be representative of their own opinion. Experts cannot be comprehensively expert in all research fields, independent members cannot be independent of all interest groups and the 'lay' members frequently are drawn from retired and/or active members of professions such as the law and the clergy or are drawn from patient/service user groups and other groups of public interest. Consequently no member can be considered truly independent in the sense of an ability to detach themselves from the research questions put to them. However, neither would we want them to be since ethical issues relate to our 'principled sensitivity to the rights of others' and the REC is there to help ensure we maintain that principle. It does mean, though, that without fully recording decisions and the rationales behind them, there can be some inconsistencies in the decisions taken – dependent on who attends any one meeting. If different people are attending the committees at different times, no two similar cases will necessarily be decided similarly.

Practice

Achieving consistency in ethical decisions is difficult for many other reasons too. Ethical concerns and awareness of ethical issues are in constant flux. It depends on evidence from new cases, transparency in research activity, publicised litigation, legislative change and changes in the membership of committees alongside inevitable changes in societal morality arising out of a large scale, and increasingly rapid, cultural change. To expect consistency in moral evaluation across a research community is to expect more than we would expect from many other spheres of society.

Similarly we expect a great deal from RECs when we expect them to be adequately comprehensive in their judgements when, increasingly, research projects address complex questions drawing upon multidisciplinary perspectives and multiprofessional teams of researchers. We should not expect them to cover all angles – since all angles cannot be covered – another reason for the field researcher taking ultimate ethical responsibility. There is, of course, a corresponding danger that members

Box 13.3   How ethics committees operate

There is very little empirical evidence about how research ethics committees operate. More recently, based on ethnographic research on REC decision-making, Adam Hedgecoe has suggested that the core role of such committees lies in assessing the trustworthiness of applicants, rather than any formal application of ethical theory. He also suggests that there is little evidence that RECs are 'ideologically biased' against qualitative research and/or particularly ill informed about social science in general. While Sue Richardson and Miriam McMullan's survey of sociologists' experiences of the process and practice of ethical review by health RECs suggests that more thought needs to be given to achieving the correct balance between the 'controlling' and the 'enabling' function of RECs.

(Richardson and McMullan 2007; Hedgecoe 2008)

of ethics committees fall back on their familiar and favoured research methods, or their personal views on popular topics or what they consider to be the more urgent research needs. Just like the rest of us, they have their preferences (see Box 13.3).

In practice what we seek from RECs is a balancing of responsibilities between individuals (field researcher and research manager) and institutions (employing organisation and professional association) – thereby achieving a form of distributed collective responsibility. Ethical research practice becomes a mutual accomplishment of all participants – research subjects, researchers, commissioners, funders and managers.

One can see the immediate challenge posed by Spicker's argument that there are some spheres of research where the participants cannot be assumed to have as many rights – to privacy and confidentiality – as in others. This implies that we can be 'selective' about the application of rights to research subjects and is but a short step from suggesting that it is ethically permissible to devalue the privacy rights of some research subjects. As with all moral judgements what matters is where we place the 'boundary' to those rights. We by no means need to suggest that these are somehow devalued as 'persons' – rather by their institutional role, position in society, public appearances and so on they have chosen to alter their own rights to privacy. As researchers we might not choose to go so far as the paparazzi or investigative journalists in 'invading' the privacy of public personalities, although, once again, such a decision remains within the ethical judgement of the individual researcher who makes their own assessment of the balances of harm and benefits.

What is the nature of the power relationship between researchers and subjects in social/behavioural science?

Social scientists may not be held in the same degree of esteem as medical researchers, and so may lack some attributed authority, but it does not mean they lack power in the research encounter. Once in the encounter it is they who could hold all the cards since they understand the main goals of the research, the limits to the data gathering required of the encounter and may even possess rhetorical and persuasive communication skills acquired as part of their training that could sustain an uneven balance of power in their favour. In being much subtler in their power applications to ensure commitment from and retention of subjects, they could do even more harm than the more formalised 'clinical' engagement of a trial biomedical intervention. A research subject might have more grounds for feeling 'duped' in such a relationship and their sense of self-esteem lowered. This would be exacerbated in a situation where the respondent mistakenly assumed that a genuine 'friendship' had been established as a consequence of the researcher's rapport-generating skills. Cotterill (1992) sees this as a particular skill of female researchers which is liable to abuse and/or misunderstanding when they are engaged with female respondents.

Dingwall (2006) warns too of the fetishising of consent. Any requirement for a formal, signed contract of consent immediately implicates both researcher and researched in an implied adversarial relationship – each having to exercise caution about the rights and obligations of the other. By seeking this sort of formalisation in social science, the ESRC REF has intervened in the research relationship in a way that has fundamental methodological consequences. Consenting can be done in many ways that respect the rights and expectations of both parties without excess formality. Indeed, there has been some recent research that suggests most participants are not excessively concerned about such matters – either not understanding the consenting process, the requirements for it to be conducted and/or that it matters that much to them in terms of their participation in research (NatCen 2007).

This problem of gaining fully informed consent once again illustrates the failure to distinguish between risk aversion and ethical engagements in research. Seeking a written and witnessed consent is a matter of damage limitation and anticipates litigation. It is disingenuous ever to claim fully informed consent when even the researcher may not, indeed cannot, be fully informed. They cannot anticipate all the things that could go wrong in research, so how can the research subjects be expected to? Even to get the subject to be 'as informed as' the researcher would theoretically require that they be educated/trained to the same level of competence. So the requirement ought to be that the subject is as informed as is necessary to ensure they remain as free as possible in making their own judgements about how engaged in the research they wish to be – from 'not at all' to 'fully', with no obstructions to their discontinuance in the research that could harm them.

RECs can only fulfil their functions fully if they possess the willingness and the ability to share the experience of difficult decisions – building a repository of research ethics knowledge. (The same is true for professional associations as discussed in Chapter 3.) The SRA has a research ethics forum drawing on senior members of the organisation from which researchers can seek specific advice about the ethical standing of their projects. Similarly the Market Research Society *codeline* uses a series of case studies and FAQs to assist in such decision-making. In this way researchers will not be left to the potential for inconsistencies lying within the REC system.

Ethics creep in general

Some academics fear the growth of ethical scrutiny as a threat to academic and, therefore, research freedom (Shea 2000) (see Box 13.4).

Box 13.4   Ethics creep

In Durham University the Dean of Arts and Humanities circulated this memo to the staff:

'All teaching that raises issues that are likely to cause offence to some … must have ethical approval from the departmental teaching and learning committee. It is anticipated that this may cover topics such as race, slavery, witchcraft, abortion, euthanasia, many gender issues etc.'

This might be seen as a risk limitation requirement in an educational environment in which students are seen as consumers with rights and protections under anti-discrimination laws. However it certainly challenges the central principle of academic freedom which supports challenging received wisdom and raising new ideas that may be seen as controversial.

(*The Times Higher*, 17 December 2004: 2)

This demonstrates potential contradictions in principle between laws supporting freedom of speech and those protecting the sensitivities of individuals – this could present a problem to the dissemination of research reports which may be seen as provocative or challenging.

The suggestion is sometimes made that the additional layers of red tape commensurate with the growth of ethical policing delays the inception of research and, necessarily, has economic consequences for all stakeholders. An interesting parallel is again offered with biomedical and pharmaceutical drugs research. There is a suggestion that the more drugs trials are regulated in Europe and the US, then the more companies, with millions to gain and lose, will transfer their research studies to countries with less rigorous regulations for research ethics. Emerging economies such as China, India and SE Asia might be less concerned to regulate research on the grounds that their developing commercial structures require support and there is a great deal of money to be made from the large pharmaceutical companies conducting trials there. The solution to such economic threats cannot be to dispense with rigorous ethical regulation but to set standards for human subjects research that can be applied internationally. Not to do so is a bit like suggesting that certain standards in human rights only apply to certain geographical regions. It is up to countries that have established and overseen systems intended to protect people to advance those standards globally. Research fields cannot only be contaminated locally in an increasingly global world. How willing would we be to learn from research conducted in what we would regard as an unethical manner on human subjects in one of these developing countries? Could our beneficence, our knowledge gain, be regarded as properly generated in this way – in fact, might we not have grounds for epistemological doubts for knowledge gained from a range of improper practices?

Nonetheless, inefficiency and lack of subtlety alone cannot be enough to remove the need for ethical scrutiny – it merely makes the case for improving the knowledge and sophistication of those serving on such committees. And although much of the relevant legislation remains untested, we might have to examine its potential consequences more carefully and ensure that the law too does not become so prohibitive that no valuable research can be conducted.

Concluding reflections on ethical review

Dingwall may not be overstating the potential for damage when he writes: 'There is, however, now abundant evidence that the corrupt have little to fear, while honest and conscientious scholars, seeking to engage in research intended to enrich the public realm, are subject to pettifogging obstacles, designed to bolster the power of the organisations charged with governance' (Dingwall 2006: 57). Yet where is the evidence that corrupt social scientists are 'getting away with' behaviour that should be censured? While there is much anecdotal evidence from honest researchers who feel their work is hampered, it is hard to judge what general damage has been done to the profession and practice of social research.

Perhaps it is the case that it has suited organisations to confuse governance with ethics. The moral legitimacy for applying regulatory governance derives from a rhetoric of ethics that appears morally reprehensible to challenge or resist. Research ethics is a complex field of study and practice (Van den Hoonaard 2006). It is hard, if not impossible, to maintain some of the key distinctions – hence the need for individual researchers to assume the major responsibility for their own ethical decision-taking. In this they need support, advice and guidance from their professional associations and, possibly, some independent oversight in the form of ethics review. And it is certainly true, even if only on the basis of reported personal experiences, that research ethics committees themselves do not always behave ethically.

But we should not assume that ethical review is necessarily adversarial (as Israel and Hay (2006) do, for example, in the final chapter of their book) and so necessarily obstructive of social science research. Such a view derives from a confusion of the need to anticipate and address ethical dilemmas with institutional risk aversion and damage limitation. The critics are right that this has arisen out of the historical dominance of biomedical professions in previous systems of ethical scrutiny and the UK's NHS has now recognised the need to keep assessment of research ethics separate from research governance – which inevitably is more concerned with the potential for institutional damage arising out of the conduct of research.

Ethics committees can tend to become principlist in their approach to ethics – adopting certain moral philosophies or standpoints in a 'purist' manner instead of the more pragmatic ethical pluralism required of empirical research. To address the adversarial problem a fuller consideration of the balance between institutional ethical requirements and the individual researcher's moral judgements is required (see Chapter 14 and Pallister et al. 1999).

Israel and Hay (2006) rightly point out that research training tends to compartmentalise ethics as somehow separate from techniques and methodology. Ethical awareness and thinking ethically must permeate the research process from design to dissemination. In this way ethical scrutiny becomes less of an obstacle to be overcome and more of a facilitative, supportive process to ensure minimum harm to research participants. In similar vein there is a need to identify interested individuals within each research organisation who can conduct preliminary reviews of proposals for ethical concerns, who keep abreast of developments in the field of research ethics – disseminating such information to colleagues – and who can act as mentors for ethical advice and guidance.

I trust this chapter and the rest of this book makes it clear that I am no defender of crude and poorly conducted ethical review. I do believe that some form of ethical scrutiny with a degree of 'independence' from the research team is vital to the maintenance of professional standards in social science. It should be done – but it must be done well and not confused by institutional and/or professional protectionism. Research ethics scrutineers should be asking – who is doing the research, what are they doing it for and how are they doing it? (Returning to the questions that were raised in Chapter 1.) If they can see it is being conducted and/or overseen by a reputable, experienced researcher with sound professional credentials, in order to answer a valuable research question that may improve human life, they are employing techniques that minimise the potential for harm to themselves and to others and, throughout the conduct of the research, they maintain an awareness of the consequences of their actions for others – then they will have assisted in accomplishing ethical research in social science.

In order to maintain a climate of trust in the practice and outcomes of social research, it is inevitable that systems of ethical assurance will be established and need to be maintained by all those engaged in work of this nature. The trust of the public, colleagues, those who commission and fund research and those being studied requires an effective system of ethical review, clear lines of responsibility and a manageable degree of independent overview (Dench et al. 2004). However it is also the case that no administrative system, no matter how well conceived, can guarantee sound ethical practice among all researchers. Similarly unnecessarily cumbersome systems of ethical review can hinder the operation of valuable research enacted in the public interest. All too often institutional caution has taken precedence over ethical concerns and ethical review has been confused with risk aversion, damage limitation and managerial line accountability. There is a continued need for vigilance – not just of researchers, but of how ethics committees also bear their responsibilities. As Richardson and McMullan (2007) have argued, we can learn a great deal from both the negative and positive aspects of the operation of NHS RECs in how ethical scrutiny of social research can be improved.

While increasing scrutiny is inevitable, it is no substitute for sustained ethical thinking and ethical awareness by individual researchers. This whole book aims at encouraging this raised ethical awareness. A pragmatic (and ethical?) response by research organisations should be to establish their own systems of ethical scrutiny in-house and/or link to their specific professional organisations and make best use of whatever scrutiny systems are available. More importantly researchers and research organisations should stay ahead of the game as much as they can by being proactive in research ethics rather than simply, even grudgingly, reactive. Since RECs are largely voluntary bodies, the profession can contribute by joining them and engaging in debate. If committee members do not inform themselves adequately, perhaps it is our duty to take the challenge to them and ensure they are informed methodologically and ethically prior to taking key decisions that affect the development of our profession.

14
Sustaining Ethical Awareness

At the start of this book I likened the journey to a moral maze. The metaphor suggests that we could easily get 'lost' with so many decisions to take and potential wrong turns and dead ends. Elsewhere the analogy adopted was that of a minefield – with potentially explosive hidden dangers just waiting to destroy us. I hope that by this point in the book such metaphors seem less appropriate. Perhaps the 'balancing act' now seems more apt. We need to acquire the skills to balance our decisions against each other to achieve the most favourable outcome.

Whatever the metaphor, we can become so enmeshed in the pragmatics of conducting research ethically and ensuring appropriate scrutiny procedures that the fundamental principles upon which ethical practices are based can be neglected. I have argued throughout that ethical decision-making is as vital a methodological skill as the facility with research instruments that makes for a productive researcher. There are many ways of sustaining ethical awareness and much of it can engage us in facing the human condition in fruitful debate and reflection, much of it beyond the more immediate concerns of social science research.

It can be difficult to discuss ethics in a practical manner without appearing to be moralising or, worse, condescending. To advise on taking ethical decisions in the spirit intended in this book is to help establish principles and set the grounds for good judgement – not determine the final outcomes of that judgement – once more, only researchers themselves can do that.

Traditional views

In the rush to develop professional 'transferable' skills there is a danger that some of the vital roots of the discipline upon which those skills are based can be forgotten. In two, now classic, lectures Max Weber confronted the ethical dilemmas of politics and of science:

> From no ethics in the world can it be concluded when and to what extent the ethically good purpose 'justifies' the ethically dangerous means and ramifications.
>
> (Weber 1918 in Gerth and Mills 1948: 121)

And when reflecting on the vocation of science:

> No science is absolutely free from presuppositions, and no science can prove its fundamental value to the man who rejects these presuppositions.
>
> (Weber 1918 in Gerth and Mills 1948: 153)

We have seen throughout this book how confronting such paradoxes is the essence of 'good' research and this search for objectivity and truth in spite of the philosophical constraints forms a thread throughout the sociological tradition. C. Wright Mills's *The Sociological Imagination* was a powerful work when published and rewards regular rereading. It offers a comprehensive but constructive critique both of grand theory and abstracted empiricism together with some of the most practical suggestions on 'intellectual craftsmanship' one could find. Wright Mills was a brilliant writer and researcher with a strong moral and political impulse, who opposed the naïve emulation of the natural sciences in the search for prediction and control in the social sciences. He saw this as revealing

> a rationalistic and empty optimism which rests upon an ignorance of the several possible roles of reason in human affairs, the nature of power and its relations to knowledge, the meaning of moral action and the place of knowledge within it, the nature of history and the fact that men are not only creatures of history but on occasion creators within it and even of it.
>
> (Wright Mills 1970: 127)

The early 1970s saw a period of self-reflection in the social sciences that challenged some basic assumptions and introduced the notion of 'reflexivity' – critical awareness of the claims that can be made and how the research act is essentially one of engagement in which the very presence of the researcher has to be seen as part of the outcomes of the research (Gouldner 1970; Schon 1983). Stanislav Andreski (1974) summed this up in a trenchant critique in which he condemned the contemporary study of human behaviour as more 'sorcery' than science. He reported on a request made prior to World War I to French figures in the social sciences – then known as *les sciences morales* – about what they regarded as the most essential method in their field; the reply from Georges Sorel was: 'honesty' (Andreski 1974: 243). Reflexivity is generally now accepted as a vital element in securing that 'honesty', but remains something that researchers are wary about fully disclosing partly due to the enduring mystique of 'objectivity' and partly in fear of the reproof of ethics committees (Blackman 2007). There is, however, an argument that an excessive concern with reflexivity bears the price of potential increased emotional harm to the researcher (Sampson et al. 2008).

Ethical pluralism – methodological pragmatism

From time to time throughout this discussion I have warned of the dangers of an ethical purism – the tendency to adopt any one particular moral philosophy and assume that it offers adequate guidance for resolving most ethical dilemmas and ensuring ethical research. But some form of ethical eclecticism is essential in practice in order to 'navigate the righteous course' (see Pallister et al. 1999).

The point about ethics is that a balance of rights and wrongs is an inevitable characteristic of moral choice – *professional 'codes'* intend to 'legislate' for professional protection, while *ethical 'guidelines'* aim to 'educate' in order to assist the individual researcher's own moral choice. But the moral layers which guide researchers' decisions also include the wider cultural environment, the culture and goals of their employing organisation and, ultimately, their personal ethical sensitivities which will be linked to their belief systems, their cognitive capacities and their personal life experiences, families and personal relationships.

Put more formally we can see how these 'layers' are related to distinct moral philosophies. We may talk of goal-based (consequentialist/ classic utilitarianism), duty-based and rights-based (deontological) moralities (Foster 2001). Goal-based moralities justify the aims of research. Duty-based morality exhorts us to practice our profession to certain standards, while rights-based morality is concerned with protecting our subjects' autonomy, dignity and well-being – as well as our own. All three moralities will have to be incorporated in establishing a pragmatic philosophy that meets the goals of social research.

Are there any taboos of method and/or topic?

Two final generic moral questions have to be addressed at this point:

1. Are there any topics that the ethical social researcher should not study?
2. Are there any methods the ethical researcher should not adopt?

The two most usually morally proscribed methods covert observation – participant or otherwise – and social experimentation have been discussed earlier and from my argument throughout the book it should be evident that my response to these questions is in the negative. No topics are inherently 'unethical' in terms of our potential for scientific interest in them, nor can any method be entirely proscribed. The ethical choices to be made when adopting a method and/or a topic for study will depend upon the scientific and social importance of the research and our views on how the subjects to be studied should be treated. If we always return to our notion of respect for the rights of others then we, and they, should be safe.

In fact, Frank Furedi has argued vehemently for anyone to have the right to the 'disinterested' quest for knowledge and information on any topic whether they are a professional researcher or not. He equally condemns the notion that special dispensation should be granted by 'authorities' for anyone to research morally repugnant topics and counsels wariness of the creation of a moral panic and ethical crusaders who aim to determine what the rest of us can legitimately research (Furedi 2003).

The question then becomes how we estimate the value or worth of our work and of the topics and the people we study.

Ecologism and the environment

One major driver of public discussion about ethics in recent years has been concern for what humans have done to the environment and the assumed consequence of global warming. I doubt that any intelligent social researcher has not equally been driven to reflect on what this means for themselves personally, but also for the subjects of their studies – people, organisations, groups, communities and society at large.

There is a broader philosophical issue here for which caution is advised; that is, the tendency to counterpose 'mankind' (meaning 'humanity') to 'nature', as if we were in competition with 'it'. Rupert Read (2007) makes an excellent case for using the term 'environment' in which human beings and nature are conjoined. We are neither 'in' the environment, nor is 'it' external to us. We *are* the environment and it is *us* (cf. the work of Ludwig Wittgenstein and of John Dewey).

An anthropocentric view would reject the notion that we share 'being' the environment with other sentient creatures (animals) and all that is 'live' (to include plants) and 'not live' (say, mineral substances). An inclusive ecological perspective requires that we think more broadly about what we share with these 'others'. As ethically aware researchers, we should be talking in terms of local, regional and global 'ecosystems'. We need to decide 'What ecosystems we wish to live in and to secure for future inhabitants of that ecosystem … this planet' (Read 2007: 22). For example, an unquestioning valuing of economic 'growth' is neglectful of a perspective of sustainability for our chosen ecosystem. Instead we should be thinking of 'development'.

Such a view is something social researchers have to contemplate since it is connected with how we view our role in the world and just how separate we can ever consider ourselves to be from the other inhabitants of our ecosystem and, therefore, how we study 'them' and 'us'.

Sources of ethical reflection

In reflecting on the Holocaust, Auschwitz and attempts to legislate against such horrors being perpetrated again, the Dalai Lama points out that no administrative scheme could have been so foolproof as to have prevented it. But what can stop it is the fundamental awareness across the population that such behaviour is not morally acceptable: 'Much more effective and important than such legislation is our regard for one another's feelings on a simple human level' (Gyatso 1999: 68). His basic premise is that an ethical act is 'one which does not harm another's experience or expectation of happiness'. '[E]thical conduct … consists in acts which take others' well being into account' (Gyatso 1999: 106). It follows that to act ethically we need to take others' feelings into consideration when we take action – we need to draw upon what he sees as an 'innate' human capacity for empathy (Gyatso 1999: 82). If we have compassion or empathy, then ethical conduct follows automatically. 'Ethically wholesome actions arise naturally in the context of compassion' (Gyatso 1999: 139).

We may condemn the Internet for the trivia it purveys. On the other hand it has become a vehicle for enhanced global public discourse which allows the exploration of global ethical visions. The growth of ethical consumer and business networks on the Internet is testimony to the growth of ethical concerns among the general public. One example is *Ethical Junction* which brings together businesses and consumers who share a commitment to ethical values. It offers direct access to products and services and a news forum, and is the source of up to date information on events as well as opinions and comments: http://www.ethical-junction.org.

Evidently the regular news media are a constant source of ethical debate. But given their power in agenda setting, developing an independent judgement can be assisted by commentators offering alternative sources of information and insights free of vested interests (see, for example, Monbiot 2000, 2003, 2006). Alternative debate on news can be found from Media Lens who explain their mission as

> a response based on our conviction that mainstream newspapers and broadcasters provide a profoundly distorted picture of our world. We are convinced that the increasingly centralised, corporate nature of the media means that it acts as a de facto propaganda system for corporate and other establishment interests. The costs incurred as a result of this propaganda, in terms of human suffering and environmental degradation, are incalculable.
>
> http://www.medialens.org/

While Media Wise in particular is concerned to promote ethical practices in journalism: http://www.mediawise.org.uk.

Scholarly writing on morality and ethics varies in its user-friendliness and pragmatic relevance to the concerns of an aware social researcher but there is a range of writing in popular philosophy that is highly accessible and thought provoking (Grayling 2003; Cohen 2007; Baggini and Fosl 2007). The fictional works of Alexander McCall Smith, a former professor of medical ethics, frequently draw upon the concept of 'moral proximity' – the idea that we are more likely to be provoked into moral action when experiencing others' problems that are physically, culturally and geographically 'close' to us.

Sharing experience is vital to successful and high quality social research. Sharing both successful work and the failures or unpredictable occurrences prompt further reflection. Researchers should be willing to allow novices or peers working in similar fields to have sight of successful proposals – at least the ways ethical issues might have been addressed in them – since there is a high degree of market sensitivity which prevents the full application of the scientific ideals of sharing. Such mentorship can be found from many of the professional associations in social research and contacted via the links provided at the end of the book (and see Rowson 2006).

Emerging arenas for ethical concern – e-science and e-research

The development of e-science depends upon interdisciplinary and international (global) collaboration. Issues of trust between researchers as well as between researchers and the public/their subjects will necessarily be raised. The usual concerns of data security, intellectual property and priority rights, and professional standards are enhanced by new technological infrastructures and advanced communicative mechanisms. The ethical considerations of e-research differ in kind not in principle. In obtaining informed consent there may be more possibility for research subjects to engage in sustained deception. Data security issues have already been touched on in Chapter 9 with portability and transfer being major threats. The distinction between public and private 'spaces' may be even harder to sustain on the Internet; and website provision for debriefing may lack the 'human' touch which can retrieve some of the most difficult stresses and strains raised by the research encounter (Hewson et al. 2002: 51–4).

E-interviewing could offer a less intrusive alternative to phone call and text messaging interviews which have both grown in order to increase response rates by recognition of the increasing ICT sophistication of the target population. Using the massively growing networking sites it is possible, through instant messaging, to interview respondents internationally and, given the 'weak relationships' established through such sites, there is a good chance that the respondents will not consider such interviews as being too intrusive (Fontes and O'Mahoney 2008).

How cross-cultural, interprofessional ethical standards are to be established and maintained in the face of new data sharing possibilities remains a problem. Perhaps in light of such developments more thought could be given to the development of establishing a more universal ethical position for social research.

Universal ethics

Our own sense of the 'rightness' of our moral standpoints leads us into thinking that a universal ethics could be possible – and so a universal

research ethics feasible too. But we tend to forget about cultural impe-
rialism and the reactions to it. Standards can be more specific and
localised than we expect. This is the reason for the existence of the 'soft
power' embedded in organisations like the British Council, the Goethe
Institute and now the Confucian Institutes being established by the
Chinese government around the world. But a universal set of moral
standards could grow in the other direction – by establishing professional standards in research we could come closer in the rest of the
values that we might share globally.

In sharing concerns about how we take ethical decisions we often
come across solutions adopted by others. They may contain a core of
ethics that draw on specific cultural traditions but in sharing their more
general applicability might be realised and applied.

Conclusion

The backcloth to this book is a concern to conduct 'good science' in
morally 'good' ways, to achieve some 'good' for society and individuals. A lot depends on what is meant by 'good' in each of these spheres
and this clearly conflates moral questions with questions of method
and purpose (see Grayling 2003). Given the impossibility of a universal
definition of 'goodness', the good researcher for me is one who strives
to adhere to their own carefully thought through set of moral standards,
while ensuring those standards do not fail to respect the rights, dignity
and well-being of others.

Discussions of standards in science raise issues of training, funding
and intent (see Box 14.1).

The consideration of ethical dilemmas in research is an exercise in
professional integrity and in the establishment, maintenance and the
raising of professional standards that is in all our interests – whether
as researchers, subjects of research or the beneficiaries of research
findings.

The problem is that all research with human subjects requires intervening in their lives – usually without invitation. That does not mean
that we are necessarily wasting people's time and we could become
overly cautious about that. There are plenty of less than useful things
people are doing in the world – admittedly of their own choosing – but
if the research intervention promotes thought, stimulates activity and,
even, generates criticism, we could claim to be of better benefit to the
general population than, say, not interrupting their favourite television soap opera. In fact, there may be times when heightened concerns

Box 14.1   Standards in science

Dr Ian Gibson, Labour MP for Norwich North, has raised such concerns for many years:

'This country suffers at the hands of a hierarchical research structure, with regard to research and the allocation of resources. The result of this is certain universities dominating the political advisory process within the scientific community. Coupled with this, a large proportion of scientists have no feel for the political process and many don't care anyway. Politicians are all too often ignorant, not only of the value of science, but its limitations as well. ... We need to throw off the aged doyens whose work gets them caught like rabbits in the headlights of a media storm, the market-orientated structures, and the interminable assessment exercises. The scientific community needs a complete re-think of science's relationship with society and to re-educate our population accordingly.'

(*The Guardian*, 13 June 2006: 31)

over ethical scrutiny leads researchers to become too 'precious' about the need to protect the population from research and the unintended consequences of their participation in it. People frequently resent being overprotected or patronised and prefer to think and act for themselves. If researchers make mistakes, the researched population should be expected and entitled to critically engage in a dialogue about that directly with the researchers or indirectly via the mass media or other avenues for redressing grievances. The researched population can comment, critique and complain and if social research is to continue to be valued we need active involvement in that dialogue. Dangers arise when we assume the researched to be unable or untitled to comment upon our activities. Researchers need to engage in publicly defending and promoting what they do to further the primary principle of the value to society of social science.

Hence there is a need for a set of principles that establish recommendations for good behaviour while not compromising professional standards in research. The complicating problem is that such principles can, and often do, contradict each other – leaving researchers to make judgements that can expose themselves and their subjects to the potential for harm. Given the need to make such judgements it is important to challenge the view that ethical, or methodological, compromise is somehow unethical. Methodological compromise is inevitable since there are fundamental unavoidable research dilemmas – between resources and objectives, between drawing out the unique characteristics of the individual case and revealing the underlying pattern, and systematic nature of human society. Similarly ethical decision-making is a matter of balancing one set of principles against another. Compromise that minimises harm and maximises benefit must, in itself, be ethical.

There appears little doubt that ethics committees and research governance will continue to grow in number and in reach. If researchers refuse to accept the general tenets of research governance, then society will be more likely to obstruct any attempt to engage the practice and the profession is thereby constrained. As with the recognition of many professional requirements it is far better that professions regulate themselves properly before inappropriate or ever more burdensome regulation is imposed by external (governmental or legal) agencies (Iphofen 2004). The consequences of an unwieldy regulatory bureaucracy for the advancement of social scientific knowledge are as yet unknown. At the same time no boundaries appear to have been transgressed sufficiently to lead research subjects to appeal to extensive legal redress.

By considering the ethics of research, practitioners are building a cumulative experience of how to address such concerns. By submitting proposals to ethical scrutiny (and by actively participating as scrutineers) researchers will gain insight and a cross-fertilisation of ideas that, once again, will enhance their ethical awareness. Moreover by engaging in such debate it might be possible to move towards a single code or set of guidelines for all ethical human subjects research – the clarity in decision-making, the comprehensiveness, and the sharing of knowledge and fundamental assumptions and so on could prove to be of immense benefit to the development of social science.

Malcolm Rigg (in an unpublished seminar paper for the Association of Research Centres in the Social Sciences (ARCISS) in 2006) has argued that ethics are ' an important element in the cluster of virtues that social research institutes must espouse'. He includes in this list of virtues: theoretical, methodological, inferential, utilitarian and accountability principles. The interesting problem is that we could subscribe to all of these principles without the virtues of ethics – but we would not be ethical without following all of these other principles.

Behaving responsibly as a researcher, as a professional and as an individual human being requires the sustained consideration of the ethical implications of one's activities – not to engage in such considerations is, in itself, unethical. The principle of researcher reflexivity has ethical as well as methodological import. The knowledge produced as a consequence of research cannot be seen as somehow detached from the many purposes for which the research was engaged in, from the multiple professional loyalties to which the researcher is tied, and from the precise ways in which the researcher engaged with the people they were studying 'with' and 'on'.

While only the individual researcher is adequately well placed during the conduct of a research project to make such judgements and to attend to their consequences for good social research, given their vested interests in research outcomes, some form of independent ethical review continues to be vital. Attempts to enhance the power of research subjects suggest also the need for their inclusion in the judgement of ethical conduct – they may choose to disengage from, criticise or seek redress for any grievance perceived as consequent on the research.

Since research outcomes do depend on a tacit partnership between all research collaborators, ethical research will necessarily be a mutual accomplishment of all these stakeholders: researchers, participants, funders, sponsors and reviewers. This joint accomplishment depends on all parties coming together to recognise the ethical dilemmas entailed in their actions and resolving them in a spirit of collaboration. Some stakeholders have more of a key role and greater insight than others – the field researcher has an overview of the direct implications on subjects of the research, and should carry a major burden of responsibility for getting it right.

All of this suggests the need for transparency – to be ethical and to be seen to be being ethical in the generation, conduct and reporting of research activity. There are complex decisions to be made and the need to persuade others of the value of our research activities is paramount. It might sound a little relativistic, even instrumental, but Charles Stevenson's view was that moral judgements are not merely descriptive, rather they express approval or disapproval and seek to influence the feelings of others. Thus '...ethical terms are 'instruments' used in the complicated interplay and readjustment of human interests' (Stevenson 1937 reprinted in Cahn and Markie 1998: 500). By revealing and discussing our own judgement calls, we further the building of a moral order underpinning the primary goals of social research activity.

There is a fundamental irony to human life and to researching it: we behave at times as if we were all the same and understand each other and, at other times, all so different that we could never understand each other. The truth is, of course, somewhere in between. We must share some elements of common humanity, but each of us is unique in biology and biography. The role of ethics is to help balance those commonalities and differences so that we can make life happy and possible – one of the goals of social research is to understand how we manage to accomplish that.

Ethical Review Checklist

How to use:

This pro forma can be used as an aide memoire, as a guide to ethical assurance for contracting parties, and as the basis for an ethical scrutiny protocol for research projects conducted by any individual researcher, research group or commissioning body. Completing this form is not only designed to help in 'thinking through' and anticipating harms and benefits at the outset of a project, but also to support ongoing monitoring of such concerns throughout the life of a project. Use tick boxes to show decisions taken and fill in comment sections briefly to record rationales for decisions.

PROJECT IDENTIFIERS: REF. No. ....

SHORT TITLE: ....

PRINCIPAL INVESTIGATOR (PI): ....

CONTACT DETAILS: ....

RESEARCH MANAGER (To whom PI is accountable): ....

CONTACT DETAILS: ....

FORM COMPLETED BY: (NAME) .... (SIGNED) ....

DECISION TREE—WHERE ETHICAL APPROVAL WILL BE SOUGHT (Separate trees for different locations will be included.)

DONE   DATE

1. Will this research be undertaken in an organisation/on subjects for which formal ethical scrutiny is legally needed?

YES ⟶ Formal ethical scrutiny by relevant review board is required.
AND
Formal research governance approval from the organisation is required.
THEN GO TO 3.

NO

2. Will this research cover other areas of health and/or community care which legally require formal review?

YES ⟶ Ethical scrutiny by appropriate ethics committee required.

NO

3. Is this research conducted by a research organisation based in a university/Higher Education Institution?

YES ⟶ Follow their institutional research governance procedures
AND
Seek scrutiny by internal university research ethics committee.

NO

4. Is this research conducted by an independent research organisation/individual?

YES ⟶ EITHER establish own ethical scrutiny procedures
using checklist to identify ethical sensitivities
— if any sensitivities identified and don't have own scrutiny
procedures seek external/independent scrutiny.

NO

5. If this research is to be conducted Ensure full completion of this checklist
internally by your organisation ⟶ AND — if any ethical sensitivities identified
seek formal means to ensure sensitivities are addressed.

Key to <u>Symbols:</u>

 = Take special care

 = Link to…

 = Possibly talk to sponsor or other adviser

D = Consider at design stage

P = Consider at proposal stage

3

D   <u>RATIONALE FOR CONDUCTING THIS RESEARCH:</u>

Is this research necessary and justified as primary research?

	Yes	No	Comment
	☐	☐	

1. Can the required information be found elsewhere? ☐ ☐

2. Could the project be conducted as secondary research? ☐ ☐

3. Does existing research answer the research question adequately? ☐ ☐

If the answer to any or all of these questions is 'Yes', strong justifications must be made above for continuing to conduct this as a primary research project.

If the project becomes secondary research many of the following criteria may still apply:

CONTINUE AS SECONDARY RESEARCH ☐

If the answer to all above is 'No':   CONTINUE AS PRIMARY RESEARCH ☐

D P CHECKLIST TO IDENTIFY SENSITIVE ETHICAL ISSUES

RESEARCH QUALITY AND DESIGN [Link to Template for Research Proposals.]

Consider the ethical implications of proposed research methods and instruments. Poor research wastes time and may produce more disbenefits.

	Yes	No	Comment
Is there a clearly stated research issue, question or hypothesis?	☐	☐	
Is there a clearly written protocol indicative of unbiased/rigorous research?	☐	☐	
Is there an adequate review of the literature/summary of existing research?	☐	☐	
Is there a reasonable prospect of the project achieving its stated aims/objectives?	☐	☐	
Is the research capable of completion within the timescale?	☐	☐	
Is the research design appropriate?	☐	☐	
Are the methods of data collection, sampling, etc. appropriate?	☐	☐	
Are the methods of data analysis appropriate?	☐	☐	
Is there opportunity for peer review of methodology?	☐	☐	
P Is the researcher(s) adequately competent/experienced to conduct this project? (Has evidence of 'track record' and/or have CVs been sought?)	☐	☐	
Has consideration been taken of any subcontracted work and/or training of fieldworkers on ethical matters – sensitivity, vulnerability, etc.?	☐	☐	

OVERALL – Are you satisfied that the research design has done all that is possible, within the limits of its methodology, to minimise harm to all participants?

5

D P RISKS ASSESSED

Potential for harm (to individual/group/society)

	Examples of harm	Possible	Unlikely	Comment
• Psychological	Lowered self-esteem; emotional distress; embarrassment; misperceptions of the research purpose could raise false expectations of gain to participants.	☐	☐	
• Physical	Illness/accident consequent on participation in study.	☐	☐	
• Social	Unwarranted exclusion from society; ostracised by neighbours/friends/family/significant reference or peer group.	☐	☐	
• Economic	Economic deprivation as consequence of answering questions.	☐	☐	
• Legal	Legal penalties ensuing from answering questions in survey.	☐	☐	

Consider harm that may be consequent on:

	Consulted	Not Consulted
• Participation	☐	☐
• Exclusion	☐	☐
• Dissemination of findings	☐	☐

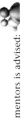 Any tick under 'possible' here – consultation with ethical sponsors/
mentors is advised:

CONTINUE TO NEXT SECTION

D P <u>Attempts made to minimise risks:</u>

With reference to potential risks assessed detail steps taken to minimise potential for harm.

Examples: **Detail:**

- Psychological   Debriefing; counselling contact information.

- Physical   Damages/reparation.

- Social   Controlled dissemination; language use; ethnic match between researcher/researched; gender matching between interviewer/interviewee.

- Economic   Rewards and incentives.

- Legal   Immunity from prosecution; compliance with law.

Yes ☐   No ☐   Comment

Have research participants/service users participated in the research design?

7

D P <u>RISKS ASSESSED</u>

Potential benefit (to individuals/groups/society)	Likely	Unlikely	Comment
<u>Examples of benefit</u>			
• Enhanced scientific knowledge — Society/community gains from knowledge about problem. Scientific progress made. Contribution made to evidence base.	☐	☐	
• Education — Knowledge is used to further curriculum development. Individual participants receive education/training they would not otherwise have gained. Information provided that enhances life style/opportunities.	☐	☐	
• Service delivery — Study enhances provision of service to community; study participants may individually gain.	☐	☐	
• Individual gains — Participants may gain personally from opportunity to air concerns; potential catharsis from sharing problems with independent observer.	☐	☐	

<u>**Attempts made to maximise benefits:**</u> With reference to potential benefits assessed detail above steps taken to maximise potential for benefit.

	YES	NO
OVERALL: Do the anticipated benefits of this project adequately outweigh the estimated potential for harm?	☐	☐

If 'NO' reconsider ways of reducing potential for harm or recommend DISCONTINUE. ☐

If 'YES' – CONTINUE.

D P <u>EQUITABLE SELECTION</u>

	Yes	No	N/A	Comment
Are research participants selected equitably?	☐	☐	☐	
• Are participants selected from groups unlikely to be among the beneficiaries of subsequent applications of the research?	☐	☐	☐	

• Are participants systematically selected from groups for reasons not directly related to the research focus of study?
 	
E.g.   easy availability
      compromised position
      manipulability				

• Are participants systematically excluded for reasons of inconvenience, not related to research focus of study?	☐	☐	☐	
• Has any consideration been given to non-participants' gains or losses?	☐			

9

P INFORMED CONSENT

	Yes	No	N/A	Comment
Suggested Information Sheet Protocols should include:				
Identify Researcher/Research Group/Research Organisation.	☐	☐	☐	
Identify Funding Source/Contracting Organisation.	☐	☐	☐	
Explain how/why subject selected.	☐	☐	☐	
Explain aims/purpose of study.	☐	☐	☐	
Explain research procedure, what their participation entails and how long study will last.	☐	☐	☐	
Identify any risks/discomfort anticipated.	☐	☐	☐	
Outline benefits of study – and who benefits.	☐	☐	☐	
Explain how study findings will be released (including feedback to participants).	☐	☐	☐	
Explain that participation is voluntary – consent can be refused.	☐	☐	☐	
Explain that withdrawal at any time is possible.	☐	☐	☐	
Explain that withdrawal and/or non-participation will not jeopardise how they are treated by any organisation involved in commissioning or conducting the study.	☐	☐	☐	
[Alternatives to non-participation should be outlined – if relevant.]	☐	☐	☐	
Steps taken for confidentiality/anonymity outlined.	☐	☐	☐	
Limits to confidentiality/anonymity disclosed.	☐	☐	☐	
Compensation offered for significant risks (e.g. counselling/advice).	☐	☐	☐	
Are the following provided:				
Contact names/numbers/addresses for information/questions/complaint/concerns.	☐	☐	☐	
Samples of proposed information sheets to ethical scrutiny committee.	☐	☐	☐	

P   <u>MANAGING INFORMED CONSENT</u>

	Yes	No	N/A	Comment
Will participants be given an information sheet?	☐	☐	☐	
Will participants be given copy of consent form?	☐	☐	☐	
Do participants have adequate capacities of intelligence/rationality/maturity/language to comprehend what is being asked of them?	☐	☐	☐	
Consent only valid if voluntary…				
…so has no unreasonable coercion to participate (implicit or explicit) been applied?	☐	☐	☐	
…and has there been no undue persuasion to participate?	☐	☐	☐	
If **NO** to any of above				
• Will consent be sought of 3rd parties?	☐	☐	☐	
(a) Parent/guardian in respect of immaturity.	☐	☐	☐	
(b) 'Representative' if mental incapacity is in question.	☐	☐	☐	
(c) For any other 'vulnerability' – a responsible person.	☐	☐	☐	
Is 3rd party competent and legally authorised to act on behalf of participant?	☐	☐	☐	
Will signed consent be sought?	☐	☐	☐	
If **NO or N/A** indicate if signed consent…..				
• … inconvenient/intrusive.	☐	☐	☐	
• … could pose additional risks to participants.	☐	☐	☐	
• … unnecessary since participants clearly refuse to part icipate by their behaviour (e.g. not completing and returning a mailed survey questionnaire).	☐	☐	☐	

11

	Yes	No	N/A	Comment

P **Exceptions to fully informed consent:**
By subject/participant.

- Information about full nature of study restricted
  Incomplete disclosure justified if …
  … demonstrably necessary to accomplish research goals
  AND   only minimal undisclosed risks to subjects
  AND   adequate debriefing is to be made available
  AND   dissemination of findings to subjects is provided for.   ☐ ☐ ☐

- For observational study …
  will retrospective consent be sought?   ☐ ☐ ☐

P **ONGOING MONITORING FOR SAFETY**

During the course of the study are provisions made for monitoring the safety of …
  … participants?   ☐ ☐ ☐

      … field researchers?   ☐ ☐ ☐

Are there any anticipated risks to field researchers for participating in the activity?   ☐ ☐ ☐

Are there any anticipated benefits for field researchers for their participation?   ☐ ☐ ☐

Are there likely to be any study-specific needs for researchers that should be met?   ☐ ☐ ☐

P STRATEGIES ADOPTED TO MAINTAIN PRIVACY/CONFIDENTIALITY

	Yes	No	N/A	Comment
Is anonymity offered to and/or sought by any of research subjects?	☐	☐	☐	
Is confidentiality promised? (High or low? Mention any threats to confidentiality.)	☐	☐	☐	
Is temporary identification of responses for subject matching required?	☐	☐	☐	
Is there a need for separately identified responses for tracking response rate?	☐	☐	☐	
Can aliases/pseudonyms be used to link data from same source?	☐	☐	☐	
Need for randomising responses (to disguise potentially incriminating information)?	☐	☐	☐	
Will identifiers be separated from responses?	☐	☐	☐	
Will identifying information be kept in locked file with (named) restricted users/access?	☐	☐	☐	
Will any identifying information be held in a foreign country (under different DP legislation)?	☐	☐	☐	
Can identifiers be destroyed if confidentiality/anonymity is under threat?	☐	☐	☐	
Can key information in reports be changed to avoid inadvertent identification?	☐	☐	☐	
Will information be reported in aggregate to minimise unwanted identification?	☐	☐	☐	
Will all research participants sign a confidentiality agreement (staff, subjects, funders, etc.)?	☐	☐	☐	
If data archiving for secondary analysis is sought, have subjects consented?	☐	☐	☐	
Any other strategies?.........Describe.				
Is there any likelihood of legal requirement to disclose information gained?	☐	☐	☐	

How to be dealt with: **Has advice of data protection officer been sought?** ☐ ☐ ☐

Are you familiar with data protection management guidance policy for your organisation? ☐ ☐ ☐

13

D P <u>VULNERABILITY</u>

Can the subject population be regarded as 'vulnerable' in any of the following ways?

	Yes	No	N/A	Comment
Children (minors)	☐	☐	☐	
People lacking mental capacity	☐	☐	☐	
Physically disabled persons	☐	☐	☐	
Pregnant women	☐	☐	☐	
Elderly persons	☐	☐	☐	
Prisoners	☐	☐	☐	
Students	☐	☐	☐	
Armed services personnel	☐	☐	☐	

Sexist (or other discriminatory) questioning/behaviour

Any other perceived/anticipated vulnerability (specify) ....

What steps taken to account for vulnerability?   Comment

- 3rd party consent
- Chaperoning
- Parent/guardian representation
- Proxies

D P DISSEMINATION OF FINDINGS/RESULTS

	Yes	No	Comment/Detail
Will research results be disseminated?	☐	☐	
If so, specify the form dissemination will take: And to whom? ...			
• Research participants	☐	☐	
• General public	☐	☐	
• Academic/professional audience	☐	☐	
• Government	☐	☐	
• Service users	☐	☐	
• Other (specify)	☐	☐	
Is there opportunity for peer review of findings?	☐	☐	
Is there any anticipated potential harm arising out of this dissemination?	☐	☐	
Is there any intention to involve research participants/service users/the community in the dissemination of research findings?	☐	☐	
Will the research result in government and/or professionals becoming committed to implementing the 'best options' emerging from the project?	☐	☐	
Has concern been given to intellectual property rights?	☐	☐	
Have all sources and contributions been acknowledged/referenced?	☐	☐	

15

A Template for Research Proposals

Introduction

This template offers a framework to help address all the elements required of a robust research proposal and hence to help deliver a quality research design.

The full proposal document should be written in such a way that an intelligent layperson can clearly understand the principles involved. Any complex issues or technical terminology should be clarified.

Project identification and rationale

Provide a succinct and clear project title.

Provide a clear statement of the research issue under investigation.

  – specifying the research 'question' or questions AND
  – if appropriate, specifying any testable hypotheses.

Justify the need for research to be conducted on this topic.

Explain why the research needs to be conducted in the chosen research site(s).

Project personnel and collaborators

Give the name and details of the PI.

Identify all collaborators/partners in the project and specify their roles.

Provide brief, targeted CVs for the PI, supervisor(s) and any collaborating partners (i.e. with relevance to the current proposal).

Clarify any consultation undertaken on project design – from research mentors, etc.

Clarify if the project has a named supervisor (normal for student projects).

Clarify if research subjects (students, patients, staff, carers, etc.) have participated in the design of the project.

Research protocol

Provide a full research protocol explaining how and why the research is to be conducted.

The protocol should .contain:

- an adequate review of the literature (see * below);
- clarification of whether the proposed study replicates prior work AND/OR
- duplicates work done elsewhere AND/OR
- has an element of originality.

Outline and give a rationale for the research design or approach.

Detail the research method(s) to be employed and any combinations of techniques or methods (e.g. self-completion questionnaire, street survey, doorstep interview).

Detail any research instruments/measuring devices to be employed (e.g. questionnaires – provide copies if available/prepared).

Detail any baseline and outcome measures that can be made.

Explain data collection procedures in full:

- providing a detailed sampling strategy;
- if sampling of a population is to be conducted explain and justify sample size;
- any calculable power and effect sizes should be provided;– the rationale for any purposive or theoretical sampling provided.

Explain the procedure for storing data and whether the data will be retained or archived for secondary analysis. If data is to be disposed of provide details of how this will happen. Ensure that the proposed project is compliant with the Data Protection Act.

Explain the data analysis procedures that will be employed:

- if qualitative data analysis, outline the procedure for coding, categorising and any data reduction;
- if quantitative data analysis, outline the procedure for grouping, collating and statistically testing data relationships – specifying the tests to be used;
- outline the use of any computer-assisted data analysis (e.g. SPSS; NVivo).

Anticipate any potential sources of bias that could compromise the rigour and/or the objectivity of the project. Detail how these problems might be addressed if they arise.

Outline the project timetable noting key stages in the project such as:

- anticipated start and completion dates;
- sequencing of interventions, baseline and outcome measures;
- period set aside for analysis and production of report;
- any anticipated obstacles to completing on schedule.

Research benefits

Outline the anticipated benefits of conducting the research. These could be benefits to subjects, participants, commissioning body, the general public, the research organisation/research site or yourself.

Explain any grounds for generalising the research findings beyond the immediate research site – for example, regionally, nationally and internationally.

Explain the intended forms of dissemination for the research findings:

- examined dissertation/thesis;
- conference/seminar presentations (local/national/international);
- self-published research report;
- scholarly/professional journals;
- popular news outlets.

Outline if any limitations to the public availability of the project's findings are anticipated.

Explain if subjects or public will be involved in dissemination/implementation of research findings in any way; if not, explain why their inclusion is not necessary/unjustified.

Outline if the research findings will help deliver better services, add value, change policy/practice or offer improved value for money.

Explain if the research will be of direct benefit to the site/organisation/community in which it is being conducted – in the form of:

- helping develop local research skills;
- contributing to the organisation/community's research infrastructure;
- providing a basis for further research and development;
- result in ways in which management, professionals and/or policy makers can improve service delivery.

Explain the feasibility of implementing any findings.

Limiting research risks

Outline any risks to researcher(s), subjects or organisations that can be anticipated.

Detail any risks to the collaborating organisation from permitting the project to be conducted.

Conduct and report a risk assessment exercise.

Specify the system for recording and reporting any serious adverse events.

Specify the indemnity/insurance provision secured against any non-negligent harm.

Specify the means whereby subjects will be informed of the nature of the project and precisely how the study will be described to potential participants (e.g. information leaflet and/or letters; copies of these should be included with your proposal).

Outline the protocol for obtaining participants' consent to gathering data and to any further archiving or secondary data analysis (e.g. consent forms; copies should be appended).

Specify how the participants will be given 'time to think' about whether they wish to participate; and how, if they wish to discontinue participation, this will be facilitated.

Project management

Outline the lines of responsibility involved in the conduct of the research.

Specify the project 'deliverables' (e.g. points of data collection and analysis, written report, examinable thesis/dissertation) and times when they are due.

For each site involved give evidence of the support of any supervisors/gatekeepers/directors.

Give evidence of your research organisation's approval, processing through its governance and ethics procedure, in the form of a letter of approval including details and signature of line manager.

Budget details

Outline the anticipated costs of conducting the research.

Indicate the itemised expenditure on:

- – human resources;
- – equipment;
- – travel;
- – computer hardware/software.

Indicate the time that will be spent on the project by researchers and collaborators.

Indicate the source(s) of funding for the project.

Note

* An 'adequate' review of the literature is required so that readers can make a judgement of the value of the proposed research. This would not have to be the kind of detailed systematic review required of a journal article or the literature review chapter in a completed thesis – nor at this stage need it fall within the 'technical' notion of systematic review. What is required is enough of a review to demonstrate that the proposer is fully acquainted with the field of study, is aware of previous work and can show how their proposal intends to build upon the existing research. Supervisors' guidance should be sought as to what constitutes 'adequacy' for present purposes.

Short Glossary of Key Terms and Concepts

This short glossary is intended as a guide to, and some justification for, the ways in which some key terms and concepts are used throughout this book.

Anonymity

This refers to the identity of the subjects taking part in a research study being only known to designated members of the research team. Funders/commissioners may also be aware of subjects' identities if this was previously agreed upon and the subjects consented (Ritchie and Lewis 2003: 67).

Commissioners and funders

I use these terms interchangeably to refer to those who request the services of social researchers and who pay for them.

Codes of practice

A 'code' is a fairly prescriptive set of instructions about what constitutes proper behaviour for those adhering to it. Professional associations usually require adherence to a code of practice as a criterion for continued membership. Thus anyone found guilty of disobeying the code can be liable to sanctions or barred from membership of the association.

Confidentiality

This refers to the avoidance of the specific attribution of comments, in any form of research dissemination, to identified participants. Direct attribution links comments to a specific name or role. Indirect attribution enables a reasonable inference based upon reported characteristics that might identify an individual or group (Ritchie and Lewis 2003: 67). 'Complete confidentiality' implies non-disclosure of anything revealed to a researcher.

Data reduction

This is a shorthand phrase for the process whereby a mass of complex data is processed or coded to permit appropriate analysis. Necessarily the 'vibrant' richness of real life is 'reduced' to categories, labels, numbers, etc. to permit more convenient analysis and/or measurement.

Guidelines for ethical practice

Unlike prescriptive codes, guidelines offer suggestions and advice for how to behave but are not sanctionable and failure to follow them is unlikely to be adopted as grounds for dismissal from or a bar to membership of a professional research association.

Social science and social research

It may be that the attempt to distinguish between these two activities is spurious. Science entails a systematic, rigorous and replicable means of investigating the world – in this case, the social world. Research into that world is the means by which this is accomplished. Research can be desk research, scholarly research or more empirical, direct investigations requiring a fully worked methodology. Thus (social) research is one of the means by which (social) science gets done. Without research it is hard to imagine there being any such science.

> Social research is the process of systematically gathering, analysing and interpreting information about the behaviour, knowledge, beliefs, attitudes and values of human populations. It both contributes to and draws from the broader social science knowledge base.
>
> (SRA 2002: 9)

Morality and ethics: Some basic principles

Moral philosophy

Philosophers have been examining the notion of 'good' behaviour for centuries. There is an extensive literature in the field and researchers are well advised to spend a little time studying it if they are to engage in ethical debate. There is insufficient space here to consider this literature fully. I do suggest reading one or two of the many excellent introductory texts in this field (see, for example, Thompson 2000; La Follette 2002).

In simple terms ethics are concerned with behaving 'properly' and making the 'right' choices.

Morality is concerned with practical problems of right and wrong thoughts and behaviour – what one ought to or ought not to do or think. When we make a decision about the rightness or wrongness of our actions and/or thoughts we have made a moral judgement. Once we make moral judgements we then become morally responsible for our actions. (That is, we have decided that a particular action or thought was 'right' or 'wrong'.)

Ethics is conventionally conceived as the study of morality. Thus it operates at a more abstract, reflective or even theoretical level than morality. While morality concerns itself with 'decisions', ethics is more concerned with 'understanding' what lies behind those decisions.

Etymologically the difference between morals and ethics is to be found in their differing Latin and Greek roots. Morals come from 'mores' – customary ways of behaving (Latin); while ethics comes from 'ethos' – principles of proper behaviour (Greek).

Ethics has been further subdivided into:

DESCRIPTIVE ETHICS:
which outlines the moral practices of different communities, groups, sects, religious organisations and so on. It is about what they consider to be right and wrong and why they consider them to be so. Thus one speaks of Christian, Buddhist or Victorian ethics for example.

NORMATIVE ETHICS:
Refers to where the proposed 'norm' comes from – the grounds of meaning or acceptance of decisions about why certain behaviour is right or wrong. The varieties of normative ethics are typified as:

Deontological ethics refers to any normative ethical theory which emphasises principles of rightness and wrongness independent of consequences. Thus, slavery is unjust even if it maximises a society's welfare; or one should keep a promise made to a dying person even if no one living gains from it. Deontologists ground moral judgements in ideas of natural rights, personal dignity and/or God's laws, etc.

Teleological (or consequential) ethics refers to any normative ethical theory which takes the goodness or badness of the consequences of an action as fundamental in determining whether it is morally right or wrong. Thus, for example, an action is considered to be morally right if it produces at least as much good as any alternative. Within this teleological perspective there are further variations. Egoists argue that it is right to produce maximum goodness for oneself (Hobbes). Utilitarians argue that rightness depends on choosing maximum goodness for <u>all</u> concerned even if that means proportionately less for oneself (J. S. Mill).

Virtue ethics
Overlaying all of this is the debate about whether there are enduring moral principles which must be absolute and/or universal – or whether there are a variety of moralities – each suited to the needs of the social circumstances in which they operate. This becomes complicated by the influence of politics in moral matters. There are differential powers among those who choose to make judgments about right and wrong behaviour. Often the most powerful determine the norms irrespective of any sense of 'higher' moralities. That is to say, the power of some social agents is higher than others and they determine acceptable moralities according to their own favoured principles.

In social research we are concerned primarily with 'normative ethics'. In other words this is about the way one *ought* to behave as a researcher. Normative principles have been established over time from considering moral choices at an abstract level in ethical theorising, from the codes of behaviour established by professional institutions and from the observation in practice of what happens when research is done for the 'wrong' reasons or in 'incorrect' ways as well as observing the benefits from doing research the 'right' way. Thus theorising about ethics can never be divorced from the application of principles in practice

(La Follette 2002: 8). The central point about normative ethics is that it entails value judgements and how one chooses to behave as a researcher can never be proven right or wrong by appealing to empirical facts. The role of normative ethics is not to recommend any particular course of action but to set out possibilities, help to assess values and assist in the making of informed, thoughtful choices (Thompson 2000: 30–2).

Primary and secondary research

Each research method tends to fall into one of two broad categories of research: primary or secondary research. Primary research refers to the direct collection of information or data with specific concepts or hypotheses in mind – it is 'first hand' research. Whereas secondary research refers to research conducted using material or data which have been collected for some other purpose and, therefore, originally with no specific concepts or hypotheses in mind. Such data might have been compiled by commercial concerns, private/independent organisations or government agencies for record keeping or to aid in planning future policies.

In primary research researchers go out and collect the information they need themselves by conducting a new investigation; in secondary research they use the information that has already been collected by someone else.

The main research methods can be seen crudely to fall into these two basic categories as listed below:

Primary research methods:

Social surveys
Interviews
Experiments
Ethnography – participant observation
Ethological observation (unobtrusive)

Secondary research methods:

Official (governments, union, corporate) statistics/data
Documents – historical, personal, public, private
Contemporary records (minutes of meetings, etc.)
Previous social research

Finally, there is a category of research which falls between the two categories. It is 'primary' in that the researchers do it themselves, but it is also 'secondary' since it relies on inferences based on the artefacts produced by social action or human behaviour – these are called 'unobtrusive methods'.

There are certain general advantages and disadvantages which are common to each of the methods which fall within the broad research categories:

Primary research

Advantages:

1. Up-to-date: It allows for the collection of fairly up-to-date information or data, whereas secondary research tends to be more outdated.

2. Novel hypotheses:	Hypotheses of sociological significance can be tested directly, since the data of particular relevance to the hypothesis can be collected.
3. Depth of study:	Researchers can investigate more subtle levels of meaning and can gain a deeper understanding of their subjects since they can make direct contact with them and personally follow up on any points on which they have insufficient data.

Disadvantages:

1. Subject reactivity:	Nearly all primary research is 'reactive' in the sense that it involves, to greater or lesser degrees, contact between research and subjects. Subjects may alter their normal behaviour as a result of such contact and thereby react to the presence of the researcher.
2. Compliance of the respondent:	Researchers have the problem of securing the compliance of the subjects they wish to study. They may try, in various ways, to conceal the fact that they are studying people, but this poses an ethical dilemma – the individual subject's right to privacy against the proposed 'benefits to science and society' gained from concealment of the researcher's identity and purpose.

Secondary research

Advantages:

1. Resource saving:	The researcher is saved the time and cost of collecting data or information that has already been collected by someone else.
2. No problem of compliance:	The researcher does not have the problem of ensuring the cooperation of individual respondents, thereby removing the problem of allowing for non-response from some of the subjects of the investigation.
3. No intrusion problem:	The data are 'given facts' before a researcher enters the scene and, therefore, are not alterable merely by the researcher's presence. Thus the investigator will not be affecting the 'normality' of the subjects merely by conducting the investigation.

Disadvantages:

1. Inappropriateness of data:	The data may not measure variables which are of precise sociological relevance. The data may not have even been collected for such a purpose. The researcher must use whatever is available regardless of the purpose for which it was originally collected. This, of course, restricts the nature of hypotheses which can be tested.

2. Unknown collection methods:
The adequacy of the methods used to collect the data may be suspect or even unknown; they could influence the data in unforeseen ways and this might undermine the validity of the results.

Defining the 'object' of our studies as 'the subject'

Some researchers, particularly those engaging in qualitative data collection and analysis, are uncomfortable with referring to the groups or individuals they study as 'subjects'. They regard this as an ethical concern in that the term suggests the kind of objectification of people one finds in more experimental or quantitative forms of research. This is more than a semantic concern and it is worth considering whether the people being studied are referred to as 'participants', 'respondents' or 'subjects' according to the precise nature of their engagement with the research project (Birch and Miller 2002). Thus if the people being studied are participating in a jointly conceived and disseminated project they are clearly 'participants'. If they are simply answering survey questions delivered on the street they are 'respondents'. Data protection legislation refers to the person about whom data are held as the 'datasubject' and, although there has been much debate about this, it seems to me to reflect that awareness that merely holding selective data about a person does not mean one 'knows' the person. Indeed data collection is a form of depersonalisation and to pretend that, by holding data, we have somehow captured the person's character is misleading. I attempt to use the appropriate term throughout my discussion and use the term 'subject' generically when the precise research engagement of those being studied is not known and/or is not central to the discussion.

The use of the term 'subjects'

I recommend this on the grounds that it is difficult to find a terminologically accurate alternative. The 'people being studied' can be an individual or a group – the term 'subject' encompasses both. Not all people being studied are genuinely 'participating'. Some research designs aim to be truly inclusive (e.g. participative action research) in which case the subjects can be regarded as much as 'participants' as the researchers. (That is to say nothing about the *precise* balance of power in the research relationship.)

In the same way, not all people under study are 'respondents' – giving answers in reply to questions in surveys, interviews, focus groups or questionnaires. Often they are simply being observed and their actions only then regarded as 'responsive' if the researcher's intervention is intended to induce a change (experimentally or quasi experimentally) in their behaviour, thoughts and/or feelings.

One of the reasons the term 'subject' is avoided is to challenge the notion that people need to be 'objectified' when being researched. In fact, it would be inaccurate not to see them as the 'subject' of study – hopefully they are deliberately chosen as the subject or as a route to the subject, they are certainly being 'subjected' to a research intervention and it remains an ethical responsibility of the researcher to ensure they are not 'objectified' in a way that denies their humanity.

All things considered, retaining the term subject is more accurate and does less injustice to those under study than if we were to imagine them as participating when they are not, when they might not see it that way and, in any case, we may be only interested in certain aspects of their life in how it relates to participation in the concerns of our study.

Any reader wishing to pursue this terminological issue further can find a fuller discussion in Oliver (2003: 3–9) and in Corrigan and Tutton (2006).

Research misconduct

Research misconduct is defined by the US Commission on Research Integrity as fabrication, falsification or plagiarism in proposing, performing or reviewing research, or in reporting research results.

'Fabrication' is making up data or results and recording or reporting them.

'Falsification' is manipulating research materials, equipment or processes, or changing or omitting data or results such that the research is not accurately represented in the research record.

'Plagiarism' is the appropriation of another person's ideas, processes, results or words without giving appropriate credit (Smith 2006).

Useful websites: Ethical Codes, Guidelines and Professional Associations

These sites were accessed during the final preparation for the book, but these pages are reproduced on the book website and updated regularly.

Professional research associations and their codes and guidelines

The EU-funded *RESPECT* project was aimed at raising professional standards in socioeconomic research across Europe. RESPECT's code and background papers are available via: www.respectproject.org.

A list of the most well-known international professional associations in social research can be found on the RESPECT project website.

The *Social Research Association*'s guidelines are intended to be educative and discursive, aimed at raising ethical awareness and ethical thinking. They can be found via the SRA home page at: www.the-sra.org.

The *Market Research Society*'s Code of Conduct and related guidelines (see http://www.mrs.org.uk/code.htm) are sanctionable, link to a complaints procedure and are based on the European Code developed by ESOMAR (http://www.esomar.org/web/show/id=43240). This includes some interesting sections on interviewing children and on marketing research for pharmaceutical companies.

The *British Psychological Society* updated their ethics code which was linked to their code of conduct in March of 2006. Theirs too has sanctions applied: http://www.bps.org.uk/the-society/ethics-rules-charter-code-of-conduct/code-of-conduct/code-of-conduct_home.cfm.

The *British Sociological Association*'s statement of ethical practice is at: http://www.britsoc.co.uk/equality/63.htm.

The *UK Evaluation Society* has a set of good practice guidelines which are a clearly stated set of principles. For a fuller consideration of what lies behind these principles they link members to other sets of international guidelines – rather than repeat the exercise of developing their own: http://www.evaluation.org.uk/Pub_library/Good_Practice.htm.

UK Government Departmental Codes of Practice

The UK Government Social Research Unit has developed guidance for the ethical assurance of government social research. This work includes a set of ethical standards for use across the government and a system to help embed these standards into daily working practice: http://www.gsr.gov.uk/professional_guidance/ethics.asp.

The Department of Work and Pensions published their guidelines to employment-related ethical and legal issues in social research in *Doing the Right Thing* (2003) by Jo Bacon and Karl Olsen. Available online at: www.dwp.gsi.gov.uk/asd/asd5.

International governmental and research council sites are essential reading

The *National Research Council* of Canada has the most systematic scheme for research ethics of research with both human and animal subjects: http://www.nrc-cnrc.gc.ca/randd/ethics/human_e.html.

The US *Department of Energy* expresses its concerns for human subjects research on: http://www.er.doe.gov/production/ober/humsubj/index.html.

The US *Department of Health and Human Services* revised its guidelines in 2005: http://www.hhs.gov/ohrp/humansubjects/guidance/45cfr46.htm.

But look more particularly at the general information site for the *Office for Human Research Protections* (OHRP): http://www.hhs.gov/ohrp/ which is a part of the US Department of Health and Human Services. It is well worth spending some time travelling around this site which is highly informative. In particular explore the 'decision charts' and the 'guidance by subject' sections.

On the obligations of research agencies for confidentiality, quality, etc. look at: http://www.census.gov/main/www/policies.html.

The US Centre for Disease Control has some useful advice on appropriate use of lay terms for writing explanatory leaflets and guidelines for writing consent forms: http://www.cdc.gov/od/ads/hsr2.htm.

The US FDA has a useful set of FAQs: http://www.fda.gov/oc/ohrt/irbs/.

Research Councils UK

The central site for the UK Research Councils: http://www.rcuk.ac.uk/default.htm has no central guidance on research ethics. But from this link you can connect to each of the Councils separately to see what they have to say. In recent years each of the Councils have been developing their ethics policies and establishing codes and/guidelines. Most are interconnected in some way now and the stimulus to these overlaps was undoubtedly the development of the ESRC's guidelines.

For the ESRC framework you should connect to: http://www.esrcsocietytoday. ac.uk/ESRCInfoCentre and then conduct a search for 'ethics framework' which will then connect you to a pdf file directly.

The ESRC also provides legal guidance on confidentiality in their 'Guidelines on Copyright and Confidentiality: Legal issues for social science researchers': http://www.esrc.ac.uk/esrccontent/DowloadDocs/wwwcopyrightand confidentiality. doc.

All councils agreed to state their position on a 'Universal Ethics Code for All Scientists' in 2006: http://www.rcuk.ac.uk/cmsweb/downloads/rcuk/documents/univethicalcode.pdf.

It is unsurprising that, given increasing public concerns about the environment the Natural Environment Research Council has been developing a fairly comprehensive policy: http://www.nerc.ac.uk/publications/corporate/ethics.asp.

The Arts and Humanities Research Council used to be the briefest – but they have realised that such issues now have to be addressed more fully although it is still hard to locate any research ethics statement from them on their website: http://www.ahrc.ac.uk/about/ahrc_policy_corporate_documents.asp.

Data archiving

UK Data Archive: http://www.data-archive.ac.uk.

Qualidata: http://www.qualidata.essex.ac.uk.

Some generic international sites can be highly informative

The interdisciplinary Association for Practical and Professional Ethics can be found on: http://www.indiana.edu/~appe/ with links to many other ethics sites.

You'll find a link here to how to construct a code of ethics: http://ethics.iit.edu/codes/.

And links to some international sources: http://courses.cs.vt.edu/%7Ecs3604/lib/WorldCodes/WorldCodes.html.

The Social Philosophy and Policy Center covers a range of ethical issues of concern to policy-oriented researchers at: http://www.bgsu.edu/offices/sppc/.

The Ethics Updates site from the University of San Diego is an extremely comprehensive source of information: http://ethics.acusd.edu/index.asp. It has some interesting materials on the moral status of animals.

There are many sites dealing with ethics in specific disciplines. For example – Ethics in chemistry: http://comp.uark.edu/~rlee/chem/links.html.

Issues discussed in the past useful discussion groups

In the past useful discussion groups within which these issues have been discussed include:

A url for discussion groups:

http://frank.mtsu.edu/~jpurcell/Ethics/ethics.html.

Those seeking advice about ethics committee approval should look at: The Intelligent Scholar's Guide to the Use of Human Subjects in Research http://www.fas.harvard.edu/~research/ISG.html.

An IRB Discussion Forum (previously known as 'MCWIRB') promotes the discussion of ethical, regulatory and policy concerns with human subjects research. There is an 'IRB Links' to other web-based resources concerning IRB's human subjects research and the ethics of scientific research in general: http://www.irbforum.org/.

UK NHS and DH Research Ethics has recently been redesigned and 'streamlined' after a lengthy consultation process.

The new National Research Ethics Service for the NHS can be found at: http://www.nres.npsa.nhs.uk/.

And the UK-wide Association for Research Ethics Committees of which UREC (the Universities Research Ethics Group) is now a member can be found at: http://www.arec.org.uk/.

References

Adèr, H. and Mellenbergh, G. J. (1999) *Research Methodology in the Social, Behavioural and Life Sciences*, London: Sage.

Aglionby, J. (2003) *The Guardian*, 10 February.

Alderson, P. (1995) *Listening to Children: Ethics and Social Research*, Barkingside: Barnardos.

Alderson, P. (2001) *On Doing Qualitative Research Linked To Ethical Healthcare*, London: Wellcome Trust.

Alderson, P. and Morrow, V. (2004) *Ethics, Social Research and Consulting Children and Young People*, Ilford, Essex: Barnardo's.

Amnesty Magazine (2008) Women's rights are human rights, *Amnesty Magazine*, March/April: 14–15.

Andreski, S. (1974) *Social Sciences as Sorcery*, Harmondsworth: Penguin.

Anthony, S. (2008) Child care matters, *Medical Protection Society Casebook*, 16 (1) January: 7.

Backhouse, G. (2002) How preserving confidentiality in qualitative health research can be compatible with preserving data for future use, *Medical Sociology News*, 28 (3) July: 32–5.

Bacon, J. and Olsen, K. (2003) *Doing the Right Thing*, Department for Work and Pensions – Research Working Paper No.11, London: HMSO (http://www.dwp.gov.uk/asd/).

Baggini, J. and Fosl, P. S. (2007) *The Ethics Toolkit: A Compendium of Ethical Concepts and Methods*, Oxford: Blackwell.

Bailey, J. M. (2003) *The Man Who Would be Queen: The Science of Gender-Bending and Transsexualism*, Washington: Joseph Henry Press.

Barnes, J. A. (1980) *Who Should Know What? Social Science, Privacy And Ethics*, Cambridge University Press.

Barron, K. (1999) Ethics in qualitative social research on marginalized groups, *Scandinavian Journal of Disability Research*, 1 (1): 38–49.

Barthes, R. (1972) *Mythologies*, Harmondsworth: Penguin.

Baty, P. (2000) Soas faces ethics row, *The Times Higher*, 22/29 December: 4.

Beatty, A. (ed.) (1920) *Twenty-Two Essays of Wm Hazlitt*, London: George Harrap and Co. Ltd.

Becker, H. S. (1964) Problems in the publication of field studies, in A. J. Vidich, J. Bensman and M. R. Stein (eds) *Reflections on Community Studies*, New York: John Wiley and Sons, pp. 267–84.

Becker, H. (1967) Whose side are we on? *Social Problems*, 3: 239–47.

Bell, L. and Nutt, L. (2002) Divided loyalties, divided expectations: Research ethics, professional and occupational responsibilities, Ch. 3, pp. 70–90, in M. Mauthner, M. Birch, J. Jessop and T. Miller (eds) *Ethics in Qualitative Research*, London: Sage.

Bhamra, S., Tinker, A., Mein, G., Ashcroft, R. and Askham, J. (2008) The retention of older people in longitudinal studies: A review of the literature, *Quality in Ageing*, 9 (4): 27–35.

Birch, M. and Miller, T. (2002) Encouraging participation: Ethics and responsibilities, Ch. 5, pp. 91–106, in M. Mauthner, M. Birch, J. Jessop and T. Miller (eds) *Ethics in Qualitative Research*, London: Sage.

Blackman, S. (2007) 'Hidden ethnography': Crossing emotional borders in qualitative accounts of young people's lives, *Sociology*, 41 (4): 699–716.

Bok, S. (1979) *Lying: Moral Choice in Public and Private Life*, New York: Vintage Books.

Boruch, R. F. and Cecil, J. S. (1979) *Assuring the Confidentiality of Social Research Data*, Philadelphia: University of Pennsylvania Press.

Boulton, M., Brown, N., Lewis, G. and Webster, A. (2004) *Implementing the ESRC Research Ethics Framework: The Case for Research Ethics Committees*, Working Paper, ESRC Research Ethics Framework: Discussion Paper No. 4 (www.york.ac.uk/res/ref/documents.htm).

Bourdieu, P., Wacquan, L. J. D. and Wacquant, L. J. (1992) *Invitation to Reflexive Sociology*, University of Chicago Press.

Bovens, M. (1998) *The Quest for Responsibility (Accountability and Citizenship in Complex Organisations)*, Cambridge: University Press.

Bower, R. T. and de Gasfaris, P. (1978) *Ethics in Social Research: Protecting the Interests of Human Subjects*, New York: Praeger.

Brent, E. and Thompson, A. (2000) *Methodologist's Toolchest for Windows (v.3) User's Guide and Manual*, Columbia: Idea Works.

Brown, N., Boulton, M., Lewis, G. and Webster, A. (2004) *Social Science Research Ethics In Developing Countries And Contexts*, Working Paper, ESRC Research Ethics Framework: Discussion Paper No. 3 (www.york.ac.uk/res/ref/documents.htm).

Bryman, A. (1988) *Quantity and Quality in Social Research*, London: Unwin Hyman.

Bulmer, M. (1992) The ethics of social research, Ch. 4, pp. 45–57, in N. Gilbert (ed.) *Researching Social Life*, London: Sage.

Cahn, S. M. and Markie, P. (eds) (1998) *Ethics: History, Theory and Contemporary Issues*, New York: Oxford University Press.

Calvey, D. (2008) The art and politics of covert research: Doing 'situated ethics' in the field, *Sociology*, 42 (5): 905–18.

Campbell, J. (2001) *The Liar's Tale: A History of Falsehood*, New York: W. W. Norton and Company.

Casey, W. F. (2006) Consent is a conversation, *MPS Casebook*, 14 (1) February: 11.

Cassell, J. (1982) Does risk benefit analysis apply to moral evaluation of social research? pp. 144–62, in T. L. Beauchamp, R. R. Faden, R. J. Wallace and L. Walters (eds) *Ethical Issues in Social Research*, Baltimore: John Hopkins University Press, xii, 436 pp.

Clark, A. (2007) *Making Observations: The Potential of Observation Methods for Gerontology*, London: Centre for Policy on Ageing.

Clarke, M., Hopewell, S. and Chalmers, I. (2007) Reports of clinical trials should begin and end with up-to-date systematic reviews of other relevant evidence: A status report, *Journal of the Royal Society of Medicine*, 100: 187–90.

Cody, A., Iphofen, R., Clarke, G. and Kelly, A. (2000) *Audit of Child Neglect Cases and Development of Likelihood of Neglect Assessment (LONA)*, School of Nursing Midwifery and Health Studies for Conwy and Denbighshire NHS Trust, University of Wales, Bangor.

Cohen, M. (2007) *101 Ethical Dilemmas*, (2nd edition), Abingdon: Routledge, (first published 2003).

Cooke, B. and Kothari, U. (2001) *Participation: The New Tyranny?* London: Zed Books.

Corbyn, Z. (2008) ESRC is criticised for 'biased' study, *Times Higher Education*, 13 March: 10.

Corrigan, O. and Tutton, R. (2006) What's in a name? Subjects, volunteers, participants and activists in clinical research, *Clinical Ethics*, 1: 101–4.

Cotterill, P. (1992) Interviewing women: Issues of friendship, vulnerability and power, *Women's Studies International Forum*, 15 (5/6): 593–606.

Craig, G., Corden, A. and Thornton, P. (2001) *A Code of Safety for Social Researchers*, London: SRA (http://www.the-sra.org.uk/staying_safe.htm).

Darbyshire, P (2008) 'Never mind the quality, feel the width': The nonsense of 'quality', 'excellence', and 'audit' in education, health and research, *Collegian: Journal of the Royal College of Nursing Australia*, Volume 15, Issue 1, February 2008, pp. 35–41.

Davies, P. C. W. and Brown, J. (1988) *Superstrings (A Theory of Everything?)*, Cambridge University Press.

Dench, S., Iphofen, R. and Huws, U. (2004) *An EU Code of Ethics for Socio-Economic Research*, Institute for Employment Studies Report 412 (http://www.respectproject.org/main/index.php).

Diener, E. and Crandall, R. (1978) *Ethics in Social and Behavioural Research*, Chicago: University of Chicago Press.

Dingwall, R. (2006) Confronting the anti-democrats: The unethical nature of ethical regulation in social science, Plenary Address to Annual BSA Medical Sociology Group Conference, Heriot-Watt University, Edinburgh, September 2006, summary in *Medical Sociology online* 1 (2006) 51–8 (http://www.medicalsociologyonline.org/).

Douglas, J. (1977) *The Nude Beach*, London: Sage.

Duncombe, J. and Jessop, J. (2002) 'Doing rapport' and the ethics of 'faking friendship', Ch. 6, pp. 107–22, in M. Mauthner, M. Birch, J. Jessop and T. Miller (eds) *Ethics in Qualitative Research*, London: Sage.

Dyer, R. (2003) Integrity matters, *The Times Higher*, 25 April: 10.

Farrar, S. (2003) Ethics fears hit tests, *The Times Higher*, 12 September: 64.

Farrar, S. and Baty, P. (2003) Exeter student wins £63,000, *The Times Higher*, 31 October: 60.

Fazackerley, A. and Tysome, T. (2004) Row rages over 'dirty money', *The Times Higher*, 28 May: 1.

Fernyhough, C. (2008) *The Baby in the Mirror: A Child's World from Birth to Three*, London: Granta.

Fincham, B. (2006) 'Ethics, risk and well-being' *Qualitative Researcher* 2 Spring 2006 1–2.

Fine, P. (2006) Ethics row hits research body, *The Times Higher*, 8 September: 4.

Fisk, M. and Wigley, V. (2000) Accessing and interviewing the oldest old in care homes, *Quality in Ageing — Policy, Practice and Research*, 1 (1): 27–33.

Flew, A. (1979) *A Dictionary of Philosophy*, London: Pan Books.

Flusfeder, H. (2007) Fury over book on blood libel, *The Times Higher*, 23 February: 11.

Fontes, T. O. and O'Mahoney, M. (2008) In-depth interviewing by instant messaging, *Social Research Update*, (53).

Foster, C. (2001) *The Ethics of Medical Research on Humans*, Cambridge University Press.

Frank, R. H. (2008) *The Economic Naturalist: Why Economics Explains Almost Everything*, London: Virgin Books Ltd.

Fullinwider, R. K. (2007) Sissela Bok on lying and moral choice in private and public life – an amplification, the encyclopaedia of informal education (www.infed.org/thinkers/bok_lying.htm).

Furedi, F. (2003) Why I believe there must not be any 'no-go' areas for research, *The Times Higher*, 24 January: 20.

Gaw, A. (2006) Beyond consent: The potential for atrocity, *Journal of the Royal Society of Medicine*, 99: 175–7.

Gerth, H. H. and Mills, C. W. (eds) (1948) *From Max Weber: Essays in Sociology*, London: Routledge and Kegan Paul.

Giddens, A. (1991) *Modernity and Self-identity: Self and Society in the Late Modern Age*, Cambridge: Polity Press.

Giles, J. (2008) Looking behind the numbers, *New Scientist*, 2643: 44–5, 16 February.

Gillies, V. and Aldred, P. (2002) The ethics of intention: Research as a political tool, Ch. 2, pp. 32–52, in M. Mauthner, M. Birch, J. Jessop and T. Miller (eds) *Ethics in Qualitative Research*, London: Sage.

GMC (2007) *0–18 years: Guidance for AllDoctors*, London: General Medical Council (http://www.gmc-uk.org/guidance/ethical_guidance/children_guidance/index.asp).

Goffman, E. (1971) *Relations in Public*, London: Allen Lane.

Gokah, T. (2006) The naïve researcher: Doing social research in Africa, *International Journal of Social Research Methodology*, 9 (1): 61–73.

Goldenberg, S. (2007) Tape 'reveals order' to shoot Vietnam protesters, *The Guardian*, 2 May: 17.

Gorard, S. (2002) Ethics and equity: Pursuing the perspective of non-participants, *Social Research Update*, (39), May, University of Surrey.

Gouldner, A. W. (1970) *The Coming Crisis of Western Sociology*, London: Heinemann.

Government Social Research Unit (2005), *GSR Professional Guidance: Ethical Assurance for Social Research in Government* (www.gsr.gov.uk).

Graham, J., Grewal, I. and Lewis, J. (2007) *Ethics in Social Research: The Views of Research Participants*, London: Government Social Research Unit, HM Treasury (http://www.natcen.ac.uk/natcen/pages/op_surveymethods.htm).

Grayling, A. C. (2003) *What is Good? – The Search for the Best Way to Live*, London: Weidenfeld and Nicolson.

Grinyer, A. and Thomas, C. (2001) Young adults with cancer: The effect on parents and families, *The International Journal of Palliative Nursing*, 7 (4): 162–70.

Grinyer, A. (2002) The anonymity of research participants: Assumptions, ethics and practicalities, *Social Research Update*, (36), Dept. of Sociology: University of Surrey.

Gyatso, T. (His Holiness the Dalai Lama) (1999) *Ancient Wisdom, Modern World: Ethics for a New Milennium*, London: Little, Brown and Co.

Haggerty, K. D. (2004) Ethics creep: Governing social science research in the name of ethics, *Qualitative Sociology*, 27 (4): 391–420.

Haigh, G. (2008) Classroom life in high definition, *The Guardian*, 6 May: 11.

Hammersley, M. (ed.) (2000) *Taking Sides in Social Research: Essays on Partisanship and Bias*, London: Routledge.

Harford, T (2008) *The Logic of Life: Uncovering the New Economics of Everything*, London: Little, Brown and Co.

Harper, T. (2008) State to snoop on your sex life with probing questions about promiscuity and contraception, *Daily Mail*, 20 April: 1.

Hedgecoe, A. (2008) Research ethics review and the sociological research relationship, *Sociology*, 42 (5): 873–86.

Hester, J. (2006) *Ethical Concerns in Lifestyle Research with Obese Children*, Leeds Metropolitan University Research Reflection (online) (http://www.leedsmet. ac.uk/the_news/research_reflections/apr06/apr3.htm).

Hester, J. R., McKenna, J. and Gately, P. J. (2008) *Experiences of Obese Children Who Attended a Residential Weight Loss Camp* (http://www.carnegieweightmanagement. com/).

Hewson, C., Yule, P., Laurent, D. and Vogel, V. (2002) *Internet Research Methods*, London: Sage.

Hoinville, G. and Jowell, R. (1978) *Survey Research Practice*, London: Heinemann Educational.

Holland, R. (1999) Reflexivity, *Human Relations*, 52 (4): 463–84.

Hornblum, A. M. (1998) *Acres of Skin: Human Experiments at Holmesburg Prison (A True Story of Abuse and Exploitation in the Name of Medical Science)*, London: Routledge.

Hulme, D. (2003a) Hand over your data! *The Times Higher*, 28 March: 16.

Hulme, D. (2003b) Whose data? 'Stealing' from the poor (http://www.id21.org/ zinter/id21zinter.exe?a=7&i=Insights46art8&u=483ecd0c).

Ioannadis, J. (2005) Why most published research findings are false, *PLoS Medicine*, 2(e): 124.

Iphofen, R. (1990) Coping with a 'perforated life': A case study in managing the stigma of petit mal epilepsy, *Sociology*, 24 (3): 447–63.

Iphofen, R. (2004) A code to keep away judges, juries and MPs, *The Times Higher*, 16 January: 24.

Iphofen, R. (2005) Ethical issues in qualitative health research, Ch. 2, pp. 17–35, in I. Holloway (ed.) *Qualitative Research in Health Care*, Maidenhead: Open University Press.

Israel, M. and Hay, I. (2006) *Research Ethics for Social Scientists*, London: Sage.

Jacobsen, K. (2008) Are we there just to help the army aim better? *The Guardian*, 13 May: 11.

Jefferson, T., Alderson, P., Wager, E. and Davidoff, F. (2002) Effects of editorial peer review: A systematic review, *JAMA*, 287: 2784–6.

Jefferson, T. and Zarra, L. (2007) Bufale spotting, part two: Assessing systematic reviews, *Journal of the Royal Society of Medicine*, 100: 180–1.

Jones, S. and McGee, P. (2007) Ethical issues in researching pregnant women: A commentary, *Research Ethics Review*, 3 (2): 51–2.

Jowell, R. (1983) A professional code for statisticians? Some ethical and technical conflicts, *Bulletin of the International Statistical Institute* (Proceedings of the 43rd session), 49 (1): 165–209.

Judt, T. (2005) *Postwar: A History of Europe Since 1945*, Harmondsworth: Penguin.

Judt, T. (2008) *Reappraisals: Reflections on the Forgotten Twentieth Century*, Harmondsworth: Penguin.

Karpf, A. (2006) *The Human Voice*, London: Bloomsbury.

Keady, J. and Williams, S. (2007) Co-constructed inquiry: A new approach to generating, disseminating and discovering knowledge in qualitative research, *Quality in Ageing — Policy, Practice and Research*, 8 (2): 27–35.

Kelman, H. C. (1967) Human use of human subjects: The problem of deception in social psychological experiments, *Psychological Bulletin*, 67: 1–11; republished in Bynner, J. and Stribley, K. M. (1979) *Social Research: Principles and Procedures*, London: Longman.

Kenyon, E. and Hawker, S. (1999) Once would be enough: Some reflections on the issue of safety of lone researchers, *International Journal of Social Research Methodology*, 2 (4): 313–27.

Kitwood, T. (1997) *Dementia Reconsidered: The Person Comes First*, Buckingham: Open University Press.

La Follette, H. (ed.) (2002) *Ethics in Practice: An Anthology*, Oxford: Blackwell.

Laity, P. (2008) A life in writing: Uncomfortable truths, *The Guardian (Review)*, 17 May: 11.

Lee, R. (1995) *Dangerous Fieldwork*, Qualitative Research Methods Series, Vol. 34, London: Sage Publications.

Lee-Treweek, G. and Linkogle, S. (eds) (2000) *Danger in the Field: Risk and Ethics in Social Research*, London: Routledge.

Levine, R. J. (1978) The role of assessment of risk benefit criteria in the determination of the appropriateness of research involving human subjects. In *United States. National Commission for the Protection of Biomedical and Behavioural Research* Appendix. *The Belmont Report: Ethical Principles and Guidelines for the Protection of Human Subjects of Research.* Washington DC, U. S. government printing office DHEW publication (OS) 78 0013, pp. 8–4.10.

Levitt, S. D. and Dubner, S. J. (2005) *Freakonomics: A Rogue Economist Explores the Hidden Side of Everything*, London: Allen Lane.

Lewis, G., Boulton, M., Brown, N. and Webster, A. (2004) *The International Dimension to Research Ethics: The Significance of International and Other Non-UK Frameworks for UK Social Science*, Working Paper, ESRC Research Ethics Framework: Discussion Paper No. 2 (www.york.ac.uk/res/ref/documents.htm).

Madge, J. (1965) *The Tools of Social Science*, London: Longmans, Green and Co.

Marcus, J. (2003) Transsexuals protest, *The Times Higher*, 1 August: 13.

Marglin, S. A. (2008) *The Dismal Science: How Thinking Like an Economist Undermines Community*, Harvard University Press.

Mauthner, M., Birch, M., Jessop, J. and Miller, T. (eds) (2002) *Ethics in Qualitative Research*, London: Sage.

Mauthner, N. S., Parry, O. and Backett-Milburn, K. (1998) The data are out there, or are they? Implications for archiving and revisiting qualitative data, *Sociology*, 32 (4): 733–45.

Meikle, J. (2004) *The Guardian*, 6 April: 9.

Miles, M. and Huberman, A. M. (1994) *Qualitative Data Analysis (2nd edition)*, London: Sage.

Milgram, S. (1965) Some conditions of obedience and disobedience to authority, *Human Relations*, 18: 57–75.

Milgram, S. (1974) Problems of ethics in research, Appendix 1: 193–202 in *Obedience to Authority*, New York: Harper Row.

Miller, T. and Bell, L. (2002) Consenting to what? Issues of access, gatekeeping and 'informed' consent, Ch. 3, pp. 53–69, in M. Mauthner, M. Birch, J. Jessop and T. Miller (eds) *Ethics in Qualitative Research*, London: Sage.

Mitchell, D. (2003) Research methodologies and the quandary of over-analysed populations, in *Using Emancipatory Methodologies in Disability Research*, proceedings of the first NDA Disability Research Conference, Dublin: NDA.

Monbiot, G. (2000) *Captive State*, London: Pan Macmillan.

Monbiot, G. (2003) *The Age of Consent: A Manifesto for a New World Order*, London: Flamingo.

Monbiot, G. (2006) *Heat: How to Stop the Planet Burning*, London: Allen Lane.

Moser, C. A. and Kalton, G. (1971) *Survey Methods in Social Investigation*, (2nd edition), Aldershot: Ashgate (2001 reprint) (first published 1958).

Murphy, E. and Dingwall, R. (2001) The ethics of ethnography, Ch. 23, in P. Atkinson, A. Coffey, S. Delamont, J. Lofland and L. Lofland (eds) *Handbook of Ethnography*, London: Sage.

National Audit Office (NAO) (2003) *Getting the Evidence: Using Research in Policy-Making*, London: The Stationery Office (http://www.nao.org.uk/publications/nao_reports/02-03/0203586-ies.pdf).

National Disability Authority (2002) *Guidelines for Including People with Disabilities in Research*, Dublin: NDA (www.nda.ie).

National Disability Authority (2004) *Ethical Guidelines for Disability Research*, Dublin: NDA (www.nda.ie).

Neuberger, J. (2005) *The Moral State We're In*, London: Harper Collins.

NRES (2007) National Research Ethics Service, Year in Review, 2007–8 (http://www.nres.npsa.nhs.uk/news-and-publications/news/nres-year-in-review/).

The Nuremberg Code (1947), in A. Mitscherlich and F. Mielke (eds) (1949) *Doctors of Infamy: The Story of the Nazi Medical Crimes*, New York: Schuman, pp. xxiii–xxv.

Oakley, A. (2000) *Experiments in Knowing: Gender and Method in the Social Sciences*, Cambridge: Polity Press.

O'Connor, M. E. (1976) Prison research: A methodological commentary on being a known observer, *Australian and New Zealand Journal of Criminology*, 9: 227–34.

Office of Public Sector Information (2007) *Mental Capacity Act 2005*, London: HM Stationery Office (http://www.opsi.gov.uk/acts/acts2005/ukpga_20050009_en_1).

Ogden, R. (2003) No ring of confidence, *The Times Higher*, 7 November: 14.

Oliver, M. (2003) Emancipatory research: A methodology for social transformation, in *Using Emancipatory Methodologies in Disability Research*, proceedings of the first NDA Disability Research Conference, Dublin: NDA.

Oliver, P. (2003) *The Student's Guide to Research Ethics*, Maidenhead: Open University Press.

Pallister, J., Nancarrow, C. and Brace, I. (1999) Navigating the righteous course: A quality issue, *Journal of the Market Research Society*, 41 (3): 327–43.

Parekh, B. (2004) Love is … desirable, but it's by no means a 'right', *The Times Higher*, 6 February: 22–3.

Paterson, B. L., Gregory, D. and Thorne, S. (1999) A protocol for researcher safety, *Qualitative Health Research*, 9 (2): 259–69.

Pearson, G. (2007) The researcher as hooligan: Where 'participant' observation means breaking the law, *International Journal of Social Research Methodology*, 99 (1): 1–11.

Petit-Zeman, S. (2005) *Doctor, What's Wrong? Making the NHS Human Again*, London: Routledge.

Popay, J., Roberts, H., Sowden, A., Petticrew, M., Arai, L., Rodgers, M. and Britten, N. (2006) *Guidance on the Conduct of Narrative Synthesis in Systematic Reviews (A Product from the ESRC Methods Programme)* (http://cpd.conted.ox.ac.uk/ healthsciences/courses/short_courses/qsr/NSguidanceV1-JNoyes.pdf).

Press Association (2006) MoD scientists will not face charges for human experiments, *The Guardian*, 13 June: 11.

Rachels, J. (1978) *Elements of Moral Philosophy*, New York: McGraw-Hill.

Read, R. (2007) *Philosophy for Life* (edited by M.A. Lavery), London: Continuum.

Reason, P. (ed.) (1994) *Participation in Human Inquiry*, London: Sage.

Reeves, A., Bryson, C., Prmston, R. and White, C. (2007) *Children's Perspectives on Participating in Survey Research*, London: National Centre for Social Research.

Reinharz, S. (1979) *On Becoming a Social Scientist*, San Francisco: Jossey Bass.

Richardson, S. and McMullan, M. (2007) Research ethics in the UK: What can sociology learn from health? *Sociology*, 41 (6): 1115–32.

Ritchie, J. and Lewis, J. (eds) (2003) *Qualitative Research Practice: A Guide for Social Science Students and Researchers*, London: Sage.

Roberts, B. (2002) *Biographical Research*, Buckingham: Open University Press.

Roberts, C. (2008) Making policy, making social research: Reflections on 30 years, *SRA News*, May: 1–2.

Robson, C. (1993) *Real World Research: A Resource for Social Scientists and Practitioner-Researchers*, Oxford: Blackwell.

Rosenhan, D. (1973) On being sane in insane places, *Science*, 179: 250–8.

Rowson, R. (2006) *Working Ethics: How to be Fair in a Culturally Complex World*, London: Jessica Kingsley.

Ruano, S. (1991) The role of the social scientist in participatory action research, Ch. 15, pp. 210–17, in W. Foote Whyte (ed.) *Participatory Action Research*, Sage, Newbury Park.

Rutstein, D. D. (1972) The ethical design of human experiments, pp. 383–401, in P. A. Freund (ed.) *Experimentation with Human Subjects*, London: George Allen and Unwin.

Sampson, H., Bloor, M. and Fincham, B. (2008) A price worth paying? Considering the 'cost' of reflexive research methods and the influence of feminist ways of 'doing', *Sociology*, 42 (5): 919–33.

Sapsford, R. (1999) *Survey Research*, London: Sage.

Schenk, K. and Williamson, J. (2005) *Ethical Approaches to Gathering Information from Children and Adolescents in International Settings: Guidelines and Resources*, Washington, DC: Population Council.

Schon, D. A. (1983) *The Reflective Practitioner: How Professionals Think in Action*, New York: Basic Books.

SCPR (1974) *Survey Research And Privacy: Report of a Working Party*, London: Social and Community Planning Research.

Shea, C. (2000) Don't talk to the humans: The crackdown on social science research, *Lingua Franca*, 10 (6) September: 1–6.

Sieber, J. (1991) *Planning Ethically Responsible Research: A Guide for Social Science Students*, London: Sage.

Sin, C. H. (2005) Seeking informed consent: Reflections on research practice, *Sociology*, 39 (2): 277–94.

Singer, P. (ed.) (1991) *A Companion to Ethics*, Oxford: Blackwell.

Singer, P. (2000) *Writings on an Ethical Life*, New York: HarperCollins.

Skinner Buzan, D. (2004) I was not a lab rat, *The Guardian*, 12 March: 7.

Slater, L. (2004) *Opening Skinner's Box (Great Psychological Experiments of the 20th Century)*, London: Bloomsbury.

Smith, J. (2001) *Moralities: Sex, Money and Power in the 21st Century*, London: Allen Lane.

Smith, R. (2006a) Peer review: A flawed process at the heart of science and journals, *Journal of the Royal Society of Medicine*, 99: 178–82.

Smith, R. (2006b) Research misconduct: The poisoning of the well, *Journal of the Royal Society of Medicine*, 99: 232–7.

Social Research Association (2002) *Commissioning Social Research: A Good Practice Guide*, (2nd edition), London: SRA.

Social Research Association (2003) *Ethical Guidelines*, London: SRA.

Sokal, A. (2008) *Beyond the Hoax: Science, Philosophy and Culture*, Oxford: University Press.

Spicker, P. (2007) The ethics of policy research, *Evidence & Policy: A Journal of Research, Debate and Practice*, 3 (1): 99–118 (20).

Springall, E. (2002) I am a researcher: Who are you?, *BSA Network*, May: 19–20.

Stevenson, C. L. (1937) The emotive meaning of ethical terms, *Mind*, 46: 496–508 reprinted in Cahn and Markie (1998).

Tad, W. (2005) Dignity and older Europeans, *Quality in Ageing — Policy, Practice and Research*, 6 (1 and 2) (special edition parts 1 and 2).

Tannen, D. (1992) *That's Not What I Meant!*, London: Virago (first published 1986).

Tannen, D. (1994) *Talking From 9 to 5 (Women and Men in the Workplace: Language, Sex and Power)*, New York: Avon Books.

Tannen, D. (1995) *Talking from 9 to 5 (How Women's and Men's Conversational Styles Affect Who Get Heard, Who Gets Credit and What Work Gets Done)*, London: Virago Press.

ten Have, P. (2004) *Understanding Qualitative Research and Ethnomethodology*, London: Sage.

Thompson, M. (2000) *Ethics (Teach Yourself Series)*, London: Hodder Headline.

Tinker, A. and Coomber, V. (2004) *University Research Ethics Committees: Their Role, Remit and Conduct*, London: King's College (Report commissioned by Nuffield Foundation) (http://www.kcl.ac.uk/phpnews/wmview.php?ArtID=674).

Tombs, S. and Whyte, D. (eds) (2003) *Unmasking the Crimes of the Powerful: Scrutinizing States and Corporations*, New York: Peter Lang.

Treleaven, L. (1994) Making a space: A collaborative inquiry with women as staff development, Ch. 9, pp. 138–62, in P. Reason (ed.) *Participation in Human Inquiry*, London: Sage.

United Nations (1993) *The Standard Rules on the Equalization of Opportunities for Persons with Disabilities*, New York: United Nations.

Van den Hoonaard, W. C. (2006) New angles and tangles in the ethics review of research, *Journal of Academic Ethics*, 4: 261–74.

Venkatesh, S. (2008) *Gang Leader for a Day*, London: Allen Lane.

Webster, A., Boulton, M., Brown, N. and Lewis, G. (2004) *Crossing Boundaries: Social Science, Health and Bioscience Research andtProcess of Ethics Review*, Working Paper — ESRC Research Ethics Framework: Discussion Paper No. 1 (www.york.ac.uk/res/ref/documents.htm).

Wells, F. and Farthing, M. (2008) *Fraud and Misconduct in Biomedical Research*, London: RSM Press.

Whyte, W. F. (ed.) (1991) *Participatory Action Research*, London: Sage.

Williams, S. (2007) Editorial, *Quality in Ageing — Policy, Practice and Research*, 8 (2): 2–4.

World Medical Association (2008) *Declaration of Helsinki* (http://www.wma.net/e/policy/b3.htm).

Wright Mills, C. (1970) *The Sociological Imagination*, Harmondsworth: Penguin (first published 1959).

Zappone, K. (ed.) (2003) *Re-Thinking Identity: The Challenge of Diversity*, Dublin: Equality Authority.

Index